Thunder Beyond The Brazos

Oil portrait of Mirabeau Buonaparte Lamar, C. B. Normann, Texas State Library, Austin, Texas

Courtesy U.T. Institute of Texan Cultures

Thunder Beyond The Brazos

Mirabeau B. Lamar
A Biography

Jack C. Ramsay, Jr.

EAKIN PRESS ⚑ Fort Worth, Texas
www.EakinPress.com

Library of Congress Cataloging in Publication Data

Ramsay, Jack C., 1922–
   Thunder beyond the Brazos.
   Bibliography: p.
   Includes index.
   1. Lamar, Mirabeau Buonaparte, 1798–1859. 2. Texas — Presidents — Biography. 3. Texas — History — Republic, 1735–1846. I. Title.
F390.L2R35   1985   976.4'04'0924 [B]   84-13835

Copyright © 1985
By Jack C. Ramsay, Jr.
Published By Eakin Press
An Imprint of Wild Horse Media Group
P.O. Box 331779
Fort Worth, Texas 76163
1-817-344-7036
www.EakinPress.com
ALL RIGHTS RESERVED
1 2 3 4 5 6 7 8 9
ISBN-13: 978-1-57168-580-3

For thou art dearer to my heart
 Than all the gems of earth and sky
  . . . Lamar to his wife, Henrietta

This book is dedicated to Karin. . .
 My sweetheart and my Henrietta

Mirabeau B. Lamar, second president of the Republic of Texas
Courtesy Library of Congress

Contents

Prologue	vii
1. Battle on the Plain	1
2. Fairfield	8
3. Soul in Desolation	17
4. Land of Fruition	23
5. The Nero of the Present Day	33
6. General for a Day	40
7. Generous Indulgence	48
8. Oak Grove on the Brazos	54
9. The Scroll of History	64
10. The Seat of Empire	73
11. The Forked Tongue	81
12. The Restless Giant	90
13. The Affair of the Pigs	100
14. Texans at Sea	111
15. Wagons Westward	121
16. The Impossible Dream	136
17. The Winter Chill	145
18. The Lost Pines	157
19. Laredo's Blooming Plain	167
20. In Search of a Home	179
21. Minister in Residence	191
Epilogue	205
Endnotes	211
Bibliography	235
Index	239

The Lamar statue in the Texas Hall of Fame, Dallas

Prologue

The guns of the Alamo lay silent.

Spring greenery was beginning to appear around the crumbling walls of the old mission temporarily turned fortress. The fierceness of battle that so recently had inundated the fields outside of San Antonio de Bexar now seemed little more than a nightmarish memory. With the change of seasons, the land was yielding to mellower influences: the hills to the west were taking on new hues; the ethereal greenness of the native mesquite could be seen everywhere; the meandering river that nourished the area was gently filling the limits of its banks. The fields of Bexar were once more a peaceful plain.

Some two hundred miles away another grass-covered prairie had been made verdant by the unusually heavy spring rains that had fallen across much of Texas. Ragged men, bone tired from forced marches and the hardships of the trail, lounged about in an oak grove where irregular sunlight streamed through the broken clouds of a partly overcast sky. Camp sounds could be heard: the clatter of utensils and equipment along with the steady noises of man and beast shattered occasionally by an oath or a shout. Animal odors strangely intermingled with the other smells of frontier life: the aroma of roasting meat and the pungent presence of strong coffee necessary to such an existence.

This was the plain of San Jacinto.

The time was late April, 1836.

Here was the Army of the Republic of Texas. It was commanded by Sam Houston, a towering figure of a man. Houston was both erratic and brilliant, unpredictable by even his closest associates, and yet highly knowledgeable of frontier life and of the men gathered at San Jacinto. He had taken the responsibility of leadership early in March just after the delegates from the various parts of the Anglo-settled Mexican province of Texas had gathered in convention at the makeshift capital, Washington-on-the-Brazos, and had solemnly declared themselves an independent nation. After accepting the title of Commander-in-chief, he had led the army of the embryonic republic in what most felt was a steady retreat from the vastly superior forces of the enemy.

This band of men was by this time the last hope for the new nation. A force of less than 200 defenders had been wiped out attempting to hold the Alamo. Shortly after that tragedy, James Fannin's army that was only slightly larger in effective strength, was marched out on the prairie where all but a handful were gunned down after having surrendered near Goliad.

Houston now had moved his men beyond the Brazos River. He was closely followed by aggressive Santa Anna who had been marching freely across the land since his conquest at Bexar. Many were convinced that this natural water barrier should have been the line of defense for the Anglo-settlers, and there was much criticism of the Texan commander when he continued to lead his men in what appeared to be a retreat to the east.

The thunder of battle, yet to be heard, would now echo beyond the Brazos.

Steadily dwindling in size, the Texas military force probably numbered no more than 900 men when they reached the plain of San Jacinto. This was a contingent barely equal in personnel to any one of the four armies that opposed them. By now the settlers on both sides of the Brazos, and well to the east, were in panic. "The Runaway Scrape" was the prosaic name they themselves gave to their predicament as family after family packed up what they could easily move, left lands and homes unattended, and headed for the safety of the United States beyond the Sabine River.

Some had left Houston's command to help evacuate those at home; others had departed simply because they had become convinced the situation was now hopeless. Obviously Santa Anna intended to settle the revolution in Texas quickly and decisively. With all of the forces that were moving to quell the hope of Texan independence, it was nothing short of a miracle that Houston was able to hold together as much of his army as he did.

As this band of determined settler–soldiers was established on the plain of San Jacinto, the army of President Santa Anna began to make camp nearby. This was the main Mexican force under the personal command of the President of Mexico; however reinforcements from three other battalion-sized detachments were not far away.

It was obvious that a showdown was imminent.

A portion of the informal notes that Lamar prepared for his inaugural address that he had intended to deliver on December 10, 1838. These same notes were probably the basis of his address to the Texas Congress on December 21. [The Lamar Papers, MS Number 914.]

Courtesy Texas State Library, Archives Division, Austin

*Their rising all at once was as the sound
of Thunder Heard Remote.*
John Milton in *Paradise Lost*

A small band of Spartan heroes created thunder on the plain of San Jacinto on April 21, 1836.

Mirabeau Buonaparte Lamar was one of that band.

But was Lamar merely *Thunder Heard Remote*. . . or did he make a significant contribution to Texas in the years that followed?

Was Lamar Thunder. . .

    Or was he Rain?

[1]

Battle on the Plain

Spring sunlight continued to filter through the trees of the plain. The two armies viewed each other across the fields separating them as each prepared for conflict.

Within the Texas ranks there was one new recruit who seemed strangely out of place: this was a Georgian who bore the name Mirabeau Buonaparte Lamar. Such an imposing appellation was enough to set him apart in an assemblage of rugged frontiersmen. Obviously a man of culture with a classical education, he was highly literate, a poet, an editor, and the scion of a Georgian plantation family.[1] A boyhood friend had described him as a person of "ardent poetical temperament . . . gentle playfulness . . . unaffected kindness . . . [whose] eyes were beautiful blue, large and round."[2] Below medium height and somewhat stout, his appearance was in sharp contrast to that of his lean and unpolished comrades.[3]

The blue-eyed poet had joined the army when the Texans had been camped near Groce's plantation, a few miles away. Although he had just arrived, this was not his first time in Texas. He had visited the province the year before; this time, however, he had come with the avowed purpose of staying and fighting for Texan independence.

He had landed in late March from the schooner *Flash*, at Velasco, just in time to hear of the massacre of James Fannin and his comrades.[4] A friend had attempted to arrange for Lamar to have a horse for his trip to join the army. A Mr. Kilgore of Brazoria was instructed by letter from Alexander Patton to let the gentleman from Georgia ". . . have the nag I left with you."[5]

However, when Lamar arrived in Brazoria, Mr. Kilgore had other plans for the horse. In those uncertain days probably no one was readily agreeable to turning loose of so valuable a commodity as that of a usable mount. Setting out on foot in the direction of Houston's encampment, the new volunteer soon encountered another Georgian, William D. Redd of Columbus, who had similar military aspirations. On April 10, the two were in Harrisburg, and shortly after that, fell into the ranks of the Army of the Republic of Texas.

Joining the Texas force was about that simple: they merely fell in. But once they were in there was serious business at hand. Hardly had the two men found a place in the erratic aggregation of professed soldiers than preparations for battle were begun. They moved with the army up the coastal plain near the San Jacinto River, and then to an oak grove; there they set up camp awaiting the enemy, who soon took a position nearby.

On April 20 the first real contact between Houston's men and the army of Santa Anna took place. It was hardly a full military maneuver: instead it was more of a spontaneous reaction by men who had long since grown weary of camp life and forced marches and were now ready to act. Santa Anna's cannon was in clear view of the oak grove. The Texan army had recently acquired artillery, two field pieces named the "Twin Sisters." More like children experimenting with new toys than *bona fide* artillerymen, the Texans began to exchange shots with the Mexicans. Infantry fire followed. But this potentially sophisticated form of military activity hardly satisfied these men of the frontier. Someone suggested that they go and get the enemy weapon. Sidney Sherman has generally been credited with issuing the call for volunteers to attempt this daring deed. Apparently his appeal was without Houston's full permission, but it was the sort of thing that the general of such a volunteer force could not have halted even if he had sought to do so. Quickly some sixty or more horses were rounded up, an impromptu cavalry company was formed, and a reckless dash was made across the open field that had become a no-man's-land.

Among those who joined in this escapade was Mirabeau Buonaparte Lamar. At last, on a horse, he was in his element — having been raised in a land where good horsemanship was considered a basic skill. But the effort, perhaps as Sam Houston had realized, was doomed to failure. Four companies of Mexican infantry appeared from a nearby wooded area to protect their cannon and opened fire on the horsemen. Aware that they were about to be cut off, the Texans began to reign in and circle back to their own lines. But before they could do so, one horseman had fallen: nineteen-year-old Walter P. Lane, later to become a Confederate general. It was Lamar who saw his comrade's danger as an enemy cavalryman bore down upon him. Wheeling about, he rode over just in time to save Lane's life and perpetuate a military career that otherwise would have been cut short. Turning away from Lane,[6] he was then able to assist another of his fellow volunteers, Secretary of War Rusk, who was surrounded by several enemy soldiers. Digging his spurs into his horse, Lamar knocked down one of the Mexicans to make a gap in the circle of attackers through which Rusk was able to escape.

The brief adventure that ended even more quickly than it had begun had no military bearing on the situation other than to create a new officer in the Army of the Republic of Texas. Because of his obvious courage and his ability to function effectively in the face of danger, Houston gave Lamar a battlefield commission and made him a colonel in the army.[7]

Lamar accepted this appointment making him the leader

of the Texas Cavalry. In his personal papers he carefully preserved a document that listed him as commander of the "Cavalry Corps," signed by "Major General Samuel Houston, Commander-in-Chief of the Texian Forces." [8]

The next day, April 21, dawned crisp and clear. There was an air of anticipation among the frontiersmen. They had made contact with the enemy and almost everyone expected action. Equipment was carefully prepared, powder and shot were checked, and saddles were adjusted. As the sun rose higher over the plain and the morning coolness turned to springtime warmth, the certainty that this was the day of battle began to ebb. A council of war was called by Houston. Exactly what happened in that council may never be fully known. One fact is clear: at least some of those present felt that the time to fight had not yet come and they argued that a more favorable battle site should be chosen. Another retreat was proposed since their dwindling numbers placed them at a numerical disadvantage to the enemy. In later years both Houston and his opponents claimed that the other had the greater reluctance to fight on that day.

Apparently the recently appointed cavalry commander was among those who ardently urged immediate attack. Lamar's account places the hesitation to do battle largely upon Houston. After the council had adjourned, Lamar later stated, "I met General Houston and expressed to him the strong desire of the army to make battle. He replied merely as follows: 'Sir, can I whip Santa Anna and his whole army by myself? Would you have me attack them alone? The officers are all opposed to fighting, and so are the men. I have always been ready to fight, but the army has not and how can I do battle?'" [9]

But even in this moment, preparations were under way for the conflict. The "lines were actually forming," commented Lamar, when "Houston came to me and said . . . 'Col. Lamar, do you really think we ought to fight?'" [10]

It is impossible to determine whether or not Houston was actually as reluctant to commence hostilities as Lamar later made him out to be. The heat of subsequent political conflicts against the background of partly remembered statements could easily make the accuracy of quoted words and remembered attitudes questionable with the passage of time.

In any case the army was ready for action. But, by now, the afternoon was half gone. Balmy breezes had replaced the early morning coolness. Mexican pickets who had stood ready for action most of the day relaxed. President Santa Anna retired to his commodious tent to spend his time of siesta with his mistress.

The hour for attack had come! Houston's sense of timing led him to recognize his opportune moment. He knew his men were now prepared for battle and the enemy was not. Quickly he gave the command to move out. Silently the lines took some semblance of military order. Lamar and his newly constituted cavalry company were dispatched to the enemy's left. The Texans' left consisted of Sherman's regiment. Burleson's men were assigned to the center. Hockley commanded the recently acquired artillery with an infantry group under Millard to its right. Eagerly the Texans crossed the plain. The ragged frontiersmen were almost at Santa Anna's tent door before Mexican pickets gave the alarm. Perhaps the erratic nature of the maneuver of the previous day had left the impression on those who first saw movement that this was no more than another futile caper on the plain. But when the fact of full attack was realized by the Army of Mexico, it was too late. It was a short and violent fight. Knives flashed, close range shots were exchanged and death came quickly to the unsuspecting soldiers from south of the Rio Grande. All of the pent-up fury of Texan exasperation was vented on those who had wiped out the garrison of the Alamo and who had some responsibility, however indirectly, for the massacre at Goliad. Houston, a few days later, wrote these words in giving his account of the battle:

> Our cavalry ... commanded by Col. Mirabeau B. Lamar (whose gallant and daring conduct on the previous day had attracted the admiration of his comrades, and called him to

that station) [was] placed on our extreme right . . . Our cavalry was first dispatched to the front of the enemy's left, for the purpose of attracting their notice, whilst an extensive island of timber afforded us an opportunity of concentrating our forces and deploying from that point, agreeably to the previous design of the troops.[11]

In a matter of minutes the battle was over and nearly half of the grand army of Santa Anna lay dead; the majority of the others were soon taken prisoner.

Santa Anna later wrote of the battle: "The enemy had surprised our advance guard, a party attacked the three chosen companies that guarded the woods to our right and took possession of them, increasing the confusion with their unfailing rifles." [12]

When he found he could not stem the tide, the president of Mexico declared in his apology for the loss at San Jacinto, that he then took horse and fled.[13]

The battle of San Jacinto that lasted only a few minutes, not only established Anglo-Saxon control over the vast domain of Texas, but it made heroes of those who had fought and won this unique contest.

Sam Houston, of course, was to become legend for his leadership in this dramatic and decisive fight. Others who were a part of the action were to reflect some vestige of that glory. The history of the Texas Republic, throughout its decade of life, was to revolve around those who had been at San Jacinto.

It was against the background of that event that Mirabeau Buonaparte Lamar was to emerge as one of the leaders of a new nation. Often neglected by recorders of Texas history, Lamar, nonetheless, came to play an increasingly important role in the life of the infant state. In spite of the fact that he was a new arrival, he was destined to become the first elected vice-president of the nation, and later serve as its second president. Lamar and his admirers soon became a powerful force in the development of the Republic. However, his leadership was generally overshadowed by the dramatic forcefulness of Sam Houston. During the days of the Texas Republic, Lamar became Houston's chief political opponent, and the Commander of San Jacinto vigorously used his energetic rhetorical ability to denounce his one time cavalry chief. This negative assessment of Lamar by Houston has greatly influenced much modern writing of Texas history by historians who have naively accepted political rhetoric for fact.[14] A more accurate approach to Lamar's contributions to Texas must now be made.

Who was the newcomer who so dramatically thrust himself upon the pages of the record of San Jacinto? It is now that this question should be fully answered.

[2]

Fairfield

Georgia dust clogged the wheels of the lumbering wagon as it made its way westward over roads hardly distinguishable from the surrounding country. On board were the initial belongings of the family of John Lamar. It was the year 1808. The Lamars were moving west to better land and increased opportunity. It was a trek of some sixty miles from the old property in Jefferson County, near Louisville, Georgia, to the new home in Putnam County, near the growing community of Milledgeville. The head of the household had supervised the building of the new plantation headquarters. Carpenters and masons had been hired in town, and as the weeks went by, the structure gradually took shape. Now, at last, it was ready for occupancy.[1]

John Lamar was thirty-nine years of age. He had lived all of his life in the area where fertile land was available near the Savannah River. Of Huguenot ancestry, the Lamars had literally hewn a livable environment from the wilderness.[2]

The removal to the new location was no easy change, but it was one that meant some improvement in both living conditions and potential income. There was a larger house and there was much more tillable land, making possible a prosperous agrarian establishment. The new plantation was given the name "Fairfield," an appellation that obviously expressed the family hopes as they first viewed the expansive fields near the bend of Georgia's Little River.

Among those who helped relocate in the new home that was still fresh with the smell of recently hewn lumber was John's brother, Zechariah, who lived with them. Among other things, he had taken upon himself the responsibility of naming the sons of the family. An avid reader in an age when few men had time to engage in such activity, Uncle Zechariah had given names to the Lamar sons that reflected his particular historical interest at the time that a name was needed: Lucius Quintus Cincinnatus, Jefferson Jackson, Thomas Randolph, and Mirabeau Buonaparte.[3]

Mirabeau, the second of the sons, had been born on August 16, 1798, at the old homestead in Jefferson County. The move to the new home must have been a big event in the life of the ten-year-old youth. The house at Fairfield was large and comfortable and was set in pleasant surroundings. It soon became a relay station on the stage route that passed through the area, and as such took on considerable importance. The farming chores necessary for the existence of the family were performed largely by slaves who were overseen by John Lamar and at times by his sons.[4]

It was in this environment that Mirabeau began to mature. He soon acquired his uncle's taste for things historical, and became interested in the books available in the Lamar home. Schools were accessible only some three or four months out of the year, and those were at some distance from home. Apparently the Lamar sons attended the nearest district school when such educational opportunities existed. The Lamars urged consistent school attendance and vowed to give their children the best possible formal education that the country afforded.[5] The effectiveness of this type of instruction depended entirely upon the ability and the character of the teacher who might be available at the moment. Mirabeau later recalled one of those who had taught him during this period, an Irishman by the name of Duffy, who not only had the ability to convey facts to his pupils, but who was capable of imparting skills interwoven with profound moral precept. Apparently the educational process did take place in spite of the primitiveness of frontier surroundings simply because there were some teachers who were determined to teach and at last some pupils who were willing to learn.

Lamar attended Powelton Academy, after the family had moved to Putnam County, for one term. This institution was a school that boasted of an excellent curriculum and a strong academic program. However, after less than a year there, he was sent to Eatonton Academy, which was closer to home and had been strengthened by the recent appointment of a new headmaster: Dr. Alonzo Church — who became principal of the school in 1816. Mirabeau enrolled there the following year.[6] This vigorous teacher, an ordained Presbyterian minister from Vermont, had a profound influence upon the young Georgian's developing interest in the classics. Under Church's tutorship, he acquired a taste for such authors as Thomas Moore, Byron, Dryden, Pope, Gibbon, and Scott.

On one occasion, he played the part of Brutus with considerable enthusiasm in a school play. The great works of both English and continental literature made a lasting impression on him. Contemporary accounts indicate that he was very much at home in Shakespearean roles.

Not only was he interested in drama and literature, but oil painting fascinated him. One biographer[7] described a painting by him that is attributed to his youthful years and once hung in the Lamar home. It was the portrayal of a beautiful woman asleep on a couch with the head of a large horse thrust through the window above her. Fencing and horseback riding were among other interests during these developing years. The composition of poetry was an avocation that began in his youth and held an increasing interest for him as the years passed. Bits of rhyme were composed by him at various stages of life, and in later years, his place as a poet was established by his publication of a book of verse.[8]

This was the plantation environment in which Mirabeau Lamar grew to manhood: one in which there was time for literature, art, drama, and poetic expression. A series of essays that he carefully preserved among his papers gives some clear indications of the character of that environment. These papers date from the period of his classical training under Alonzo Church, and allow a fascinating insight into the nature of an education available to the son of an early nineteenth century Georgia plantation owner. They are on such subjects as "Was Brutus Justifiable in Assassinating Caesar?" "Were the Europeans Justifiable in Conquering and Taking Possession of America in the Manner They Did?" and "True Happiness." [9] All show the impact of neoclassicism on the learning of the period and indicate the Greco-Roman basis of the liberal arts concept. Mirabeau grew to manhood immersed in the educational process that sought to educate the total person in relationship to a magnificent cultural heritage.

The older Lamar son, Lucius, began to read law with an able lawyer of the area, Joel Crawford.[10] Apparently the same course was a possibility for Mirabeau after he had finished the basic education that was available for him nearer to home. However, this did not appeal to him at the time: instead, he decided to begin adult life by opening a general store in the new town of Cahawba, just west of the Georgia boundary. This village had been recently laid out and designated as the capital of the state of Alabama.

In 1819 he set out for Cahawba in Dallas County, Alabama, where he joined a friend, Willis Roberts, as a partner in the general mercantile business. In May of that year, he was on hand to bid for lots for a location for a store. The store was opened, and during the remainder of the year, Mirabeau lived with Roberts in his home as the two sold goods in the new community. However, the business did not thrive, and Lamar soon sold out his interest to Roberts.[11]

He then turned to journalism. A newspaper had been

founded in the town in 1819 by William Allen which he called the *Cahawba Press*. Mirabeau joined him as a co-publisher and part-time editor. His duties included not only that of news gathering and assisting in the publication of the paper, but of contributing poems. Among his extant poetic works, there is one entitled "The Source of Strife" that dates from his period. In this he chided the several religious denominations of the community for their rivalry and called for a spirit of brotherliness. "Love" and "The Ruling Passion" are the titles of two other poetic works by Lamar that he published in the *Press*, in which he gave expression to his own innate spirit of romanticism.[12]

However, he was not content to exercise his literary ability through a standard news sheet: he proposed to produce a publication of his own. Evidence of this personal attempt at journalism is among his preserved papers in the form of an interesting manuscript entitled "Prospectus of the Village Miscellany." Dated March 8, 1821, it proports to be written by a "Mr. Lanternbalvon," but the original document that has been preserved in the Texas State Archives is obviously in Lamar's handwriting. In it he stated:

> I really possess a daring mind, a lofty conception and an unbounded wit . . . when I once get fairly under sail, I can proceed with extraordinary ease to myself and to the infinite amusement of my readers, and such indeed is my happy fluency that I am frequently able to get through a whole sentence and a half without stopping more than a dozen times . . .[13]

The "Miscellany" was to have made "its appearance every Friday noon, containing such matters as the author conceived best calculated to amuse the fancy and correct the follies of the town . . . [and] no labor will be spared to render my sheets as agreeable as possible." [14]

No further copies of such a paper are extant and there is no evidence that it ever became an established publication.

However, Lamar's work with the *Cahawba Press* continued at least for a time. The New Year's day edition of the paper in 1822 contained these lines penned by him:

> Yearly doth the Laureate sing
> In honor of his country's king
> And poets annually raise
> To patrons tributary lays
>
> I'll make some rhymes
> To the fair patrons of the press.[15]

On the back of the copy of this publication that he preserved in his personal papers, the editor wrote a note home:

> I am here in Cahawba without any business or likelihood to obtain any shortly — you need not be disappointed if you see me back in Georgia again in a few weeks, in great haste, your's, etc.
>
> M.B. Lamar

To this note he added:

> I pen'ed this address in "with a running quill," for the *Cahawba Press* — you will find many typographical errors in this sheet, and as many more errors of the head.[16]

The dream of independently establishing himself on the Alabama frontier had collapsed. Early in the year 1822, Mirabeau Lamar went home to the plantation in Georgia.

Here was a young man who was too creative to be happy behind the counter of a country store, too steeped in the classics to be content with the comfortable life-style of the plantation, and too excited about the course of events in the rapidly developing world about him to be satisfied with using his talents and training as a backwoods schoolteacher. What was the future of such a youth? Clearly this was the problem of the Lamars in the year 1822. However, the family was soon able to provide a solution.

Carefully preserved in the Lamar papers is this letter of introduction:

> Dear Sir: Permit me to recommend to your confidence and patronage, my young friend Mirabeau Lamar. He is a

gentleman not more distinguished by the loftiest sentiments of honor, than by mental superiority and devotion to Republican politics — Mr. Lamar asks the appointment of Secretary to the Executive Department.[17]

The note was signed by Joel Crawford, the law partner of Lucius Lamar, and it was addressed to George MacIntosh Troup, governor of the state.

Troup had been elected to his executive post by the very close margin of only two votes in the state legislature. The influential standing of the Lamar family would very likely have been of some value to him. In addition, Crawford was a man of increasing importance. This letter of introduction would not go unheeded: Mirabeau Lamar became secretary to the Governor of Georgia.

Troup served as chief state executive for a three-year term from early 1823 through 1825.[18] His primary problem at the time was that of the Indian question. Whites were pushing into Indian territory. The Creek Indians, who inhabited the land along the Alabama, Coosa and Tallapoosa rivers, threatened trouble. In 1802, the United States government had agreed to extinguish Indian titles to lands in northwest Georgia, but nothing had been done. In 1823, the Georgia legislature had instructed the new governor to secure prompt settlement of the matter. In 1825 the federal government made a treaty with the chiefs of the Lower Creek Indians at Indian Springs. The Upper Creeks, however, withdrew, giving those who opposed the treaty some grounds for considering the pact negated. Troup decided to ignore this agreement altogether, and since popular opinion was strongly against the federal treaty, he followed the wishes of his own state legislators. In 1826 Troup ordered the districts ceded by the Indian Springs concord to Indian owners to be surveyed in preparation for opening the land to white settlers. A showdown seemed to be developing between state government and national authority. The president sought at first to prosecute the surveyors, but no arrests were made; in 1827, the federal government gave in to the demands of the state and the surveyed land was divided by lottery.[19]

Lamar joined the staff of Governor Troup in 1823. Although no date was attached to his note of recommendation, the Calendar of Lamar Papers assigned it to 1823, a date that fits the other information available concerning the inauguration of Lamar's career in Georgia politics.

His own background made him able to accept enthusiastically the plantation-oriented thinking of his employer: vigorous support of state authority that could not be overridden by a central government in Washington. Four years later Lamar wrote a review of Troup's administration in which he staunchly defended his mentor's leadership and his policies as governor during this period.[20]

One of the documents that can be found among his papers that gives some indication of the direction of his thinking during these years, is a printed broadside he authored entitled "Proposals for Organizing a Volunteer Corps of Mounted Riflemen." This paper asked the question: "Is it not high time that the work of improvement in our discipline should begin?" In what he called "these hasty observations," he proposed "the organization of a volunteer corps of mounted riflemen." Undated and unsigned this was an effort to establish a militia "willing to discharge . . . the military obligations due to our country . . ."[21] Possibly it was also to be a protection against the growing threat of serious trouble with the Indians who were being defrauded of their lands. The uncertain role of federal authority in this issue was likely a part of the motivation for such a local militia: here, then, were the seeds of 1861 that were already deeply planted in Georgian soil.

It was during this time that Lamar became commander of a corps of military volunteers, probably the organization that he had proposed in his anonymously written declaration. The occasion for the unit's first muster was that of welcoming the aged Marquis de Lafayette, who was visiting the area.

Lamar later recounted that he had a new sword: "I placed it at my side when voluntarily called upon to command a corps on the memorable occasion of giving welcome to the glorious Lafayette in my native state." However, this was more for Lamar than a ceremonial event: "I continued to wear it so long as I had the honor of guiding that corps in the defense of the noblest principles of the noblest man of Georgia — George M. Troup." [22]

This line of political thinking was set forth in a manuscript that he prepared during this period:

> It is a common remark that Monarchy is the natural government for man. This observation has grown out of the fact that all nations thrown into anarchy and confusion have invariably in emerging from that condition settled down into Monarchy . . . it is best adapted to the government of the wicked portion of the human race and its probable that Deity designed it specially for this class of mankind.[23]

His deep seated allegiance to the democratic ideal is apparent in this document. "Republican institutions," he concluded, "are the natural ones for the government of the virtuous and the wise." [24]

This was a conviction that he shared with most of his southern contemporaries. It was a peculiar kind of democracy: essential to its nature were concepts from the classical literature that Lamar loved. Indeed, it was Grecian in form; there was the ideal of ample liberty for all. But this abundant freedom did not in reality extend to the helots: for them, brown, black, Indian or slave, there was none.

He shared a belief that was common in his region: that this neo-Grecian society could only exist upon the foundation of a strong state government. He equated any positive form of federal authority with tyranny. In his extant writings of this period, this theme became increasingly dominant. The phrase that was emerging with a growing crescendo in the South was prominent in his thought: states' rights. For him, patriotism required loyalty to one's own state rather than to any union of states. It was this postulate that was to lead to the tragedy that would shatter a nation three decades later.[25]

[3]

Soul in Desolation

Tabitha B. Jordan had the pallid complexion and fragile build that made her a wistfully charming young lady. In an age that put a premium on delicate femininity, her lack of robust strength added to her appeal. Mirabeau Lamar had met her during his Cahawba days; later, when he saw her again as a young woman of seventeen, he became intrigued with her haunting loveliness. The courtship took place during his last days as a secretary to Governor Troup; it was during this time that he proposed marriage.

On January 1, 1826, Tabitha, still in her teens, became Lamar's wife in a ceremony that took place in her home in Georgia.[1]

Even then there were the forebodings of tragedy to come: the warm flush of her wedding day could not hide the fact that she was in poor health. But there were plans for an extended trip, and the couple were soon on their way for a holiday together. When the honeymoon was over, they sought the peaceful quiet of a home in the nearby countryside to wait out the chill of winter that had always been difficult for the youthful bride.

With the end of his employer's term of office in December, 1825, Lamar no longer had a place in state government.[2] He and Tabitha took up residence on a farm owned by her brother-in-law in Twiggs County, Georgia. There they lived in relative seclusion for nearly two years.

Late in the year 1827, a daughter, Rebecca, named for her two grandmothers, was born to the couple.[3] But the joy of a first birth was offset by the increasing poor health of the mother. It was at this time that Tabitha Lamar became a confirmed tubercular patient.[4]

However, much was happening in the country. New townsites were being laid out and whole communities were coming into being almost overnight. When the town of Columbus was established in Muscogee County, Georgia, by action of the legislature in 1827, Lamar was on hand preparing to establish a newspaper in the new city.[5]

A carefully preserved printed sheet among his papers is entitled "Columbus Enquirer." It is dated January, 1828, and is signed "Mirabeau B. Lamar." It declared:

> Under the above title the subscriber proposes to publish a newspaper in the town of Columbus . . . attached to the Republican creed as exemplified in the administration of Thomas Jefferson; and in the State politics, adhering to the principles that characterized the late able administration of Governor Troup, it will defend "the union of the States and the sovereignty of the States" . . . On the great subject of the next presidential election, its influence will be given to the democratic candidate most formidable to the men now in office . . . the Editor, desirous to move in a "noiseless tenor" will provoke no personal controversy . . . Terms: The Enquirer will be printed on a large sheet, with new type, once a week, at Three Dollars per ann. in advance, or Four Dollars at the end of the year.[6]

The paper began to appear on a regular basis later in the year. Each issue, while Lamar was editor, contained at least one poem, and followed the political direction that he had announced. He bought one of the original lots of the township of Chattahoochee River, and built a wide, one-story cottage with the newspaper office on the same lot. Lamar declared the trail from his home to the nearby stream to be "the handsomest and most romantic walk in the State." [7]

In spite of his declaration to move at a "noiseless tenor," such was not easy for the new editor. Several preserved documents indicate that he soon found himself deeply involved in controversy in more than one area. A letter dated August 3, 1829, from the *Atlanta Chronicle* of Athens, Georgia, questioned his paper's accuracy.[8] Lamar answered this attack vigorously displaying a fiery zeal to defend himself and his publication.[9]

A controversy over the leadership of nearby Franklin College brought Lamar into conflict with the Reverend William T. Brantley, a potential candidate for the presidency of the institution. The editor objected to the clergyman for his "bold avowal of a most unpatriotic doctrine," which apparently meant that Brantley was a "Federalist." "The reader is invited to the consideration of one important truth," stated Lamar. "It is this, that religion and civil liberty are inseparable . . ." He then assured his readers that although he felt obligated to attack the principles of the man, he certainly intended nothing against the "Baptists of which Brantley is an unworthy member." [10]

Urged repeatedly to run for office, Lamar announced in 1829 that he would seek to win election as state senator from Muscogee County. His opponent was a Columbus merchant named Sowell Woolfolk, who had already served one term. Lamar was victorious in this, his first attempt to hold elected office. The election was held in October.[11] Immediately after this he sold a half interest in the paper to Richard T. Marks, and for a time was senator and part-time editor.

The next summer he was a candidate for a second term, but he withdrew from the political contest when personal tragedy struck.

Tabitha Lamar had continued in ill health. Apparently the tubercular condition was steadily growing worse.

On August 20, 1830, the fragile, young girl, now barely twenty-one years of age, died.[12]

Lamar not only withdrew from the senatorial race, but he closed up the cottage where he and Tabitha had lived, and he disposed of his remaining interest in the *Enquirer*.[13]

He wrote these plantive words:

> When she died and left me here
> My soul in desolation —
> I broke the shell she loved so well
> Destroyed the songs I wrote her.[14]

For a time he drew into himself to coddle his grief. He spent much of the next two years in travel: he apparently visited friends and relatives, and at least on one occasion traveled as far as Mobile, Alabama.[15] During these months he sought relief from his sorrow by indulging in poetical expression. One of his works of this period reflected his deep mood of melancholia:

> She sleepeth in the valley's shade,
> A dweller with the dead
> And I am here with ruined mind
> Left lingering on the strand
> To pour my music to the wind
> My tears upon the sand.[16]

However, in 1832, he was back in Georgia and had recovered sufficiently from his sense of depression to make another attempt in the world of politics. He announced for Congress. His candidacy was immediately fraught with difficulty. He could not gain endorsement from those in control of the state political machinery. His absence from the field for a time had perhaps had something to do with this; some alterations had taken place in the leadership of Georgia. He then sought to gain popular support by appealing to the public in a statement that he published in which he denounced the "attempted dictation of the late Legislative Caucus at Milledgeville and the Committee of Seven." This system, he declared, placed "too much power in the hands of a few." He assured his readers that his politics "have been consistent with the letter and the spirit of the Constitution and . . . uniformly in accordance with the rights of the State." [17]

However, without the endorsement of the state political leadership, he had little chance. He lost the race.

Again in 1833, he announced for Congress. This time he made vigorous preparation for a determined campaign. He bought back half interest in the *Enquirer*, giving him a voice that could readily be heard.

He then had a strong hand in the establishment of a new political organization that was to be known as the States' Rights Party. The principles of the proprietors of the new structure were set forth at a meeting held in Milledgeville on November 13, 1833. There was vigorous objection to the Federalist concept "that a State . . . has not the right to decide upon the constitutionality of an act of congress . . ." The gathering also protested against the belief that a State does not have the "right to secede from the union under any circumstances whatever." These principles, the States' Righters declared, are "a gross outrage upon the liberties of the people." [18]

Lamar also sought and secured a license to practice law. For years he had been reading in this field, and in 1833, he was admitted to the Georgia bar.[19]

However, in spite of these efforts, and the backing of a party organization, again he was defeated. It was a frenzied campaign in the midst of which one of Lamar's opponents, John Milton, shot down a political enemy in the streets of Columbus. But neither Milton or Lamar were victors. Seaborn Jones, who had served with Lamar on Troup's staff a few years earlier, won the race.[20]

The months that surrounded his second failure to gain public office brought deep personal tragedy. His sister Evaline Harvey had died in the spring of 1833, and his father, John, died that summer.[21] On July 4, 1834, his brother Lucius committed suicide, a "victim of melancholia." [22]

The two brothers had been close since early boyhood,

and Mirabeau had been an ardent admirer of Lucius. So strong was the emotional bond between the two, that in later years, he could not stand the mention of his brother's name. When the body of the older Lamar son was placed in the grave in Town Cemetery in Milledgeville, Mirabeau Lamar was indeed a stricken man.[23]

He had sold his remaining interest in the *Enquirer* after his political defeat. His own failure in politics, the loss of his wife, and now the death of a sister, his father, and the brother with whom he had been so close made a profound impact upon this man of deeply sensitive spirit.

In addition to all of this, his own health was not good. It was a generally accepted belief of the time that one's physical condition could be improved by a change of surroundings. Lamar subscribed to this conviction and determined that he was ready to travel both as a balm to his spirit and to his physique. He described himself during this period as "miserably dyspeptic and melancholy." [24]

Long fascinated by the reports that had come to him about the country that lay beyond the Sabine River, he began to take an increasing interest in that new land. Claimed by Mexico that had not many years before thrown off its allegiance to Spain, the vast areas north of the Rio Grande River still were sparsely settled. The Mexican government had agreed to permit Anglo settlers to establish themselves in that territory known as Texas, and in growing number, they were doing so.

Lamar's inquisitiveness about that land to the west suddenly became a passion: he was now ready to put an end to his melancholy and go to Texas.

[4]

Land of Fruition

A stagecoach made its way along the winding road from Columbus, Georgia, to Montgomery, Alabama. The darkness of a June night created an uncertain passage for the vehicle. Some object, real or imagined, up ahead in the flickering shadows near a narrow bridge caused the driver to pull suddenly on the reins and the equipage went careening off the road into the darkness below. Lamar was on board as one of the passengers. He later wrote that inside he "felt a sudden jerk and jolt," but all were relieved to discover that the coach had "bounded from the bridge like a living quadruped and safely landed on its four wheels." The driver with some difficulty, was able to get the conveyance back on the road and the travelers arrived in Montgomery, "without further adventure." [1]

Lamar described his first trip to Texas which began with this near mishap in a sixty-eight page document that he called a "Journal of My Travels." He related that he took leave of his friends and relatives in Macon, went on to Columbus, and there "on the 15th of June, 1835, about ten o'clock at night" boarded the stage for Montgomery.[2]

He whimsically recorded much of the detail of this first leg of his journey: the efforts to gain a few minutes of sleep were "interrupted occasionally by a violent collision of skulls" with three other passengers "which only made them 'swear a prayer or two and sleep again.' "[3]

He described his fellow travelers in his trip record: one passenger had been in Texas, but was "so unprepossessing a personage — so full of assumacy[sic] — that I could not brook his acquaintance." The second was an army lieutenant who was "a gentleman of good sense, politeness and handsome attainments."[4] The third was "a warm and generous stranger whose name I wish I could recall."[5]

Thirteen miles out of Columbus, the mishap occurred that nearly caused disaster. However, the travel-accustomed passengers took it all in good spirit, helped get the vehicle back on the road and continued on their way.

Lamar took careful note of the country through which he was passing. Apparently he was already convinced that his destination was a place of tremendous potential. He later wrote that, based on his observations on this trip, the area near Montgomery was much poorer than "Texas, the land of promise and fruition."[6]

It is interesting to observe that his personal papers during this period contain more and more information about Texas. One such document is entitled "Information Obtained From Captain Gaines," which dealt with Nolan's expedition and consists of lengthy notes in Lamar's own hand on the taking of San Antonio in 1813, and the fighting that took place in 1814. He wrote at the conclusion of this paper: "These notes were taken in 1832 — how wonderfully exact do they correspond with those taken from Col. Hall some 15 years afterwards."[7]

There are other papers in the Lamar collection of a similar sort. One concerns the buccaneer, Lafitte, and his activities in Texas.[8] Another was headed "The Origin of the Revo-

Land of Fruition

lution in Texas in 1812.." ⁹ Still another is a sixteen-page letter addressed to Lamar, dated September 3, 1835, signed by J. P. Cole, in which he described the rivers of Texas, the town of San Antonio, and the general terrain and geography of the land.[10]

Mirabeau's own journal of his travels toward Texas continued with a description of Montgomery which he stated was "in a flourishing condition . . . a population upwards of three thousand." [11]

He arrived in Montgomery on June 16, and spent three days in the city with a landlord "whose punch was preferable to his principles." He then took passage on a small steamer, the *Little Rock*, down the Alabama River to Mobile.[12]

In reminiscing about this voyage he later wrote: "A steamboat . . . is not the most favorable place for the formation of friendship or the indulgence of social affection . . . it is different in stage-traveling. For there the passengers are thrown about in such intimate juxtaposition . . . that it is impossible to indulge in haughtiness. I have always found that when the formalities of artificial life are once broken through . . . the heart never fails to develop benevolent and generous passions." [13]

However, the disappointment over lack of sociability on the initial stage of the voyage was corrected when the steamer put into Washington, Alabama. There they picked up a passenger from Putnam County, Georgia, who proved to be a congenial companion with whom Mirabeau was able to recall mutual acquaintances.[14]

The voyage on the *Little Rock* ended when the vessel approached Mobile on a peaceful Sabbath evening after a "heavy storm of rain and lighting had just passed . . . All was silent, tranquil and placid." [15]

In Mobile he had some difficulty securing accommodations. He could not get into the Mansion House, but finally "as the clock struck twelve" was able to get to bed in another hostelry, the Alabama Hotel. He noted that a companion who held military rank had less difficulty than he in securing quarters.[16]

He described Mobile as a town with "a population of ten thousand souls." "A few years ago," he commented, "I found here a little dirty town . . . and now I behold a populous city, reared up as if by magic, like one in a fairy land, with beauty unrivaled." [17]

While awaiting transportation on the next stage of his journey, he spent an evening in nearby Summerville with a friend where he attended a meeting of the Franklin Society. This, he commented, was the "first attempt to establish a literary and scientific institution in the place." He was deeply impressed by what he saw: the society could boast a membership of 100 and a library of 600 volumes and periodicals as well as "a galvanic battery of considerable power and other philosophical apparatus." [18]

However, he could not completely out-travel his own sense of melancholy. On seeing a cemetery, he wrote: "I never pass by a graveyard without stopping to peruse those pathetic records of bereaved friendship and affection." [19] "I mourn afresh the loss of my own sweet flower . . . to forget is guilt and not to weep is worse than ingratitude." [20]

He was finally able to secure a stage from Mobile bound for New Orleans. He recorded that he mounted the box beside the driver apparently better to view the countryside. The coach passed through Summerville, Springhill, and finally reached Portersville on Lake Pontchartrain. There they met a steamboat that took them across the lake to a railroad station where he found, on June 25, that he could ride in only twenty minutes to the "heart of a populous city, destined to be the emporium of half the world." [21]

However, he was disappointed in New Orleans. He was struck by "the extreme filthiness of the place." "It is improbable that a residence in New Orleans in the autumn months can ever be less hazardous than a battle of Waterloo." [22] Obviously the fear of epidemic that did frequently sweep the city was paramount in his mind.

Not only did the lack of cleanliness in the Louisiana metropolis depress him, but he found the city dull. The theaters were closed except for one in the French Quarter. The only play he was able to attend was not to his liking.

However, he found a rather unique form of entertainment in a visit to a local bookstore: there he purchased a copy of John Newland Moffitt's address on the laying of the cornerstone of the Methodist Church in New Orleans. He later sought out this church with the hope of hearing the celebrated pastor who often spoke to packed houses; however, he was disappointed in this, for the Reverend Mr. Moffitt was not in the pulpit that Sunday. He later wrote warmly of his visit to the church: "I felt for the first time that I was among my own Southern countrymen . . . even for the negroes I felt a partiality because they wore the manners of those of my native state." [23] He did not comment in his journal, however, as to whether or not he met the family of the Reverend Mr. Moffitt during his visit. If he had, he would have seen the nine-year-old Henrietta, the pastor's daughter, who was to become his wife some sixteen years later.

He soon made preparations to leave New Orleans and press on toward the west. He commented that the Mississippi River city was then the "home of fifty thousand souls" but that it was destined to soon contain "five hundred thousand." [24]

He decided to go to Texas by the Red River route rather than take the Gulf passage. Apparently his desire to see as much of the land as possible influenced this decision.

On June 30 he took passage on the steamboat *Romeo*, and steamed up the Mississippi toward the mouth of the Red River. His ship, he commented, was "commanded by a *gentleman* named Gurrey. I italicize the word because it can be seldom applied with propriety to persons in his vocation." On the passage up river they could see both "magnificent mansions" and many "indifferent dwellings." [25]

On July 4 they arrived at Natchitoches. There he found that the "Sons of thunder were whooping and carousing . . . drunk as deacons. . . ." He was somewhat taken back by the boisterous welcome he and his fellow travelers received, but he was relieved to find that "the people were only keeping the Fourth of July." However, he did not feel at home with the inhabitants of the town even after he had accepted the unique style of his initial reception. "Never met I with a community more selfish, unfeeling and ready to prey upon the necessities of fellow creatures." [26] His antipathy for the citizens of Natchitoches was likely influenced by his own loss of good health. He became ill with a severe fever, apparently a case of malaria that he had contacted in the Louisiana country. He seems to have blamed his troubles on the city where he became sick, which, he lamented, was a good four hundred miles from New Orleans. He was seriously ill for some time with the chills and fever and other discomforts characteristic of the malady of the swamplands. At last, however, the fever subsided.

"As soon as I was able to ride, I purchased of a stranger from Bastrop an excellent traveling animal and shook from my shoes the dust of this town," wrote Lamar.[27]

He then struck out across land. The first day he was able to travel nine miles to a place where a Mr. Feeman charged him "a bill of one dollar and a quarter" for food and lodging."[28] The next day he was able to travel twenty-five miles to the habitation of "an antiquated lady by the name of Brown." On the third day he crossed the Sabine and lodged with a Mr. Anderson, who had twenty-five children and had been married but twice. "I cannot look upon his achievements in any other light than [as] a praiseworthy effort to settle the southwestern wilds," commented Lamar.[29]

His illness continued to give him difficulty: the fever recurred from time to time. However, he continued on his westward journey sometimes making only a few miles a day. At one point, well within Texas, he stayed with a Mr. Thompson and attended a Methodist camp meeting where "some were in favor of immediate war with the Mexican government." [30]

Still suffering from his illness, he passed through San Augustine, which he noted, was a town that had a population of four hundred. Two days later, on July 22, he reached the city of Nacogdoches.[31] In his journal he recorded the fact that he had traveled 120 miles in one week and that he was now thirty-seven days away from Columbus.³²

He remained in Nacogdoches long enough to recover completely from his fever. He seemed almost convinced that his very presence on Texan soil would bring healing. Then he went on to New Washington, where he claimed that he "was the first to declare publicly in favor of independence of Texas." ³³ Apparently this was an open gathering of the townspeople, and Lamar had an opportunity to exercise his ability as an orator.³⁴

He made it clear in his journal that he was enamored with the country through which he was traveling; he stated that he was ready to stay there and make it his home. He considered himself a citizen of Texas from that time forward, later claiming citizenship based on public statements he had made at the time. In order to qualify for his candidacy for president of the Republic, he was able to produce affidavits proving three years residency from those who had heard him make a declaration of Texan nationality.

However, he felt compelled to return to Georgia at least long enough to settle his affairs there. But he had found the land of promise for which he had been searching!

He staked out a land claim near Cole's settlement and employed a surveyor, Horatio Criesman, to survey his headright. He found the land office closed at San Felipe, but he was able to get assurance from Austin himself, before he left Texas, that he would not forfeit his claim. It was while he was in San Felipe that he met Anson Jones, who was also destined to play a leading role in Texas politics in the years to come. Jones was in the city to attend the General Convention that met soon after Lamar's visit.³⁵

From there he went to Brazoria, where he met the editor of the *Texas Republican* and contributed three poems to the newspaper: "Arms for Your Injured Land," which was an adaptation of "Arms for the Southern Land" that he had written two years before; "Give to the Poet His Well Earned Praise," and a republication of his elegy to Tabitha, "At Evening on the Banks of the Chattahoochee." ³⁶

From Brazoria he went to Velasco, where he helped build a fort in preparation for the military action that was soon to come. While he was there, he received a letter from his brother, Thomas, from Macon, expressing concern over his health and his situation: "I beseech, entreat, implore . . . delay not a moment in writing to us." [37] This plea from home helped hasten his return to Georgia, and he sailed from Velasco in late October, planning an early return to Texas. Even then the battle of San Antonio was in the making, but he did not know this until he was to hear of it after he had reached Georgia.[38]

John T. Lamar wrote home from Velasco, Texas, telling of the conquest of San Antonio by the victorious Texan forces in late 1835 and advising immediate investment in Texas lands.[39] This news must have shortened Mirabeau's stay in Georgia, and he quickly made his preparations to return.

By early April he was back in Velasco. On April 10, 1836, he wrote his brother Jefferson from Harrisburg declaring:

> I leave this place in the morning for the army; a dreadful battle is to be fought in three or four days on the Brazos decisive of the fate of Texas; I shall, of course, have to be in it . . . Texas is in a dreadful state of confusion; the Mexicans thus far are invading . . .[40]

He then told of the reversal of Texan fortunes and the fall of the Alamo; he also related the tragic story of the massacre of Fannin and his army near Goliad. He continued his account:

> I shall reach Houston day after tomorrow, a distance from this place about 50 miles — in the event of my falling in battle, you will find my trunks, papers, etc. in the possession of Mrs. Jane Long who has temporarily fled from Brazoria to Bolivar point at Galveston Bay. The money brought by me to be paid out in lands, I have, of course, in the present confused state of things, not been able to lay out. Government has no authority to sell lands, and from individuals no purchase can be yet made safely. I have therefore been much embarrassed to know what to do with so large a sum of money; it is too dangerous to keep it about me, especially as

I am going into battle. After due consideration, I have placed it in the hands of Lorenzo Zavala, the vice president of the Government, the most responsible and probably the most honest among them. His receipt for the money I know not how to dispose of other than to keep it about me with instructions to Wm. D. Redd to take it to you in the event of my falling and his escaping. The amt. placed in Zavala's hands is six thousand dollars . . . It is true I might fly precipitately to the U.S. and return them their money without trusting it to anyone here or exposing myself to danger — but a course so unpatriotic and disgraceful I know they (the gentlemen) would not require of me . . . I also peril my life, I am confident they will acquit me of any selfish disregard of their interest.[41]

Lamar was the bearer of land investment funds put together by his brothers and friends in the hope of gaining early access to valuable Texas lands.

However, he had other concerns in his return to Texas: "If I fall I shall leave . . . a will which you will have to execute . . . my health at present is good," he continued. "I feel much solicitude for my mother; if she was well and cheerful and could hear of affliction with fortitude I should be happy. Tell Rebecca Ann that she must learn to write, read and spell well and that is the best education." [42]

Lamar's interest in owning a portion of Texas and in becoming a permanent resident was clear in this letter. "I have petitioned to Government for my league of land as a citizen of Texas in 1835," he stated. "But the Gov[ernment] will do nothing in it. I think, however, the testimony of Hoxey and Christman, the Surveyor, of my intention to return to the Country as a citizen, will hereafter secure the land when the war is over." [43]

Lamar was now ready for battle. He had written these words a few months earlier when he became aware that he would likely be involved in military conflict:

> I only sigh for the laurel-wreath
>   That a patriot wins in DANGER
> Speed, speed the day when to war I hie
>   The fame of the field is waiting.[44]

The field that was waiting would be that of the plain of San Jacinto.

But Lamar was back in Texas and he was willing to live — or die if need be — in what he had sometime before declared to be "the land of fruition."

[5]

The Nero of the Present Day

Darkness did not bring serenity when the sun finally set on that April evening on the plain of San Jacinto; it merely lessened the confusion which followed the battle. The bitter exasperation that had turned the Texans into fiendish seekers of revenge waned as exhaustion overtook them. However, the horror of the aftermath of the conflict remained.

There was a bright moon over the plain that night: its pale glow intensified the fearsome terror apparent there. The bodies of over six hundred slain Mexicans lay in disarray at and near the field. There were perhaps another two hundred who had been severely wounded, many of whom were writhing in death agony; their moans added to the disquietude of the night. Some had made their escape from the battle site toward a bridge cut on Houston's command that had spanned Vince's Bayou several miles distant. There in the brush many had been run down by the pursuing Texans. It was a place of eeriness as the dead and the dying lay where they had fallen. Packs of wolves roamed about and raised their howls to the moonlit sky as they sought after and occasionally fought for the carcasses of the slain. There was little rest for either the exhausted victors or the conquered.

Houston himself had received a serious wound in his foot. However, his victory was complete in military terms: the opposing army had been destroyed and only a handful of his men had been killed or wounded.

But the army of Santa Anna was not the only Mexican force that had been in the field. Somewhere beyond the bayous were other detachments commanded by able and experienced soldiers such as the Italian Filisola and General Urrea. Sam Houston's army numbered no more than 900 Texans. Some estimates range as high as 4,000 for the total size of the Mexican force still in Texas and potentially ready to confront the victors of San Jacinto.

Houston gave the order to find Santa Anna: this would be the key to Texan security. Victory could only be assured if the wily Mexican dictator could be captured.

As the morning of the day after the battle dawned, no accounting had yet been made for the fugitive general. Could he have escaped and somehow made his way through the ranging Texan patrols to join his fellow countrymen? Would it not then be possible for him to unite his divided forces and bring the full power of his wrath to bear upon them? These were certainly frightening possibilities that could have made the victory at San Jacinto short-lived and meaningless.

Prisoners were still being rounded up during the morning hours of April 22. Hastily built stockades had been erected to hold these stunned soldiers from the south. Aware that their lives could easily be forfeited to the men who had shouted "*Remember the Alamo! Remember Goliad!*" on the day before, they surrendered meekly, singly and in small groups.

The briskness of morning had given way to the warmth of a spring afternoon when the hoped for happened. One of the Texan guards heard a prisoner exclaim: "El Presidente!" An unimposing soldier had been captured and brought with other prisoners to the stockade. The imprudent exclamation of the Mexican had betrayed the identity of the newly captured prisoner.

At last Santa Anna, the president of Mexico, was in Texan hands. When the news was known, a cheer went up from the guards and was soon taken up by the entire army. The Mexican commander was quickly brought to Sam Houston, who had propped himself up on a mattress nearby to nurse his wounded foot. Antonio Lopez de Santa Anna now stood before the victor of San Jacinto.

Here was the guarantee for the Texans that the carnage of the day before would not have been in vain. Filisola and Urrea would hardly dare attack as long as the *Comandante* was a prisoner.

But what do you do with a captured president? This was the question that had to be decided.

The first task, however, was that of bringing some sort of order out of the disarray of battle. The field had to be cleared of dead and wounded. Military equipment and supplies that could be highly valuable to the poorly equipped Texans were sought. Some 600 muskets, 300 sabers, 200 pistols and several hundred mules were added to Texan resources. In addition nearly $12,000 in specie was discovered in the discarded baggage of the enemy. There were also ample supplies of ammunition and powder. These were catalogued hurriedly and stored near the prisoner's stockade.

Lamar must have been active in these operations. But the tragedy of battle had had its impact upon him in a personal way. One of his close friends, Benjamin Bringham, had been severly wounded and became one of the few Texans to die as a result of the fighting. After his burial on April 24, Lamar wrote these words as a final tribute to his comrade in arms:

> Beautiful in death
> The soldier's corpse appears,
> Embalmed by fond affection's breath,
> And bathed in his country's tears.[1]

Even after the dead had been buried, there was still much that had to be done. David G. Burnet had been named provisional president of the Republic and Lorenzo de Zavala vice-president by the delegates who had assembled in early March at Washington-on-the-Brazos. These two men arrived at San Jacinto soon after the battle, and began to make preparations to cull from the confusion of events some sort of official order.

Sam Houston's leadership had been paramount up to this point; now this was temporarily suspended by the severity of his wound. Since there were no means of adequately treating him in Texas, Doctor Ewing, his physician, recommended that he should be taken to New Orleans as soon as possible for surgery. By May 11, a schooner had been located that could take the wounded commander back to the United States. There he received adequate treatment and by June 4 he was able to write to Lamar: "My wound has improved. Some twenty or more pieces of bone have been taken out of it." [2]

In the meantime important decisions had to be made in Texas. Burnet enlarged his cabinet by inviting Lamar to become Secretary of War.[3] The cabinet then moved to nearby Velasco, where discussions began with Santa Anna that were to lead to the treaty that Texans were to consider an end to the war with Mexico. Lamar expressed his convictions over the serious problems before them in a letter that he addressed to the president and the cabinet on May 12.

While Santa Anna "has been considered by most of the Cabinet exclusively as a prisoner of war, I have been disposed," declared the newly named War Secretary, "to regard him more as an apprehended murderer."[4] He believed that the Mexican president "has forfeited his life by the greatest of all crimes and is not a suitable object for the exercise of our pardoning prerogative."[5] However, he felt that he and the other prisoners could be held until the end of hostilities in order to negotiate "an exchange of prisoners according to rank and number."[6]

His practical recognition of the complexities of the situation, however, made him add this statement:

> If they [the prisoners] can be of any possible use in bringing about a recognition of our independence, it must be in this way . . . as prisoners of war; it is to their interest to forward our views . . . but if we should release them upon the

strength of any pledges which they might make, we turn loose an inveterate enemy . . . Hence I vote for their detention as prisoners.[7]

He stated his convictions about Santa Anna in strong terms: the Mexican president was "the Nero of the present day . . . the foe of all virtue . . . the cold blooded butcherer of our friends and brethren." [8]

He concluded that all captives should be treated as prisoners of war except Santa Anna, who "is guilty of the most exalted crimes —perfidy and murder" and he should "hang upon a gallows as high as Haman's . . . his crimes being sanguinary I would read his punishment from the code of DRACO." [9]

Two days later the Treaty of Velasco was signed between Burnet's cabinet and Santa Anna. The Mexican president acknowledged in this agreement that the war was ended, all Mexican troops were to be withdrawn beyond the Rio Grande, and private property taken from Texans was to be restored.

But the discussions at Velasco went further than the openly acknowledged pact. There was a proposal that Santa Anna be allowed to return to Mexico and use his influence there to secure Mexican recognition for Texan independence. This was in keeping with a pledge for the Mexican's personal safety that Sam Houston was supposed to have given him before he had departed for New Orleans. It was this that Lamar violently opposed. He believed that as a prisoner Santa Anna should be retained until all hostilities were over and then be tried as a war criminal. It was because of his opposition to this part of the agreement that he refused to sign the treaty when he was asked to do so. However, a majority of the cabinet agreed to it and only Lamar and Zavala withheld their signatures.[10]

The treaty, along with the continued detention of Santa Anna, did end the immediate threat of hostility. Early in June the battalions which had been awaiting developments in

Texas returned to Mexico. For the time, at least, the threat of Mexican military power was abated.

Two schools of thought quickly developed in regard to the disposition of the imprisoned general. One was the view that was endorsed by Houston, which contended that Santa Anna back in Mexico would aid Texas since that land was then given to frequent disorder: the general would only add to the instability of the situation. Being discredited by his defeat at San Jacinto, he could not immediately resume leadership, but he could foment difficulty that would result in greater security for Texas by the simple fact that a nation with internal turmoil cannot readily invade another. The other line of thinking was one which held that the Mexican dictator should be put to death for his crimes. While Lamar agreed with this point of view, he wanted proper judicial process. When a mob stormed the prison seeking to lynch Santa Anna, Lamar personally helped save the dictator's life. He later wrote about this incident: "I jumped up immediately and rebuked the mob for their outrage."[11] He was able to calm the passions of the potential assassins and help restore peace.[12]

It was almost certainly because of this event that Santa Anna asked Lamar to come and talk with him in his prison near Columbia. Stephen Austin arranged the meeting between the two and urged Lamar to converse with the captive president. When the two met, the Mexican asked that the Texan direct a letter to the army urging that he be granted freedom. After a few moments of silence, Lamar replied with a strong refusal to do so. Austin reported that as he left, Santa Anna, remembering a vice-president who had betrayed him, remarked, "There goes the shadow of Farias."[13]

Later, when consideration was being given to sending Santa Anna to the United States, Lamar presided over the Senate as vice-president where the matter was vigorously debated. "Send him to Washington with an Escort and the moment he sets foot on the soil of the U.S. . . . he is free . . ." declared S.H. Everitt.[14] The Senate then passed a resolution requiring that Houston consult with the Senate on the terms of releasing Santa Anna. This Houston did not do. He ignored the Senate action, gave the defeated general a good horse, and sent him to the United States escorted by Colonel Barnard E. Bee. Once he was out of Texas he immediately borrowed two thousand dollars from Bee to improve his wardrobe: this made it possible for him to travel back to Mexico in a style in keeping with the dignity of the office of president of a nation. But once back in his homeland, the thoroughly discredited dictator could not muster sufficient strength to ever again be a serious threat to the youthful Republic of Texas.

[6]

General For a Day

The Guadalupe River begins in the rocky hill country of Texas. It winds its way past rugged bluffs in uneven uplands, then gently pours itself into rolling country to finally emerge as a placid effluence as it reaches the coastal plain. In the year 1836, because of the heavy spring rains, it had become a mighty stream. The army of Texas had moved from San Jacinto, across the Brazos and the Colorado rivers toward the direction from which enemy troops might be expected to come: it encamped on the banks of the Guadalupe near the frontier village of Victoria.

By June this was no longer the rugged force of daring men who had withstood the Mexican tide at San Jacinto. Many of that original band of some 900 men had left to go back home and repair the damage done to land and homes during their months of absence. In the meantime news of the fantastic victory in Texas had spread to the United States. By the hundreds, new recruits had come. They had landed at Velasco, Galveston, and at other Texas ports. Some had traveled overland. They had come by ship, by wagon, by foot. By now the Army of Texas was more than double its number when it had engaged in its brief moment of bloody conflict; but few of these men had participated in the event of April 21.

When Houston had left Texas, he had entrusted the leadership of his command to Thomas Rusk. Rusk, in turn, had turned to Burnet, asking that some sort of official government action be taken toward the army. The constantly increasing hordes of volunteers were rapidly precipitating a crisis. Many of those who came wanted to see something happen and were willing to create action even when the necessity of such did not exist. Here was a band of adventurers flushed with the excitement of a victory in which most of them had no part, seeking some form of diversion from the humdrum activities of life back home. Clearly this was a potentially volatile situation.

This mob of men camped on the banks of the Guadalupe had to be fed in some fashion, they had to be given some sort of supplies, and above all else, there had to be some form of disciplinary control.

Burnet looked about for a solution and decided that his answer was Mirabeau Lamar. He was Secretary of War and was well aware of the problems that the burgeoning Texas military establishment possessed. Rusk had written Lamar at length on June 1 about the needs of the army, and he ended his communication with a request that he be given information on just how the government planned to raise funds for the militia.[1]

Lamar had considered returning to the United States. A friend in Victoria, William Redd, had heard rumors that the Secretary of War was about to leave Texas; he wrote strongly urging him to delay his trip to Georgia because of the critical situation in the army of the newly born republic.[2]

On June 25, Burnet commissioned Lamar "to the rank and office of Major General in the Army and Commander-in-chief of all the forces in the service of Texas." [3]

"We have appointed the late Secty of War, the Hon. M.B. Lamar to command the army," stated Burnet in a letter dated July 8. He went on to indicate the reason for his decision: "He acquired a deserved popularity in camp and I believe his appointment will meet with general satisfaction."[4]

Lamar accepted the position and began almost immediately to receive suggestions for handling his new responsibility. John Chenoweth and a John Turner wrote to Lamar asking that army forces be deterred from driving away their cattle for the use of the Texan military force and their Mexican prisoners. Apparently they were especially unhappy that their beef was being used to feed the enemy.[5] Lamar responded to Chenoweth's protest by stating that he had ordered a stop to the practice of driving cattle out of the area for any purpose: at the time, however, it is doubtful that this order meant much of anything to anyone.[6]

Lamar made preparations for personally taking over the leadership of the army. A Colonel Macomb wrote to him on July 13 accepting appointment to Lamar's staff.[7] The tone of the papers in his personal files indicates that he already considered himself as functioning as the army's field marshal.

The rumors of a fresh Mexican invasion were still flying about. Burnet himself wrote Lamar on June 27, only two days after he had appointed him commander-in-chief, informing him that there was news of armies from south of the Rio Grande moving into Texas.[8]

As a response to Burnet's warning, Lamar prepared a communiqué to the army that he planned soon to join as its leader:

> On assuming the glorious responsibility of leading Texas to the field of battle, I feel deeply, vividly aware . . . that to command an army of heroes is the highest honor that can be conferred upon a soldier because it is the highest privilege a soldier can enjoy and the highest aspiration a soldier can make. The enemy are about to countermarch upon our territory. They come with the foul purpose of again desolating our beautiful country. The Spirits of Travis, of Fannin and their gallant company whose blood has consecrated [words obscured] the foundations of our freedom summons you to the field . . . Soldiers your country calls you to her

defense . . . the call is *en masse*: let all obey and all will be well.⁹

Before he left to take active command of the army, Lamar handled considerable correspondence as Secretary of War. Memucan Hunt, a friend from Georgia, wrote from on board a schooner in Galveston Bay. He sought high military appointment and urged the Secretary's assistance in this. He then urged that Lamar "remain in Texas until the storm is over." [10] This was obviously another reference to Lamar's plan to go back to Georgia for a visit. However, at this time, he had no thought of such a journey.

Another interesting piece of correspondence of this time was a letter from James Hamilton, dated in late June, in which he introduced Barnard E. Bee to "Colonel Mirabeau Lamar, Secretary of War." [11] This was an introduction that was to have a profound effect upon both Lamar and the Republic in the years ahead as the two would play important roles in the later history of the nation. Bee was the man who would escort Santa Anna out of Texas, an act that Lamar opposed. However, in the years ahead, Bee became a trusted servant of the government that Lamar would later head.

But by late June, the secretary was ready to become a field general. In early July he packed his saddle bags and began the trip through the warm coastal plains amid mesquite and brush to the Texas camp on the Guadalupe. By July 14 he was with the army that he had been appointed to command.

His first impression upon arriving in camp was a highly negative one. He later reported that there he found a motley band of undisciplined recruits rather than either a determined army of heroes or an effective militia. He complained about what was apparently open insubordination and the complete absence of any form of discipline among the men who were carousing on the Guadalupe.[12] Texas was in dire straits if this was the army that would have to withstand a well organized countermarch of the enemy troops who had so recently left Texas.

Rusk was still on hand and maintained no more than a

tenuous command over the rapidly deteriorating situation. Lamar conferred with him and with Felix Huston. It was now clear that the camp leaders at Victoria did not fully recognize the authority of Burnet's government. The action of appointing a commander of the army was considered "unceremonious interference" in the affairs of the military even though this had been done by the only government that Texas then had.[13] There was a tradition that was operative particularly among militia units of the southern United States that permitted soldiers to select their own leaders; this concept influenced the situation. Lamar accepted this postulate and agreed that the validity of his generalship of the army would be put to a vote by the men in the ranks.

An assembly was called in the camp. Lamar was presented to his men; he was allowed to speak. Then a vote was taken to accept or reject him as commander of the army. The tellers were able to count 179 votes in his favor; the oposition to him could only be estimated at something in excess of 1,500.[14]

Some years later crusty old Sam Houston was to chuckle over this event. He gave Lamar credit for only 116 votes out of some 2,000 and commented sarcastically in a letter that he wrote for publication: "Thus was unGeneraled the veritable 'hero of San Jacinto.' "[15]

Apparently by now the rumors of immediate attack by a powerful enemy had proved to be false. Lamar accepted the vote of the men in the ranks of the citizen army and withdrew his claim to command. He wrote Rusk a letter "with a view to restoring private friendship and public tranquility."[16] Apparently he did not blame Rusk for his rejection by the men encamped at Victoria.

On July 17 he reported to Burnet about "insubordination in the Army." He related that he had been told upon his arrival in camp that he would not be accepted as commander. He did state that "Rusk, Green and Felix Huston . . . [had] . . . carried the popular currant against me." He was convinced that he had worked out his relationship to Rusk, but he believed that courts-martial should be meted out to Green and Felix Huston.[17]

Lamar had been general for a day — if that! He left camp and for the time being resolved to give up public life. The immediate crisis seemed to have passed, and he was ready to turn to personal concerns. He took up residence in Brazoria in a rooming house run by a Mrs. Long and turned his attention to acquiring Texas land for himself and his friends with the money that he had brought to Texas earlier in the year.[18] He had received several letters in May from acquaintances asking that he help them in investments in the real estate of the new republic.[19] His advice was sought later by those who were seeking to purchase land both for speculative purposes and for permanent homesites.[20] Although there is considerable correspondence in this portion of his personal papers concerning land purchase and the value of Texas properties, there is no indication that he made serious efforts to acquire any sizable tracts of real estate for himself. Almost certainly his own lack of capital was the reason for this; however, his advice was widely sought by those who trusted his judgment in such potential transactions. His chief concern was simply that of establishing himself in Texas and assisting as many of his friends as possible to become a part of a new nation.

In 1835 he had begun a collection of papers about Texas. This was eventually to result in the massive Lamar Papers that are preserved today in the Texas State Archives and that constitute a major source of information about the formative years of Texas as a nation. His continuing interest in history is apparent in the wide range of materials that he collected: it includes accounts by others about past events, current information and a host of letters and notes that had come to him. Battles and events relating to Texas in the past, geographical information gathered from many sources about the region, records of early settlements along with many personal documents are among these papers. The collection includes Lamar's own personal correspondence, information about family matters, official letters and documents relating both to significant and to relatively unimportant matters. It was during his less active periods that he generally added the largest number of materials to this interesting compilation.[21]

A new avenue of service, however, was soon to develop for Lamar. Burnet wrote to him on August 8 suggesting that he consider the possibility of running for office.[22] A few days before, on July 23, the provisional president had issued a proclamation calling for an election to choose a president, a vice-president, a congress and to ratify a constitution. This was in keeping with the provisions specified by the delegates to the gathering at Washington-on-the-Brazos in March when Texas had been declared to be an independent nation.

In spite of his rejection by the recruits to the army in camp, Lamar was still a prominent figure and he could boast of having many influential friends. Thomas Buford had written to him from Nacogdoches just before this that the former Georgian was "very popular in all Texas."[23] Richard Royall had penned a similar letter at about the same time expressing the high regard in which he believed the former secretary of war was held in the Republic.[24]

Lamar consulted with Burnet about the possibility of his becoming a candidate for the office of vice-president of the Republic. The provisional president replied:

> Yours was received last evening. I have been writing all the morn and my digits of the dexter hand really ache with over much fatigue — I have not heard of any one for V.P. — and would be well pleased to see you in that honorable position. But the newness of your migration to this land of immigrants, may present an obstacle to your success — many people would prefer an old Settler to a new one without reference to qualifications — Austin I doubt not will be elected and will do well . . . I have no later news of much interest from the army . . . they are much bothered there . . . in great haste . . .[25]

In spite of the fact that the immediate threat of invasion had subsided, there was widespread concern about the situation that existed in the army. P.H. Bell wrote to Lamar in early September that the Texas militia was in a "disorgan-

General for a Day 47

ized, unsettled condition." He urged Lamar to seek office as a means of remedying the problem before the new nation; he promised to work in his behalf.[26] His friends believed that he was needed in office even though he was still a newcomer. Apparently there were many who were convinced that Lamar could lend a steadying hand to the uncertain tossings and turnings of the Republic of Texas.

Convinced that he could render a service to Texas, he decided to accept the challenge and run for office. Once having made this decision, he began to actively seek the vice-presidency. His only serious opponent was Thomas Rusk, who made little effort to support his own candidacy. When all of the votes had been counted, Lamar won over the man who had been partly responsible for his loss of the position of commander-in-chief of the Texan armies by a margin of ten to one.[27]

Sam Houston won easily as president of the new nation and Lamar received a total of 2,699 votes as vice-president.[28] For the next two years he was to serve in that capacity under the presidency of the man who had been his commander at San Jacinto.

[7]

Generous Indulgence

Two small frame buildings stood beneath live oak trees at the end of a muddy lane. It was the fall of 1836. The heavy rains that had been an unusual characteristic of that year in a land that often knew prolonged droughts continued to make travel difficult. But, in spite of that fact and the distances to be traversed, this tiny village which had been given the impressive name "Columbia" was soon full of visitors. It was here that the first constitutionally established government of a nation was about to assemble.

Nearby the Brazos River cut a wide swath in the land. Rising in the rugged breaks just below the high plains, this stream was one of the dominant features of the geography of Texas. When Houston had chosen to take his remnant army across the Brazos to the coastal plains in the face of an advancing enemy earlier that year, there were many who felt that the Texan cause was forever lost. Perhaps it was appropriate that the new nation should inaugurate itself near the banks of that surging and muddy stream.

The election that had been held in September had not

only produced a president and a vice-president, but fourteen senators and twenty-nine congressmen. They gathered in the new capital on October 3, and prepared to begin the gigantic task of creating a stable government from the raw materials of a frontier society.

In spite of the diverse personalities of the men involved in this venture and the differences that they had already exhibited, there seemed to be an initial spirit of cooperation. All were well aware that the undertaking before them was tremendous in scope and full of countless difficulties. Within two weeks of the first assemblage of congress, the ad interim president and vice-president had duly submitted their resignations, and a ceremony of inauguration was set for the newly elected leaders of the nation.

This event was scheduled for four o'clock in the afternoon of October 22. The fall sunshine that shown that day after weeks of stormy weather was symbolic of the high hopes of those who gathered there; this appeared to many present as something of an omen of hope.

Just after Sam Houston was ceremoniously installed as the chief executive, Mirabeau B. Lamar stepped forward to accept his position in the new government.

Lamar was given an opportunity to speak and he took advantage of the occasion: "Permit me to embrace this opportunity of expressing my unfeigned acknowledgement of the free suffrages of my fellow citizens in having elected me to the honorable situation of vice president of this Republic," he stated.[1]

He then enthusiastically entered into the theme of common cooperation for the good of Texas: "Let all private feuds be buried in the public good," he continued. He then gave a bit of sober advice: "Let unbiased reason be your guide — moral rectitude your only policy — and the public good your only object . . ." He concluded his relatively brief statement with these words: "Let our bright motto be God and our Country."[2]

Two days later Lamar made his first address to the newly

constituted Senate. Apparently the first press corps of Texas was on hand, for this speech was printed in an early November edition of the *Telegraph and Texas Register*. In this statement the vice-president voiced a dramatic warning against what he considered one of the great evils of sound government: "Do you ask what it is?" he rhetorically inquired. "I answer PARTY; by which I mean the organization of a greater or smaller number of people for the political elevation of favorite individuals and for the support of measures, originating in passion or interest . . . Liberty has not a greater foe, nor despotism a better friend." The existence of partisan politics, he declared, "always implies something selfish . . . Party is as cruel as the grave . . . let us all profit by the lesson and flee the danger." [3] This was, indeed, an uncluttered age and Lamar was an idealistic politician.

The congress continued in session only long enough to take care of the necessary task of setting up some form of national government; then they adjourned to get back to the more immediate business of hewing an existence from the unsettled land.

Lamar began to make immediate plans to return to the United States. He had seriously considered doing this soon after the Battle of San Jacinto, but his appointment as general of the army, and his later venture into the political arena, had caused him to delay these plans. Possibly he now felt he could make the trip he had long considered important to his personal affairs.

In November 1836, Thomas Rusk knew about Lamar's plans for the journey to Georgia. He wrote promising "the notes" that the new vice-president had wanted. These were probably historical data that he was continually adding to his collection of papers. "If you come by Nacogdoches," wrote Rusk, "I will hand them to you then. If you do not, I will enclose them to you to Milledgeville, Georgia." [4] This letter is also interesting in that it clearly indicates that whatever breach there may have appeared to be between the two over the question of the commandership of the army was now healed. The two men remained friends: this despite the fact that they had been nominal opponents for the office Lamar then held.

Lamar was still in Columbia in early December when he received a letter from J.T. Fanning who wrote from Louisiana urging him "to make such arrangements as to take New Orleans on your route to the East." [5]

Although there is no extant record of Lamar's whereabouts in the early weeks of 1837, it is highly probable that he did accept the invitation to visit New Orleans. Friends in Georgia and Alabama were uncertain as to his activities during this time. In March 1837, Thomas Wilson addressed a letter to him from Marion, Alabama, in a rather interesting form: "General M.B. Lamar, Texas, care of Col. Houston." [6] If old Sam had seen that salutation, he would have doubtless had some pungent remarks to make as to just who held the higher rank! However, the contents of this epistle are equally intriguing. "I have been extremely anxious to hear from you," Wilson wrote. Lamar's arrival in Augusta had been announced in the papers, he stated, but then he had heard that the Texan vice-president was still in the Republic. He then declared rumor "has you bound hand and foot by the silken chain of Hymen!" [7]

Probably Lamar had begun his journey eastward, but had tarried in New Orleans. That city had both intrigued and frightened him on his first visit. He had formed friendships there and had found the southern Louisiana city congenial to his way of life. The letter from Fanning, Wilson's letter, and the obscurity of events in this period of Lamar's life would indicate a protracted stay in the Cresent City.[8] Possibly the lonely widower had interests there had nothing to do with either politics or business! Personable and outgoing, he could readily charm the opposite sex. Apparently this he did in the romantic city of New Orleans.

However, by May he had shaken off the silken chain and had reached Columbus, Georgia. Considerable correspondence was addressed to him there during the month and throughout the summer.

During these months in the United States, Lamar was invited to public dinners on frequent occasions and given the opportunity to exercise his oratorical abilities.[9]

A public dinner in his honor was held on July 4, 1837, in Columbus. A nineteen-page manuscript carefully written and stitched together, records his speech at this event. It began with these words: "Friends, and Fellow citizens, surely I have great reason to love the people of Columbus. They have been ever indulgent to my errors and more than just to all my virtues . . ." He declared that he had "no treasure but a quiet conscience . . ." He praised "the country of my adoption . . . Texas" that is "well worthy of all the sympathies which have been excited in her behalf. . ." "I feel it my duty to be there," he continued. He related at some length the injustices he believed Mexico had perpetrated on Texas, and then told in glowing terms the story of the successful revolution in which, he claimed, "ten thousand disciplined veterans" were defeated by "a little band of Spartan heroes." [10] Perhaps this apparent exaggeration of the odds could be excused as a bit of poetic license.

On July 6 the *Columbus Enquirer* described the day: "The thunder of deep mouthed cannon announced that the National jubilee had come." There was a parade with fife and drum music, a prayer, the reading of the Declaration of Independence and an oration with a dinner in Lamar's honor.

His speech was described as one that "for vivid and descriptive eloquence, poetic imagery and patriotic sentiment, was unsurpassed by any similar event." "It received," declared the reporter, "immense cheering." [11]

While Lamar was enjoying this attention as a favorite son who had made good in a new nation, he was receiving letters urging him to return to Texas.

Sam Houston wrote asking him to return so that he could be relieved of responsibilities in order that he could attend to some personal affairs.[12] This letter from his superior was immediately acknowledged; he replied on July 7 stating, "your polite and friendly letter recalling me to Texas . . . [was received] . . . I have not arranged my unsettled business, but there is no sacrifice I am not willing to make for our common country." [13]

Another letter written by a P. Grayson just before this had urged Lamar's return as soon as practical and stated that the vice-president was needed in Texas because of the "confusion of public affairs" and the "inaction of congress." [14]

In September, the Senate took formal, but secret action authorizing the president pro tem to write Lamar "requesting and enjoining" his return. [15]

Other letters about this same time made the same request. [16] "Your friends desire your immediate return . . . [and] . . . your country demands it," wrote Major Handy on October 4. [17]

Apparently there were many who considered Lamar's presence to be a steadying and calming influence upon the affairs of the youthful nation.

Lamar canceled some invitations for public dinners and engagements and made his way back to Texas. He went first to Mobile, and by October 14, he was on his way to the west. He missed his boat at New Orleans and once more tarried there for a time. While in the Louisiana city he received a letter in which there was a hint of danger to his life: the rumor was that a gang of desperadoes employed by his enemies was lurking in wait for him along the overland route. [18] However, Lamar did not take this seriously. He traveled by way of San Augustine, where a banquet was held in his honor, and then went on to the newly established capital city, Houston.

On November 9, he made a speech "on resuming his seat as president of the Senate." He thanked them for their "kind and generous indulgence" for the time he had taken in "settling my private affairs preparatory to a final removal of my interest to this, the beautiful land of my adoption and affection." [19]

He concluded with these words: "For our country God hath done much; let us not be written in the history of these times that we have done nothing." [20]

[8]

Oak Grove on the Brazos

Robert Eden Handy had found an oak grove on the banks of the Brazos River that he thought would be to Lamar's liking. It was a pleasant spot on the edge of the flourishing town of Richmond. Vaguely reminiscent of similar scenes in the Georgian's home state, it had about it the comfortable atmosphere necessary for the setting of a gracious home. Ever since his first journey to Texas, the newly elected vice-president had been looking for a place to build a permanent residence. The boarding house in Brazoria had been headquarters for him during his early months in the new Republic. But he longed for some place where he could feel that he had become an established part of the land. He had asked his friend, Handy, to locate a plot of ground for him, and had entrusted him with the responsibility of finding one to his liking.

On February 17, 1838, Handy wrote from Richmond to Lamar, who was then in Houston, describing the site he had chosen: "I . . . have consulted a mechanic in regard to your house . . . I will, if possible, have it finished for you within two months — I have selected your lot near the River — a little removed from the bustle of our Village. We hope however to see you shortly." [1]

Handy superintended the building of the low frame house; this was the principal residence on the property that Lamar later called "The Oak Grove." This structure was under construction in the early months of 1838 and was occupied before summer. When Rebecca, Lamar's daughter, visited there later in the year, she wrote in her diary: "The place where Papa lives is beautiful, it has a great many shady trees in the yard." [2]

Finances were always a problem for Lamar. He had a small inheritance that had come to him after the death of his brother Jefferson. However, in order to build the new home and buy the land, he had to borrow $2,000 from his cousin Gazaway Lamar. With this he was able to establish a small plantation type home complete with slaves who worked the fields nearby and performed other necessary chores. At first he had a female slave and one male, Black John. Later he added two others.[3]

In his correspondence with R.E. Handy concerning the construction of the home near Richmond, he frankly admitted the problems of his financial condition. Handy replied with the confident words of a staunch admirer: "You say that you are a 'bankrupt' — I am happy to know that you are at least rich in the affections of the people." [4] In any case Lamar settled in the home on the Brazos and made the Oak Grove his headquarters.

Lamar's wide variety of interests was apparent in his activities at this time. One of these was that of establishing a newspaper in Texas. A letter from a friend in Georgia in October of 1837 wished Lamar success in such a project and stated: "I hope that your Press may promote the cause of Liberty and Truth in Texas . . ." [5]

Printing equipment was secured by Lamar, but he was never able to begin publication. On January 25, 1838, he entered into a contract with Leger and Thompson in which he loaned them "the press, printing materials and paper now at

Velasco" on the condition that they be returned when demanded.[6] Perhaps his financial situation had much to do with postponing his plans to reenter the publication field.

However, another project that did not involve ready capital was being promoted by him. Shortly after his return to Texas in 1837, he had issued a call for a gathering of interested persons for the purpose of establishing a philosophical society in Texas. His visit with the association operating in Mobile, Alabama, some two years before, undoubtedly inspired this action.

The organization was formally constituted on December 5, 1837. Lamar was elected president and Congressman Anson Jones was made vice-president along with other such notables as Surgeon General Ashbell Smith, Secretary of State Irion, Speaker of the House Joseph Rowe. Smith, Irion, and Rowe were men who had been trained as physicians. David S. Kaufman, a Nacogdoches lawyer, was also named to the top echelon of the society. Former president Burnet and W. Fairfax Gray, clerk of the Supreme Court, were secretaries; Attorney General Birdsall was librarian.

There were twenty-six charter members of the society; this constituted most of the intelligentsia of the young Republic. The majority of these men were extremely well educated for their time and most were professional men.

They drew up an impressive statement about their aims in which they called upon

> Intelligent and patriotic citizens to furnish to the rising generation the means of instruction within our own borders, where our children . . . may be indoctrinated in sound principles and inbibe with their education respect for their country's laws, love of her soil and veneration for her institutions. We have endeavored to respond to this call by the formation of this society, with the hope that if not to us, to our sons and successors it may be given to make the star, the single star of the west, as resplendent for all the acts that adorn civilized life as it is now glorious in military renown. Texas has her captains, let her have her wise men![7]

This flowing statement has about it the Lamarian touch.

It was his conviction that the time had come to establish within the frontier nation a strong basis for learning and culture. This became a recurrent theme in his orations and his written statements.

A fascinating description of Lamar was written by Francis R. Lubbock during this period, giving an interesting indication of the life-style of the vice-president. Lubbock declared him to be "in the prime of life and [with] the halo of his glory won at San Jacinto." He recorded this picture of Lamar:

> He was a man of French type, five feet seven or eight inches high, with dark complexion, black long hair inclined to curl, and gray eyes, Lamar was peculiar in his dress; wore his clothes very loose, his pants being of that old style, very baggy and with large pleats, looking odd, as he was the only person I ever saw in Texas in that style of dress. I found the Vice-President rather reserved in conversation; it was said, however, that he was quite companionable with his intimate friends. He had proved his soldiership at San Jacinto — he was now trying the role of statesman.[8]

Lamar did not consider his responsibilities as vice-president as very demanding, and spent little time at the capital which then was the city of Houston. His newly established home at Richmond was not too far distant; he could reach the political center of the nation in a reasonable time if necessary. On one occasion he wrote that he felt that his position was "plain and simple . . . of easy execution." [9]

His reluctance to stay in Houston may indicate the growing breach that was becoming apparent between him and the president. In spite of this, however, Houston wrote these words in January 1838, to Lamar: "I pray that you may soon be able to come to the seat of Government. It is very important for me to leave here for the East. My affairs are going to wreck." [10]

However, when the Senate was in session he was on hand to preside. In April 1838, he delivered an address to that body in which he greeted them on the "resumption of your legislative duties." He expressed concern in this statement over what he declared to be "manifestations on the part of the

Mexican government to resume hostilities." He concluded with "confidence in your integrity, patriotism and abilities." [11]

A later address delivered in Houston, probably at a public dinner, echoed these same sentiments in which he called for men of consistent and honorable character. Perhaps here he was feeling the pinch of the obvious breach with his chief executive. He concluded this statement with these words:

> What constitutes a State? Not high raised battlements, labored mount . . . [but] men, high minded men, men who their duties know, but know their rights and knowing dare maintain them.[12]

In the midst of these activities a pleasant interlude occurred for Lamar when his eleven-year-old daughter, Rebecca Ann, came to visit him in his Richmond home. She had been living with various aunts and uncles in Georgia and Alabama since 1830. A frail girl that must have brought to Lamar memories of his dead Tabitha, Rebecca left Georgia on July 22, 1838, in company with an uncle and an aunt, John and Amelia Randle. A diary in the possession of her descendants gives details of the trip. The three made the journey by way of Montgomery, Mobile, and New Orleans. By ship they went to Galveston and then to the City of Houston.[13]

Rebecca enjoyed the days with her father quite conscious of "dear papa's high position." She was delighted with the situation of the home on the Brazos and recorded that "Papa receives a great deal of company at Oak Grove."

Her presence there, along with the visit of the Randles, became a newsworthy item for the Texan press. Isaac Burton wrote in late August from Nacogdoches to Lamar: "I know by the papers of the arrival of your family — accept my congratulations on the occasion." [14]

In October Rebecca and her two adult companions returned to the United States: "I cannot express the sorrow I feel at being separated from my beloved parent," she wrote in her diary.[15]

One other interesting note appeared in Lamar's correspondence at this time. This is a letter from the famed Gail Borden, who wrote to him from Galveston on August 16, 1838, concerning land development in the area.[16] His personal papers, however, shed no further light on Lamar's relationship to the father of modern food and milk preservation methodology.

However, in spite of the seeming tranquility of these days, the vice-president had a continuing political interest. Lamar's passion for home, family, and friends was secondary during the year 1838 to one great concern: that of becoming president of the Republic of Texas.

His initial campaign for the presidency had begun during the closing days of 1837. S.H. Everitt had written to Lamar on December 1 of that year asking permission to use Lamar's name as a candidate for that office.[17] Friends had urged him to consider running for some months prior to that, but the vice-president had been reluctant to acknowledge his own candidacy. He knew that one man could marshall strong forces against him should he choose to run: that man was Thomas Rusk. He remembered the pride-deflating vote that resulted from his readiness to accept the appointment to the rank of general of the army. He could not easily forget how he had been so humiliatedly out-voted by the Texas militia camped on the banks of the River Guadalupe.

However, the requests that he become a candidate for office continued to come to him. Those who were unhappy with the free wheeling individuality of Sam Houston's leadership were increasingly anxious to have a man like Lamar at the head of the Republic. No two personalities could have contrasted more dramatically than those: Houston was the charismatic leader of the rough and rugged frontiersman; Lamar was the cultured gentleman whose more moderate leadership would appeal to the growing ranks of the educated and the genteel of Texas. Those who favored one brand of helmsmanship generally opposed the other. Houston could not run again for another consecutive term; however, his endorsement of any candidate would carry much weight. He was still the hero of Texan independence and the recognized father of a nation.

It was in December that the vice-president made his first move toward actively seeking office. He asked Rusk about the matter; the potential opponent denied any interest whatsoever in holding the highest position in the nation. He even went so far as to urge Lamar to run.[18]

The way was now clear: Lamar announced as a candidate for the presidency. He indicated in a letter written on December 7, 1837, to Everitt[19] that he was interested in openly seeking the office, and he later assisted Everitt in composing an editorial backing his candidacy in the *Houston Banner*.[20] A formal petition had been drawn up in December signed by eleven of the senators endorsing him. Only three of those in the capital city at the time had failed to attach their names to the paper: those were Richard Ellis, Alexander Sommervell, and Robert Wilson.[21] However, these men were in a minority and the Lamar bandwagon was beginning to roll.

In March, Everitt reported to Lamar that his district was in favor of the candidate.[22] Shortly after that, a letter from Memucan Hunt reached Lamar referring to the senatorial endorsement that congratulated him on his nomination.[23] Everitt wrote later that prospects were good for his election in Galveston,[24] R.M. Williamson reported on his strength in Washington and in Austin County,[25] and James Jones assured Lamar of his victory based on reports for his area.[26]

However, there were some indications of opposition in the correspondence that reached the vice-president: Thomas Green urged him to visit Velasco to help overcome problems there.[27] One of the basic issues that began to immerge was that of the question of Lamar's eligibility since he was still considered a newcomer and had not resided continuously in Texas the full three years that the constitution required. Since there was very little else upon which to question his aptness for office, this became an important question. Lamar answered this by recalling his declaration of intent to citizenship in 1835 during his first trip to Texas: this, he contended, was the beginning of his residency and clearly made him eligible for the office of President of the Republic.[28] The electorate generally accepted this thesis and no legal procedure was ever instigated against him on this issue. His claim to having been a legal resident in 1835 was probably as sound a claim as most could make at such a fluid time in the history of Texas.

On April 17 his campaign received a boost when a large public meeting was held in Richmond, the town where Lamar had recently settled, and his nomination was proclaimed by his fellow townsmen for the highest office of the land. Later that month similar meetings were held in Columbia and in Galveston; in June the citizens of the capital city of Houston and the residents of Matagorda pronounced Lamar to be "the universal candidate of the people of this country!" [29]

Another candidate for the office was now in the field: this was Peter W. Grayson who had served as attorney general in Burnet's cabinet and had later been commissioner to the United States. Grayson received the backing of those who supported Sam Houston and who shared his outlook.

A strong campaign began to be organized in behalf of the new candidate by attacking Lamar on two counts: one was that he had gained more than his share of the public land; the other was a renewal of the contention that his claim to residency in Texas was not strong enough to make him eligible for the office that he sought. The first criticism he largely ignored; but the second charge was too serious to be overlooked. Lamar produced affidavits showing that he had declared his purpose of becoming a citizen in the summer of 1835.[30] He held tenaciously to this claim, which continued to be a basic issue in the election.

However, there were other attacks directed against him. *The Galveston Civilian* went so far as to claim that the vice-president was afflicted with partial insanity. To this the *Telegraph and Texas Register* that strongly supported Lamar's candidacy replied: "We sincerely regret that his disorder is not contagious, in order that the country might reap some benefit from it even before election." [31]

The campaign took a grotesque turn when Grayson removed himself from contention by committing suicide. On July 9, he killed himself at Bean's Station in eastern Tennessee leaving a note complaining of "melancholia."

Quickly the Houston men settled on a new candidate: James W. Collingsworth. Some question exists as to whether or not he could have served if he had been elected for he was only thirty-two at the time. He never became a serious candidate, however, for soon after his nomination, he, too, committed suicide. He varied from Grayson's example only by choosing to destroy himself by jumping into the waters of Galveston bay from a steamer.

Once more the search for an opponent to Lamar began. This time the Houston backers were able to come up with the name of Robert Wilson, a prominent businessman who had served as a senator. He was one of the three who had refused to support Lamar earlier in the year. However, his entry into the presidential race was too late.

Reports on the progress of his candidacy continued to flow into Lamar's Richmond headquarters: Everitt reported in July that "all things . . . bear the most prosperous and flattering appearance."[32] In late August both Isaac Burton and Hugh McLeod were able to declare that Lamar's strength in east Texas and the Nacogdoches area was overwhelming.[33]

The election was held on September 3. Lamar received 6,995 votes and his opponent drew only 252. Lamar's running mate, David Burnet, won by a much closer margin defeating his two opponents A.C. Hoxton and Joseph Rowe by 776 votes.[34]

During October notes of congratulation poured into the Oak Grove.[35] Typical of these was one by W. Ray Gillmer in which he declared his pleasure on "your triumphant election."[36] The people had spoken — aided by a strange series of events that had eliminated strong opposition. But Mirabeau Lamar was now the president-elect.

On November 5, he made a farewell address to the Senate stating that he had been "called by a liberal and confiding people to a station upon which I shall shortly have to enter." He asked their support and expressed his confidence "in your attachment to the constitution." [37] He was now prepared to face the greatest challenge of his career.

[9]

The Scroll of History

The coastal plains of Texas can have about them a penetrating mid-winter dampness that belies the relatively mild nature of the climate. Only a few miles of swamp-like fields separated the village of Houston that had been proclaimed capital of a nation and the waters of Galveston Bay.

In December 1838, there was little to recommend the place. It was no more than a sprawling frontier settlement set on flat alluvial lands stretching drearily toward the horizon. Those who came there generally complained about the peculiar qualities of the weather or the monotony of the terrain. In spite of the unimpressiveness of the site, however, it was a truly prophetic location, for here, in time, would develop in a more industrialized age, the largest metropolitan area of Texas. But in that year, it was no more than a ragged collection of frontier dwellings.

A capitol building had been constructed on the main thoroughfare of the community, which, during much of the winter, was nothing but a mass of mud. Other structures were

The Scroll of History

simple in design — making use of the raw materials that could easily be brought from Galveston.

The town began to take on something of a festive air as preparations for the second presidential inauguration of the Republic were begun. People were arriving from nearby communities in considerable number, and a few were there from distant points. The first president had served the two-year term the constitution had allowed him: for some time now, at cross purposes with the majority of his congress, the crusty chief executive had sulked on one side of the small capitol building while his vice-president and much of the congress had gone their way with little reference to his leadership.

The ceremony for installing the new president was to take place on December 10: benches and seats were set up in front of the crude building housing the government for participants and for some of the observers of the event.

Lamar had prepared his inaugural address with great care. Well aware that he did have considerable ability as a public speaker, he was determined to take advantage of the occasion. However, he had not counted on the antics of the outgoing president. Sam Houston had done everything that he could to prevent the election of Lamar; he was determined to give visible and dramatic evidence of his displeasure.

As onlookers gathered about the site of the ceremony, Houston appeared dressed in knee breeches and wearing a powdered wig: he was father of his country and he was prepared to look the part. His tall frame adorned in a fashion quite contrary to his usual mode of attire made him look very much like a reincarnation of George Washington. He asked for permission to make a few farewell remarks, and then he proceeded to take advantage of the situation making use of his unique flair for the bombastic. For the next three hours he continued to remind his hearers, most of whom were admirers of his successor, of the important place that he himself had played in the brief history of the Republic of Texas.

"The Scroll of History was unrolled," declared Houston. There seemed to be no way to get him to re-roll it! Lest the part he had played in that unfurling be too readily forgotten, he spelled out his accomplishments in considerable detail as Lamar squirmed in exasperation and the minutes turned to hours and finally lengthened into a good portion of the day.

When at last Lamar did have his chance to speak, he realized that his patience was too far gone for him to be capable of effective delivery. He handed the manuscript of his address to a friend who then proceeded to read it in calm and uninspired terms. The Victor of San Jacinto had upstaged him and the recently elected president wisely chose not to contest the claims of his former commander on that particular day.

However, once installed as president of a nation, Lamar knew he would have his due opportunity for a rejoinder. A few days later, on December 21, when the newly elected congress assembled, he had that chance: it was now the time to deliver his first presidential message to the Republic's senate and house of representatives. His own personal papers indicate that his statements on this occasion were the same as those that he had planned to present eleven days earlier at his inauguration.[1]

"The character of my administration may be anticipated in the domestic nature of our government and peaceful habits of the people," he declared. He wanted to make it plain that Texas was no longer merely a state involved in rebellion; it had now matured to nationhood. He wanted the world to know that the new Republic had no relationship to the erratic and swashbuckling attempts that had been made to control Texas earlier in the century. The government he would lead would be one that was concerned with peaceful pursuits, would be a responsible nation among nations and would follow a course far removed from the rough and tumble approach of his immediate predecessor. His administration would be interested in such matters as "agriculture, commerce and the useful arts."[2]

He then made a statement that was a complete reversal of the policy of the first president: as leader of the Republic of Texas, he would no longer seek annexation to the United

States of America. This was something of a second declaration of independence. The new nation had broken the chains that had bound it to Mexico; Lamar believed that there need be no bondage to any other nation, not even the country from which most of the Texans had come. Nothing could have been more contradictory of the policies of Sam Houston than this, for the first president had seen his responsibility as nothing more than that of caretaker until the political climate in the United States would make it possible for Texas to become a part of the union of states.

Lamar carefully outlined his thinking in relationship to this important question. Annexation had been favored by the people after San Jacinto since Texas was then "feeble and exhausted." However, he continued, "these imposing considerations which at one time rendered his proposed political connection seemingly desirable have lost their validity and force; indeed they exist no longer." [3]

He was fully prepared for Texas to go it alone and become a completely independent and self-sufficient nation. There was every reason that this was possible: "Never were a people so favorably situated as we are for the establishment of a wise and happy government," [4] he protested. They had the strength, the will, and the ability to do so. It was only necessary that they "stand by their constitution." He himself pledged to do the same.[5]

The question of annexation had been constantly before the leadership of Texas ever since the day that it was clear that Texans would have a viable opportunity for determining their own future. Houston and his followers had vigorously pursued such a union. It was their conviction that the Republic should hold on to its territory until some change should take place in the United States permitting the admission of another state. However, Lamar's approach to the matter was more realistic. There was simply no immediate likelihood that the door to statehood would be open. Therefore, since the knocking at the door had been ignored, there was simply no point in pursuing the matter further. Instead, he was prepared to build a new nation which would stretch westward from the Sabine. The dream of a Texas extending as far as the Pacific Ocean was not an impossibility: if such had happened, it would have produced a country greater in extent than the United States east of the Mississippi. Some historians have written off this Lamarian concept as visionary and impractical. However, to do so would be to ignore the reality of the situation that existed in 1838. In many ways, it was the most honest and completely practical approach possible made at the time. In any case, this concept was the basis of the new administration and the actions of the second president would be posited on the belief that the youthful Republic could and would become a strong and truly independent nation.

The remainder of Lamar's statement to congress spelled out policy concepts based on this conviction. He urged that plans be made as quickly as possible for the appropriation of public land for a national school system and a university. If Texas was to be self-sufficient, such an undergirding would be essential, he believed, for the nation to remain free and to grow in strength. He called for a uniform municipal code and for the establishment of the common law of England by statute. Clearly defined legal procedures were essential to a strong Texas. He made one recommendation that was not popular but that was certainly essential to the concept of a continuing Texas: there must be direct taxation in substitution of dependence merely on import duties. A matter that was directly related to this was the necessity of the establishment of a national bank in order that normal commercial development go forward in the Republic. He also called for a favorable commercial treaty with the United States.

Two other matters were a part of his declaration to congress: there must be a much stronger Indian policy and a vigorous defense of the Texas settlements against the continuing raids that were being made by the original inhabitants of the land; he also urged that every effort be made to gain recognition of Texas by the European nations.

All of these carefully thought through policies were necessary for the sort of independent state Lamar envisioned. His administration was not to be a mere caretaker of a political entity that would soon cease to exist by merger. His program was neither the visionary or the impractical concept that his enemies would later make it out to be — a charge that some modern historians have naively accepted. It was, instead, a practical plan for the building of a nation based on the one certain political reality that then existed: that the United States of America would not accept the recently formed Republic as a part of the union at that particular point in history.

Having once set forth his program for an independent Texas, Lamar turned to more mundane needs. A simple white house had been built in the capital city that had been the residence of the first president. It was estimated that $5000 was needed to repair the building that had sections of the floor pulled up for firewood by Houston's rough-and-ready admirers. However, that sum of money was not available and the presidential secretary recorded that a total of $116.50 was spent in order to make it possible to occupy the house.[6]

The new president then turned to the task of establishing a cabinet to administer the government. He made appointments that were readily ratified by a sympathetic congress drawing upon the best talent that was available within a frontier nation.

Only one member of Houston's cabinet was retained: that was Robert Barr, who was continued in the position of postmaster general. Obviously this was not an area that involved the execution of public policy. At the time postal service was little more than a dream. The first regular mail route came into being when the capital was moved from Houston to Austin and there was a necessity of regular communication between the coast and the newly established interior capital. Even then the casualness with which mail service was regarded was indicated by a contemporary account that related that the mule had escaped from the carrier and had disappeared into the Texas countryside with all correspondence attached. The situation was covered by simply announcing "those who sent letters . . . must write them again."⁷ In any case it was politic to keep at least one member of the previous government in office. Barr had been in Texas for over five years, and he was generally well liked; he was considered inoffensive to all. He was succeeded the following year by Edwin Waller, who in turn gave up the task of maintaining a frontier mail service after a short tenure. John Jones held the office in 1840 and was taken to task by Lamar for allowing a clerk to "publish an insolent paper traducing the motives of the President."⁸

Lamar began his administration by naming men to the remainder of the cabinet whom he believed would be responsive to his policy of Texan self-sufficiency. The important office of attorney general went to a recently arrived Mississippian named James G. Watrous. He served in this capacity for a time and was later succeeded by James Webb.

Richard G. Dunlap received the initial appointment to the secretaryship of the treasury. He did not remain in this position long, and Lamar offered the post to John Hemphill in February 1839.⁹ Dunlap later went to Washington as minister to the United States, but late in 1839 his appointment was rejected by the Senate in a divided vote, and Barnard E. Bee was named as Chargé with the authority necessary for the duties of that important responsibility. Dunlap had succeeded Anson Jones in Washington, who took his replacement by Lamar as a personal affront, never forgiving him for the act.¹⁰

Memucan Hunt was made secretary of the navy. He was a North Carolinian, and like most of the others in the government, was a man with military experience. He had been in Washington attempting to work for annexation during Houston's regime. However, by this time he apparently agreed with Lamar that union with the mother country was no longer a viable option. Louis P. Cooke later took this post which was to become both an important and a difficult position as the young nation made a serious effort to build a navy.

Albert Sidney Johnston, who had been a second lieutenant in the United States Army, and who later became one of the important military figures of the Confederacy, received appointment to the cabinet post of secretary of the army.

Another highly talented man selected to serve in Lamar's cabinet was Barnard E. Bee who was named secretary of state. He was a South Carolinian; he had served in Houston's cabinet, and had the dubious honor of escorting Santa Anna to the United States. He later held high military rank in the Confederacy. He served in the cabinet for only about two months; his talents, however, were needed elsewhere, and he was sent to Mexico to attempt to work out relations with that country.

This important post then passed through many hands. Lamar asked David Burnet to accept the responsibility of secretary of state in May 1839, on a temporary basis.[11] James Webb, Nathaniel Amory, and James Mayfield also acted as ad interim secretaries.[12] Lamar sought, at least for a time, to keep this position open for J. Pinckney Henderson, who had served during Houston's administration, and had been in Paris and London representing Texas. In January 1840, Lamar nominated, and the Senate confirmed unanimously, Abner S. Lipscomb, who held the office for some four months, one of the longer tenures of this secretaryship. Over a dozen changes took place in this post during the three years of Lamar's leadership of the nation, alternating so often that the president was accused of being his own secretary of state, a charge that was not without some justification. However, the men who could fill this position ably at home, were often needed in foreign negotiations and were generally transferred to the capitals where their talents could best be used in the essential efforts to secure Texan recognition.[13]

The official family was rounded out with two other important positions: Lamar's old friend David Burnet was vice-president and presided over the Senate; Thomas Rusk was chief justice of the supreme court. All in all this was an able body of men, and without a doubt they were among the better choices available for the posts to which they had been named in a country with little experience in the formulation of government. In general they were a credit to the president who appointed them and the talent and ability evident in Lamar's cabinet speak well of his ability as an administrator and practical leader in a difficult political situation.

On January 25, 1839, Texas adopted its flag. A drawn design showing a lone white star on a field of blue with two broad stripes, white above red, was officially prepared. This document is in the Texas Archives with the notation that it was approved with Lamar's signature and the names of "John M. Hansford, Speaker of the House of Representatives and David G. Burnet, President of the Senate." With it there is also a paper signed by Lamar entitled "An Act Amending the Act entitled 'An Act Adopting a National Seal and Standard for the Republic of Texas' Approved the 10th of December Eighteen Hundred and Thirty Six."

All of this would clearly indicate that Lamar and his associates were deeply serious about building a new and permanent nation. In any case Texas now had a new president, a new cabinet and a new flag. It was ready to take its place among the nations of the world.

[10]

The Seat of Empire

Crisp fall air lent exhilaration to the chase. Eight mounted men followed a rocky trail over a steep hill which sloped upward from the Colorado River. Autumn's tints of brownish yellows interlaced with rusty reds and occasional shades of gold could be seen in the rising land beyond the river; the brighter colors softened into hues of blue blending into the early morning haze. The river at that point ran broad and serene through a valley covered with wild rye. Its calm waters caught the glint of sunlight and sparkled with moments of shimmering glory that complimented the grandeur of the more distant landscape.

But the men on horseback did not pause to consider the beauty of the scene. A herd of buffalo was between them and the river and they were hunters. Immediately they spurred their horses and gave chase. Shots rang out as puffs of acrid smoke filled the early morning air. The party charged down the slope and immediately several of the great beasts fell to the ground. After the initial slaughter had ended, in order to prevent the over zealous from riding too far in pursuit, and becoming separated from the group, a bugler rode to the top of the hill and recalled the hunters. They then gathered to view their prizes and prepare to preserve as much of the results of the hunt as possible.

The leader of the party was Mirabeau Lamar, then vice-president of the Republic of Texas. It was the fall of 1838 when his duties in the capital city of Houston were extremely light. He had gone to the western fringe of the Texas settlements with his private secretary, Edward Fontaine, to hunt buffalo. However, seeking this prey was likely not his only motive in this expedition. Before he was to take up the duties of president of the young nation, he wanted to see more of the country to the west. Knowing that settlement would have to move in that direction, he undoubtedly was anxious to survey at firsthand what lay beyond the inhabited areas of Texas.

This was dangerous country still dominated by Indian tribes often far from friendly to the Anglo pioneers. Six men familiar with the area joined Lamar and his companion for the hunt, providing the president-elect some protection from potential disaster. The group made their way up the valley of the Colorado River, and came at last to the cabin of Jake Harrell, one of those solitary frontiersmen who insisted on living beyond the fringes of civilization. There they camped for the night. Early the next morning, Harrell's young son ran to awaken the hunters with the news that the prairie was full of buffalo. The party was soon mounted and the hunt was under way.

With the excitement of the chase over, Lamar, who had shot one of the animals himself, turned to survey the land. Making his way to the crest of a hill that rose gradually from the banks of the river, he looked out across the valley and declared: "This should be the seat of future empire." [1]

It was on this spot that the capitol building of Texas would someday stand.

The search for a permanent capital site for Texas had been in progress for some time. A commission had been appointed early in the history of the Republic to find a location for the government; but when a site near La Grange was recommended, the congress, led by Houston, rejected the suggestion in favor of establishing the capital in the city that was to bear the name of the first president.

Soon after Lamar's inauguration, a five-man commission was appointed to select a seat of government between the Trinity and the Colorado rivers. Two of these men were from the area east of the Trinity and three from the lands to the west. Before the group set out to look at possible sites, Lamar himself suggested that they give consideration to the place where he and his party had hunted buffalo on the Colorado the previous fall. They visited the site, and immediately brought back the recommendation that the new capital should be located there. Within twenty days, the land was routinely condemned and plans begun for building a new city.[2]

On May 11, 1839, W.H. Hunt reported to Lamar that the work party he accompanied, led by Edwin Waller, was on its way to the Colorado River.[3] Soon after that the expedition arrived at the spot near Harrell's cabin and began work. On May 23, Waller wrote to the president describing the topography of the land and their progress.[4] By June 2 he was able to report that the site had been properly laid out and that the construction of necessary edifices was under way.[5]

"The public buildings shall be in readiness for the next Congress. I have two 16 foot square rooms up now," he declared. During the summer months work went forward rapidly.

Waller's mid-July report declared: "I have all the timbers got out for the capitol and shall raise it in a short time. I have to pay very high for hands ... I am getting short of money."[6]

Financial problems must have plagued the operation from the beginning because Waller wrote only four days later requesting "fifteen thousand dollars for present uses" and urging Lamar to "send the amount soon as possible."[7]

By the end of the summer, twenty or thirty buildings had been completed, and a Lamar supporter declared that "they are better buildings than were built during the first year in Houston . . ."⁸

By October, all of the structures were complete and the inhabitants of the new city of Austin were making preparations to become a capital and receive the government of the nation.⁹

In the meantime, the president and his cabinet in Houston were making plans for the relocation. Lamar was already being subjected to severe criticism for leading his administration in building a new seat of government. So vigorous were the attacks upon him that two of his supporters, T.J. Green and B.T. Archer, proposed a testimonial dinner in his honor to be held in Velasco in August. The extent of the opposition developing over the issue is evident in the formal invitation drawn up for the dinner, which, Lamar was informed, would be "in testimony of your private character and public service." They have heard from your enemies, since the organization of your administration the most indiscriminate abuse of all of your public acts as well as individual character."¹⁰

However, in spite of the fact that he usually responded enthusiastically to such invitations, Lamar declined this one because of the impending change of capital locations.¹¹

The actual removal of governmental operations took place during the month of October. About forty ox wagons were required to carry the cargoes of papers and furniture from Houston to the new capital where offices were set up in the recently constructed buildings.

The structure designated as a meeting place for the representatives of the Republic was appropriately decorated with portraits of Washington and Austin, and contained the following appointments:

> Sixteen ink stands, five candlesticks, ten sand boxes, three benches, one large table and stand for the speaker and some old chairs. The Senate chamber listed as its equipage seven benches, two tables, one table and stand for the speaker and three good chairs.¹²

The president's offices were located in a double log cabin

just south of the capitol; this building faced the broad and impressive thoroughfare that had been laid out running northward up the slope from the river. This street still bears the name Congress Avenue. Other national offices were nearby.

On October 17 the city officially became a national headquarters. It was on that date that the president and his party arrived. Everyone then resident in Austin who could secure a horse went out some two miles to meet him where a double line of welcome was formed for his entry.

Albert Sidney Johnston, Secretary of War, preceded the president, and led the procession that moved into the city with considerable ceremony.[13]

Edwin Waller had been designated as the orator of the day. He gave three reasons for the selection of the new site in his welcoming statement: "Beauty of scenery, centrality of location and purity of atmosphere . . ." [14] He concluded his oration with these words addressed to Lamar: "Under your fostering care may it [Austin] flourish, and aided by its salubrity of climate and the beauty of situation, become famous among the cities of the New World." [15]

The president replied in a brief speech and then paused for lengthy cheering to take place. With that his party crossed the city line and a salute of twenty-one guns was fired by a six-pounder. The nation's leaders next moved to Bullock's Hotel, where all crowded into the small dining area for an official dinner that lasted five hours. As was customary for such occasions, glasses were raised and flowery toasts were offered during the lengthy meal: a total of thirty-seven toasts were recorded during the marathon talk fest. It was the sort of occasion at which Lamar was at his best. Standing in the rough building surrounded by the newly built log shacks, he lifted his glass for one of the toasts and proclaimed that here "has sprung up, like the work of magic, a beautiful city, whose glory is destined, in a few years, to overshadow the ancient magnificence of Mexico." [16]

This enthusiasm over the establishment of the new capital was certainly not shared by all. By this time the city of

Houston had become a thriving town of some 2,000 residents with steamboats plying the waters between the city and the port of Galveston on regular schedules. The Houston paper, *The Morning Star*, bemoaned the loss of the government's presence protesting that in 1839 there were "hundreds of buildings, neat and comfortable, large stores well filled with the conveniences and many of the luxuries of life, fine hotels offering accommodations for a hundred boarders and two theatres in successful operation." [17]

Anson Jones remonstrated that "no policy could possibly have been more unwise than the removal of the seat of Govt. to Austin." He believed that "corrupt means were used to place it there." [18]

If Jones and the leaders of the former capital city were unhappy with the change, Sam Houston's anger over the removal was beyond expression in either printable or repeatable language. His reaction took the form of a bit of Houstonian buffoonery: he and his admirers planned another entry into the City of Austin that would parody the president's arrival.

Preparations were made for Houston to enter the city on the very day the Fourth Congress was called to convene. Anson Jones was named the orator of the day; he was escorted by a cavalcade marshaled by three colonels. This assemblage rode out three miles from the capital, a mile farther than Lamar's welcomers had gone, to meet the victor of San Jacinto. There, with many flourishes, the crusty old general was welcomed. He, like Lamar, made a brief reply, and then was escorted into the city with considerable pomp.

Later a banquet was scheduled in his honor with Jones acting as toastmaster. Some two hundred persons attended the banquet that was designed to outdo the earlier affair at Bullock's Hotel. Contemporary accounts indicate that a larger number was anticipated than those who appeared; however, this fact was attributed to bad weather.

One of the absentees was the president. As at the previous gathering, which had honored Lamar, glasses were again lifted and toasts were proposed: the first one went significantly to the United States since the continued seeking of early annexation was one of the themes of the Houston party. This brought three cheers. The second toast was for old Sam; the response was "three times three" cheers. He acknowledged this honor in what an admirer described as "one of the most eloquent speeches we ever remembered to have heard." [19]

A third toast was dutifully offered to the president of the Republic. This produced no cheers. The rest of the evening involved drinking to such themes as "freedom of opinion and liberty of speech," and "currency based upon agriculture and commerce." Toasting had to continue past the thirty-seven mark: Anson Jones received a toast, "retrenchment and reform" was toasted; and the final and forty-first toast was to Sam Houston as the "next president" of the Republic.[20]

But the new capital had been established. Admittedly it was not easy for those who inhabited that frontier settlement during those early days to find the normal conveniences of life. However, Lamar was convinced that his stout Texans would forego personal comforts for the good of the nation, which he believed was best served by the new location of the seat of government. In any case new settlers were pouring into the area, and by the beginning of the next year, Austin could boast a population of 856, including thirty-five mechanics (carpenters), nine stores, nine groceries, six Fargo banks, two lawyers, six physicians, and "only about 20 gamblers." However, this was a frontier town, and the chaplain of the Senate, who made the census, stated that of the entire population only seventy-two were church members.[21]

Houston's admirers made great sport of the new capital. With wry humor they pretended to be fearful of attacks by hostile Indians. They would post guards at the windows of the House Chamber to watch for the invasion that they insisted would occur.[22] Houston wrote: "This is the most unfortunate site upon earth for a seat of Government." [23]

He later made the location of the capital a major issue when he returned to the presidency. In his second inaugural address, he urged the Sixth Congress to restore the town of Houston as the national capital. By that time he had strong opposition on that issue, and could not get a bill through congress for moving back to the east. He contended, however, that the removal of the capitol to Austin had not been done legally in the first place. For much of his second term of office, he insisted upon operating from the coastal city in spite of the fact that Austin was still designated as the nation's capital. When he tried to remove the archives from the western site, the citizens of Austin armed themselves with artillery and prevented him from doing so. A resident later wrote Lamar that "we have . . . held on to the 'archives' and will battle for them to the death." [24] Austin did remain the capital, and in time the reasonableness of its central location became more apparent. It was thus that the most violent of the conflicts between Lamar and Houston finally resulted in a victory for the Republic's second president. But the egotistical old Sam would neither forget nor forgive those who had removed the capital of Texas from the city named in his honor.

In 1839, Lamar had his new seat of empire, and he was now ready to look out across the broad expanses of unsettled frontier and make of Texas a nation that would take its place among the great states of the world.

[11]

The Forked Tongue

The Hill Country of Texas is a rugged series of uplands stretching to the south and the west of the site where Lamar had established his national capital. On still evenings when the prevailing winds had subsided, it was often possible for those early Austin residents to see the gently spiraling smoke of Indian campfires. Several streams bisect the area creating rocky promontories that often give way to sudden precipices. Noted for its many springs and watering places, it was a favorite haunt of roving native tribes.

The possibility of Indian raids on Austin was more than the imaginings of Houston's men. The new capital was on the edge of a country that not only afforded water and pasturage, but security from counterattack for the various nomadic bands that moved through the area. Fortunately for Lamar's government, the early period of his administration was a relatively peaceful time among the Indians of that part of Texas. However, that situation was soon to change, and even as the new capital was being established, there were other parts of the Republic deeply embroiled in the problems that resulted from conflict between the natives and the settlers. This was one of the more serious difficulties that the second president had to face.

Inherent to the very nature of this problem was the fact that Anglo settlers in North America had never been able to comprehend the way of life of the native inhabitants of the land. South of the Rio Grande, the Spanish conquerors had come, in time, to make broad allowances for the living styles of those who had been there before them. In many cases there came to be peaceful coexistence resulting in the blending and the merging of both cultural patterns and racial strains.

But the settlers moving in great waves to the west from the Atlantic coast across the major portion of the North American continent had their roots in Britain. The English, Scottish, Welch, and later Irish immigrants were determined to perpetuate an agrarian mode of life that had been fashioned in their ancestral islands. In addition to this fact, they came in great numbers and they came as family units seeking tillable land. Here they sought to establish farms and plantations, towns and villages, homes and institutions that were not unlike those that they or their ancestors had left. They had come to settle and possess the land.

However, the Indian thought of the land quite differently. For him it was not necessary to cultivate or fence the land in order to establish a valid claim to its use. It was a common heritage and he believed that he was entitled to live upon it and to move about without restriction. His nomadic concept was very much a part of the life-style of the native tribes that inhabited Texas, and was in direct conflict with the agrarian philosophy of the Anglo settler. There was simply no easy solution to the problem that this enmity produced.

Sam Houston, despite his egocentricities, was one of the few of the newcomers to Texas who had some ability to understand the Indian. At one time he had lived among the native Americans, and this contact made it possible for him to deal personally with the Texas nomads in a way that few other white men could.

The Forked Tongue

However, even his ability to parley with the natives was not enough to prevent all difficulties as the embroilment between the westward moving settlers and the Indians grew in intensity.

The large standing army that had existed when Lamar had been rejected as commander in the camp near Victoria had nearly ceased to exist. When the first president assumed the responsibility of full leadership of Texas, he had appointed Albert Sidney Johnston to command the army. Felix Huston, who had been so largely responsible for Lamar's rejection, then challenged Johnston to a duel, wounded him, and kept control of the army. President Houston, realizing that the military situation was out of hand, furloughed the army with the exception of a small band of less than 600 men in May, 1837. With this act there was, in effect, no army for the remainder of his administration. It was during this period that the Indian situation became more severe. Raids continued to increase in frequency as settler after settler reported depredations on both person and property.[1]

When Lamar became president, he immediately urged Congress to move to protect the "northern and western frontier." On January 1, 1839, the legislators responded by authorizing the president to accept eight companies of mounted volunteers for six months and appropriated $75,000 for that force and another $5000 for fifty-six rangers.[2] The citizen soldiers who joined the ranks of the newly created militia were, at best, a temporary solution to the problem. However, the more significant action was the authorization of a ranger company that in time became an efficient, and in later years, a highly romantic fighting unit that did have a definite place in limiting the perils of frontier life.

Apparently a part of the difficulty was the fact that agents from Mexico were taking advantage of the weakness of the Texas situation to stir up trouble among the native inhabitants of the land.[3] On August 20, 1838, evidence of this sort of an operation had been discovered when incriminating papers were found on the body of a Mexican national named Pedro

Miracle who had been killed in a raid on Texas settlers: his diary indicated that he had already visited several Indian tribes following the instructions of General Vinente Filisola who had urged him to foment animosity among them against the Texans.[4]

Lamar was deeply concerned with this matter. In his statement to the Congress he declared that "protection is commensurate with allegiance . . . the poorest citizen . . . holds as sacred a claim upon the government for safety and security as does the man who lives in ease."[5] It was with this declaration that the second president began his administration.

The immediate crisis for the new government was to come in the form of the existence of a strong and well led band of Cherokees that claimed rights to a sizable tract of land in East Texas. The tribal chief, a man named Bowles, had negotiated a treaty with Sam Houston in February, 1836, when the outcome of the Texas revolution was still very much in doubt. Houston agreed to grant land rights to the Cherokees on the grounds that they had occupied that territory since 1820. However, when the Texans met in March, the Convention that had declared Texas an independent nation refused to ratify the treaty Houston had negotiated.

But Houston's concern at this time was that the natives of the region remain peaceful, and just before the Battle of San Jacinto, he wrote to the Cherokee chief a letter declaring, "you will get your land."[6] However, when the battle was over the Republic had become something of an established nation. Even though the first president had urged ratification of the treaty he had negotiated, the Texas Senate, meeting in December, declared the agreement null and void.

Throughout Houston's administration, Bowles was able to keep his restless braves in line in the hope that the man who occupied the position of president would be able to come through on his promises. However, the increasing numbers of white settlers and their constant encroachment on Indian-claimed territory continued to make the situation more and more volatile.[7]

When Lamar came to power, he had difficulty in understanding how an independent state, which the Cherokee nation claimed to be, could exist within the bounds of the Republic of Texas. His Anglo comprehension of nationhood did not allow for the acceptance of the type of coexistence that Houston had been able to tolerate.

Immediately after Congress had authorized a militia to deal with the Indian problem, the second president issued a call for volunteers.[8] There was an enthusiastic response that quickly produced an army for the Republic. In April, Major B.G. Waters received presidential instructions to build a military fort in Cherokee territory at Grand Saline. Bowles reacted by mobilizing his warriors and then proceeded to order Waters out of the area. To Lamar, this was nothing less than a declaration of war.

He responded by writing to the Cherokee leadership: his letter was addressed to "Col. Bowles and other head men of the Cherokees." The document was printed and ordered to be circulated by the Senate of the Republic. In this statement Lamar indicated concern over evidence that the Indian antagonism toward white settlers appeared to be the result of Mexican interference: "You and your people have been deceived by evil counsellors. The forked tongue[s] of Mexicans has beguiled you." [9]

He then stated his political philosophy: "You have no right to maintain within the Republic an independent government . . . the treaty of February 20, 1836, with the provisional government has been nullified." [10]

He further charged that the Indians were in collusion with the foes of the nation and stated that if they should "put in jeopardy the lives and property of our citizens . . . the inevitable consequence will be a prompt and sanguinary war which can terminate only in [your] destruction and expulsion." [11]

He concluded his public statement with words that were certainly sincere in terms of his own understanding of the situation, but that were nonetheless one more chapter in the tragic story of the bitter clash between red and white men in North America:

> This government has no desire to wrong the Indian, or to shed his blood, but it will not hesitate to adopt the most vigorous and decisive measures for the defence of its rights and the protection of its people.[12]

The stage was now set for the disaster that was to follow.

An event occurred in May 1839, that added fuel to the already volatile situation. A band of Indian marauders, apparently led by a person of Mexican ancestry, struck between Sequin and Bexar killing several settlers. The invaders were ruthlessly hunted down, and put to death, but this was simply one more occurrence in the chain of events that helped to convince Texans of the necessity of strong action toward all Indians living in the bounds of the Republic.

Lamar did make an effort to negotiate with the leadership of the Cherokees. He sent Burnet and Albert Sidney Johnston to consult with Chief Bowles with the power to act as a commission of the Texan government. They proposed that the Cherokees be paid for the land and for all improvements they had made and that they be reimbursed for their transportation out of Texas on the condition that they return to Arkansas. Bowles and the Cherokee leadership initially agreed to this proposal.[13]

On July 9, Lamar wrote to the settlers in the area "enjoining them to abstain from acts of violence toward the Indians," indicating that he planned a policy of ultimate removal.[14]

However, the Cherokees made no immediate plans to leave the territory. Lamar assembled a force of some five hundred militiamen led by General Kelsey Douglass to enforce his demand for the departure of the Indians from Texas soil.

On July 15, fighting erupted between the Cherokee warriors and the whites on the banks of the Neches River. Bowles sought to drive back the Texans, but was shot down in the fighting. From that time on there was no restraint. The Indians fought in desperation but were no match for the superior Texan forces of Kelsey Douglass. By the end of the month, the Cherokee resistance had been completely broken and the remnants of the tribe were driven out of the land claimed by the Republic. The Texan general reported to Johnston that the major battle of the campaign had occurred on July 15 and that only three of his men had been killed and five wounded. The remainder of the operation was largely that of rounding up those who still defied his forces. By the end of the month the last elements of resistance had been ruthlessly crushed, and the Cherokee survivors were unceremoniously marched out of Texas.[15]

The land that had been occupied by the Cherokees later became the subject of legislative debate. It was Houston himself who introduced into the Texan Congress the Cherokee Land Bill that provided for the survey and the sale of the property. Revenue from the sale would go to alleviate the needs of the Texan treasury. The bill passed both houses and was approved by Lamar on February 1, 1840.[16]

Eradicating the legal claims of the Cherokees and removing them as a tribe from Texas, however, did not end the Indian problem. There is some evidence to indicate that this event merely intensified the difficulties between the two races. There were reports of scalpings by marauding tribes in the vicinity of Austin in March of 1840.[17] In August, James Kerr wrote of a "large party of Indians . . . Comanches, Cherokees and others" had appeared at Victoria where "many of the citizens have been killed and all the horses taken . . . the town of Linnville has been burnt to the ground." [18]

These depredations were probably inspired both by the Cherokee expulsion and by an event that occurred early in 1840, later known as the "Council House Fight." In January, three Comanche chiefs entered San Antonio and approached the Texan militia commander, Henry Karnes, with a request for a treaty. Claiming that they wanted peace, they inquired as to what terms were necessary for an agreement. Karnes told them that no peace could be considered unless all white prisoners were released. The visiting chiefs agreed to this and returned with a lone fifteen-year-old girl captive named Matilda Lockhart. When she was brought to San Antonio, it was apparent that she had been tortured by having flesh burned away from her face. The militia leaders in the council house meeting reacted by insisting that other prisoners be brought. The Indians agreed that other prisoners may have been taken by other bands of Indians, but that Matilda was the only one for whom they were responsible: "The others belong to other tribes" was the reply.[19]

One Indian brave spoke up insolently: "How do you like that answer?" With this the exasperation of the Texans gave way to violent action. The command was given to cordon off the area and make prisoners of the assembled chiefs and their aides. One of the Indians sprang at the militia commander with a knife and immediately bedlam broke loose. Even the squaws outside entered into the fight that finally resulted in the extermination of almost the entire Comanche contingent. Three women, one child and all of the men were killed and twenty-seven wailing squaws and their children were taken prisoner while seven whites were killed and eight wounded.[20]

This tragic event left a continuing legacy of hatred and bad will on both sides. The results of this can be seen in a letter written by a would-be settler in Texas to Lamar in August 1840:

> I am now ready to move my family on my land 12 miles below Little River fort but hearing that station is now evacuated I am at a loss to know what to do. I can't possibly settle there without some assurance of protection . . . I hope your Excellency will let me know quickly as possible what I am to depend on.[21]

Lamar had claimed in a formal statement to the citizens of Galveston shortly before this that his expulsion of the Cherokee meant that "liberty was acquired and a happy government established." [22] However, this sixteen-page defense of his Indian policy was obviously written against the background of severe criticism of what had been done and the general failure of his government either to pacify the native inhabitants of the land or to completely satisfy the fearful setters.

Late in his administration, Lamar sought to deal with this problem by requesting that a treaty relationship with the United States for mutual control of the Indians be established. Apparently some of those who had been driven into Arkansas did not choose to remain there peacefully. Nathaniel Amory of the Texan legation in Washington pursued such a possibility on April 23, 1841, but no concluding action was taken during Lamar's term of office. It was not until 1843 that such negotiations were finally completed and a treaty between the two nations was adopted that helped settle the matter.[23]

During his term of office, however, the second president of Texas was unable to offer any sort of a satisfactory solution for the Indian problem, and although he accused others of speaking with the forked tongue, there were at least some that felt that his government had done so.

[12]

The Restless Giant

There were two rivers south of San Antonio.

One was the modest Nueces with beginnings in the rocky uplands that bordered the Edwards Plateau. It was a stream that gathered strength from several lesser tributaries as it flowed south-eastward to finally merge its waters in those of the Bay of Corpus Christi.

Further to the south lay the Rio Grande. In keeping with its name, it was a massive stream that had cut its way into deep chasms through towering mountains; it nourished broad plains and brought life to arid hill lands. On occasion it had been known to change its course and cut new channels through the land it watered. It was a restless giant.

For the people of Texas during the days of the Republic there was little interest in the great river; their concern lay with the country that existed beyond the Rio Grande.

Like the river, Mexico, too, was a restless giant. It was a nation that had its roots in the ancient cultural heritage of the proud Aztecs. The effluence of Spanish civilization had merged with the vigor of the native races to produce a new,

The Restless Giant

and in many ways, a unique country. After centuries of rule under the Spanish crown, Mexico had overthrown the Iberian power to become a free and separate nation. That revolution had reached a climax in 1821, but the struggle for authentic independence was to continue for some time.

In the year 1838 Mexico was still in adolescence. It had fluctuated during its brief period of nationhood between experimentation with a concept of power which assumed strong centralization along the lines of the pattern established by the Spanish overlords, and efforts at democracy that took the form of self-sufficient provincialism. It was a nation that was a proud giant. Like the river that ran north of most of its population centers, it was, in that early period of nationhood, still flowing toward the greatness that was yet to be.

For Lamar, one of the primary questions before his government was how to deal with the country that existed to the south. Since the treaty that had been signed by Santa Anna had never been ratified by any of the several governments that had ruled Mexico, the very existence of Texas as a republic was related to this question. Mexico still claimed Texas as a part of its domain, and a state of war, or at least of insurrection, still existed.

As time went by, however, it became more and more obvious that Mexico would never again be able to mount a serious military attack against its neighbor to the north that would bring Texas back under the Mexican flag. Her own instability in this period made such a reconquest impossible. But Lamar knew that in order to clearly establish Texas as an independent nation, it would be necessary to determine a boundary between the two states.

The Nueces had generally been regarded as the southern edge of Texas. But that river disappeared into the rocky uplands only a little over two hundred miles inland. Where, then, was the boundary from that point westward?

Since the Rio Grande was a more natural barrier, one that could be easily defended against an invading force, Lamar and his associates began to propose that stream as the southern edge of Texas. It was the only logical dividing line between the Sierra Madre to the south and San Antonio to the north. Then, too, it would mean greater territory for the Republic. In addition it would provide a clear line of demarcation all the way to El Paso. From that point Texas could then claim territory westward to the Pacific.

Lamar was determined to establish Texas on just such a basis. Even before his inauguration as president, he prepared to send a peace commission to Mexico to negotiate for a settlement of the war and establish a boundary between the two states.[1]

The time seemed to be ripe for such an action. Mexico was still in the throe of uprisings which had resulted, at least in part, from the discrediting of Santa Anna after the Battle of San Jacinto.

Barnard E. Bee was to go to Mexico in secret mission. No better choice could have been made for such an important responsibility. Bee had the characteristics of a diplomat: he had been able to get along with the Houston men as well as with Lamar. He had once handled the ticklish job of escorting Santa Anna out of Texas, and had even gone so far with his assignment that he had loaned the ex-president of Mexico the money that he needed to properly refurnish his personal wardrobe. If anyone could successfully undertake this important assignment, Bee was the man for the job.

He was to go to Mexico as minister plenipotentiary. If he should be received by the authorities there, he could assume that position. If he was not received, then he was simply to act as an agent of the Texas government.

Of course the primary objective of his mission was to secure a peace treaty between Texas and Mexico that would recognize the Republic's independence. But he had instructions also to settle the boundary between the two nations — if necessary, he was to agree to the Nueces as the boundary and then offer to buy the land between that river and the Rio Grande for the sum of $5 million dollars.[2] It was an impressive plan and one that made sense in terms of a continued Texas as a nation apart from the United States. Although the finances of the infant Republic could hardly support such a sum at the time, doubtless Lamar and his associates were confident that a satisfactory treaty with Mexico would mean future revenues for Texas that could in time pay off such a debt. If such a proposal had gone through, it was certainly not unreasonable to believe that Texas could lay claim to the entire southwest with what is today southern California as the western limits of her territory.

In the meantime Lamar made every move possible to extend Texan influence southward to the Rio Grande. On February 21, 1839, he issued a proclamation opening trade with Mexican citizens living along that river.[3]

Bee made his preparations for the trip to Mexico. He left Texas for New Orleans, and there he found a ship bound for Veracruz in early May.[4] At the Mexican port, he sought permission to go to Mexico City, but he was refused.

Bee had a delightful optimism about his obviously difficult assignment. One letter is extant that he penned from Veracruz on May 28, in which he asked James Webb to "tell Gen'l Lamar I will carry it through, but if not we can whip them!"[5] He went on to describe the Mexican coastal city as "full of soldiers," but he believed that their military bearing indicated to him that "the planters of Georgia might as well expect to conquer that state with their slaves as Mexico to reconquer Texas."[6] Bee obviously was thinking of his mission as primarily one that would end the state of war between Texas and Mexico: this was his basic task, but closely related to this was the question of the boundary itself.

He returned to New Orleans shortly after his rejection at Veracruz and there set up a base of operations. His brief sojourn in Mexico had not discouraged him. He wrote Webb on July 5 that he should "say to Gen'l Lamar he shall have peace by Novr!"[7]

He had received information by this time that Lamar intended to enlarge the diplomatic mission by sending James Treat to Mexico to work toward the Texan objectives. Bee wrote to Lamar in July that he hoped that "the first news from Mexico will render Mr. Treat's visit to that country wholly unnecessary."[8]

Treat did accomplish more than Bee had been able to do: he did at least get to Mexico City. There he was able to make far more progress than had previously been made simply because of his relationship to the British Minister to Mexico, Richard Packenham. It was through Packenham's intercession and his knowledge of the proper channels in the Mexican capital that Treat was finally able to gain the ear of officials in the government. The Texas Agent eventually had a conference with the Mexican Secretary of State, and in March, 1840, submitted a proposal for a treaty between the two countries. Evidence of Packenham's support of Treat is extant in diplomatic correspondence between Lamar's government and the Texan that was sent by ship to Veracruz under cover of "Her Britannic Majesty's Minister there, Richard Packenham, Esq."[9]

For a time it looked as though Treat was going to be able to accomplish much of what he had been assigned to do; however, a revolution broke out in Mexico that unseated the government with whom he was dealing and ended the chances of the completion of the agreement that seemed amazingly near consummation. Treat's nearly successful mission was one of those might-have-beens of history which could have changed the whole prospect for the Texan Republic. Although it was an effort that ended in failure, the fact that it came so close to success goes far to demonstrate the basic soundness of Lamar's foreign policy.

Treat finally left Mexico in discouragement only to die on board a ship of the Texas Navy enroute back to his home.[10]

In December, 1839, Lamar took his Congress into his confidence regarding these negotiations that up to this point had been carried out with considerable secrecy. On December 19, a special session of Congress was held in which the president reported to the elected representatives of the nation that a mission was in Mexico seeking to negotiate a peace with that country. On that occasion he discussed the objectives of his efforts revealing everything except the names of his agents. The fact such an event could take place, indicates the informality of the government process that existed, and which would be impossible at a later time. Congress responded to this confidence that the president placed in them by voting to approve his continuing efforts in the very complex matter of the Texan relationship to Mexico.[11]

During this time, Bee had been in the United States seeking help there for securing a treaty of peace with Mexico. Lamar was determined to spare no effort in this project and sent Dunlop to assist Bee in this task. Earlier in the year, May 1839, the Texan emissaries could only report that the Washington government would be "very happy to interpose, should it be the wish of Mexico." [12] This attitude of cautious neutrality continued to be the official position of the United States.

But there were now forces within Mexico which would soon bring the nearly successful treaty negotiations to a stop. During the later months of 1839, the revolutionary army of General Antonio Canales was operating in northern Mexico. Early in 1840 Canales led his troops, who had opposed the central government of Mexico, across the Rio Grande where he set up headquarters on the river's nothern bank at Laredo. He then proceeded to send out a call to the towns and villages on both sides of the river to gather for a convention to organize a new nation in opposition to the centralists. On January 18, a group of separatists proclaimed the Republic of the Rio Grande as an independent and sovereign state. The movement imitated the Texas Revolution in some respect, and the leadership fully expected support from the government in Austin, which they might well have received, had Lamar not been in the midst of negotiating a peace with the central government of Mexico.

Jesus Cardenas was named provisional president of the new nation, and he attempted to establish Laredo as his national headquarters with a capitol building situated on the high bluffs on the northern bank of the Rio Grande. Its simple one-story form looked out on the central plaza of the town and could be seen clearly from the sprawling village which constituted the southern part of Laredo across the river. A number of Texans joined Cardenas and Canales: Ruben Ross and S.W. Jordan both brought bands of settlers from the north to support the newly proclaimed republic.[13]

However, Lamar knew that this movement could completely upset the negotiations that were still in progress in Mexico City. He had to be cautious and he acted with considerable discretion. He made an official proclamation of neutrality, and he attempted to avoid any overt support for the Republic of the Rio Grande. However, his personal sympathies were certainly with the movement. When Canales was defeated at the Battle of Morales by the centralists, and he and Cardenas fled to Texas, Lamar personally met with him. He could not even then display open support, but there is every indication that the Texan president granted the separatists every possible unofficial encouragement.[14] It was partly on the basis of Lamar's approbation that Canales was able to reorganize his army, and with the aid of men like S.W. Jordan, William Fisher, Juan Seguin, and some three hundred volunteers, make a new effort to establish his fledgling republic. However, in October 1840, Jordan was betrayed near Saltillo and was barely able to fight his way back north across the Rio Grande. In November, Canales finally surrendered to the forces of the central government of Camargo, thus ending the short-lived Republic of the Rio Grande.[15]

If that nation had ever come into existence as actual fact, it would have served as a potent buffer against possible invasion from Mexico. However, before the year 1840 was half over, it was obvious that hope of the secure establishment of such a state was a futile one.

In the meantime relations between Texas and the giant to the south continued to deteriorate as rumors of a large scale Mexican invasion became more frequent. Early in the year Lamar had received a letter from José Navarro commenting upon what he considered well-founded tidings of invasion. He stated "I trust that the government will take immediate steps to relieve us from our threatened and dangerous position." [16] Lamar's personal files include correspondence dated in March 1840, making similar references to the possibility of attack from the south.[17]

However, one of the factors that served to strengthen the Texan position and prevent overt military operations by the Mexicans against Texas was the fact of the French presence in the area in the form of a fleet in Mexican waters. Admiral Baudin, commander of the naval force representing France in the Gulf of Mexico, sought Lamar's cooperation in the event of the resumption of open hostilities between his country and Mexico. Lamar's response to this communication is significant: he indicated his willingness to raise an army in Texas if the negotiations then in progress failed to succeed. He added, though, in his reply to the French admiral, that he would be able to provide men should France be able to advance funds for the support of such a military operation.[18] Perhaps this was a fair statement of the continuing problem of the Texan government: men, morale, but no money.

But at the time there were others who were talking about war with Mexico. There were those who looked forward with considerable enthusiasm to a resumption of open hostilities. In August, 1840, Albert Sidney Johnston wrote to Lamar making reference to a conversation with a friend who had spoken of the imminent possibility of hostilities: he declared that if such were the case, "I will be much gratified to contribute . . . and with much pleasure place myself at your disposition for that purpose." [19]

Later in the year Lamar turned over the duties of the presidency to his vice-president, Burnet, because of illness. Shortly after that on December 15, 1840, the acting president delivered a fiery message to Congress in which he taunted the pride and the patriotism of its members and urged them to consider organizing an expeditionary force against Mexico and to make a declaration of war. This was no longer a call for defense. The Republic of the Rio Grande had failed; diplomacy had brought no satisfactory results. There were many who felt that some offensive move should be made. It is interesting, however, that this hawkishness reached its highest level when Lamar was not actively administering the government. There is every evidence that, at least to some degree, he was a moderating influence and had little to do with the drive for a reckless plunge into a war with a powerful neighbor.

As a result of Burnet's speech, a joint committee of Congress was formed to consider an actual invasion of Mexico. However, the committee recognized that funds were simply not available for the support of such a military operation. Their recommendation was that since financial credit was not available — the only army possible as an invasion army would be one that would live off of the land. There, they declared, "the war would be made to support the war." [20] However, there were some cooler heads who remembered how barren the deserts of northern Mexico actually were and how impractical such an effort would certainly have been. It was finally agreed that only defensive measures should be taken at the time and the immediate war fever died down.[21]

Lamar made one more effort to settle the problem of Texas's relationship to Mexico after he returned to active leadership of the government during his last year in office. He commissioned James Webb, then secretary of state, to go to Mexico and attempt to do what both Bee and Treat had failed to do. Britain's Lord Palmerston had supported the move and had instructed Packenham to again aid the mission in every possible way. Webb was given instructions in March that were similar to those of his predecessors. In May he wrote to Lamar from Houston explaining that he had been delayed in his plans to go to Veracruz, but that he planned to set out soon. "I feel some confidence in the success of the mission," he declared. He was pleased with the fact that he already had assurances of British assistance. He stated that Packenham was working for two goals: that Mexico "recognize Texas or promptly . . . pay the British debt — the one she can do, the other she cannot." [22]

However, Webb was refused permission to land in Veracruz. He then sought to go to Yucatan to negotiate an alliance with the federalists there, but his ship was caught in a storm and he was forced back to Galveston.[23] Thus ended Lamar's last effort to work out the difficult problem of the Texan relationship to Mexico. The Restless Giant to the south continued to flex its muscles. However, Lamar's efforts to contain the giant had been wise efforts, and they came amazingly close to success.

[13]

The Affair Of The Pigs

There was much that was unusual about the wagon train that wound its way over the rough roads of the Republic of Texas en route to Austin in January of the year 1840. It had come up from Houston. It rumbled to a stop amid the scattered buildings of the recently proclaimed capital. It was not like other cargo carriers on the frontier: it was manned by teamsters who had about them a regal air. These transporters carefully protected the contents of their vehicles with a caution one would expect from the guardians of a royal household. As a matter of fact this was very nearly the case, for this was the arrival of the possessions of Count Alphonse de Saligny, Chargé d'affaires of the King of France.

Saligny was moving to Austin to establish the first foreign legation the Texan capital had seen. Among his possessions were carpets, tapestries, paintings, books, fine wines and bric-a-brac from Europe. The unloading of the goods of a French nobleman was a unique sight in the village. One can well imagine the stares and the nods the bystanders gave as this unusual event took place.

The Affair of the Pigs

The arrival of the chargé meant that at last Texas was being recognized as a nation among nations. It may have taken a bit of indulgence on the part of some, but the count's presence was at first accepted, and in general the outgoing and somewhat overbearing Frenchman became a part of the community.

But one day the inevitable occurred: the conflict of cultures took the form of an invasion of French property by Texas pigs. The chargé kept a string of fine horses that were accustomed to eating only the best of food; corn had been carefully stored for that purpose alone. Some fifteen to twenty-five pigs belonging to the proprietor of Bullock's Hotel managed to get into the area where the special corn was stored, and then proceeded to gorge themselves on the elite feed. One of Saligny's servants responded to this invasion by "most maliciously and wantonly" killing the pigs.[1] Bullock retaliated by asserting that the rights of his pigs had been violated and then felt called upon to explain the situation to the French servant by a vigorous beating. The count took the matter to the Texan government and demanded Bullock's arrest. He was arrested and charged, but immediately released. The Frenchman protested further and Bullock was bound over to the court, but no punishment was meted out to him.

Saligny felt that this incident indicated that he could not contend with the ways of the frontier. He believed justice had not been done and that he could not continue to live in such an environment. He withdrew both his prestigious presence and his household from the capital and moved to Galveston where he felt he could exist in a somewhat more civilized situation. He then proceeded to use his influence to undermine the integrity of the young nation. His influence was considerable: his brother-in-law was then the French Minister of Finance, who, partly on the recommendation of the Texas chargé, opposed the proposed loan which was being negotiated in France. The loan failed, and this ended the hope that Lamar's government had of attaining financial solvency and a realistic political stability.

The loss of this loan was to have considerable effect upon Texas for the remaining days of its existence as an independent state. The loan had been the most promising prospect that the Republic of Texas had in dealing with its inherent financial difficulties.

From the outset money was the most serious problem Lamar and his government faced. It even overrode the complexities of relations with Mexico, since a well-financed army could have guaranteed a reasonably strong border at almost any point that Texas may have chosen.

Texas was not alone in its money problems: the Panic of 1837 had struck the United States and had developed into a worldwide phenomenon. This meant that there was no easy money available from east of the Sabine to help solve the financial dilemma of the young Republic.

During Houston's term of office, it had been recognized that revenue sources had to be developed in spite of the frontier reluctance to levy any form of taxation. Two tariff acts had been signed into law by the first president in June of 1837 and in May, 1838. One was an ad valorem tax that was assessed on property; the other was a levy of one dollar per head established against all cattle belonging to citizens of the United States. This not only appealed to Texans but made citizenship in the Republic more attractive. However, even these somewhat innocuous forms of taxation aroused considerable opposition. In time, though, the necessity of the inevitable was recognized and a direct tax law was passed in 1840 and a strong ad valorem tax was established in February, 1841.[2]

The taxing procedures and the collection of customs in the Republic were highly uncertain and often inconsistent. At best this meant for Texas an indefinite and generally sporadic income. However, one fact continued to be obvious: the young nation needed money and that money was necessary in large amounts if the nation was to continue to exist. Lamar's Indian policy and the threat of invasion from Mexico as well as the necessities inherent in the general operation of government demanded some sort of adequate funding. Texas could not wait for a gradual development of economic stability that would someday come through the consistent collection of taxes and custom revenues.

When Lamar came to office there was already a sizable debt. In order to carry on the necessary functions of government and pursue any constructive activities, he had no choice but to go deeper into debt. However, he believed in the future of Texas, and he was convinced that in time these financial problems could be solved. In the meantime Texas needed foreign credit.

As one step in this program of eventual fiscal stability, he urged the establishment of a Texas National Bank at the very beginning of his administration.[3] This was a project that would require adequate funds which could only be secured through a foreign loan.

In the meantime he did what most modern governments have done: he issued paper money. There was already a total of some $800,000 of the Republic's currency in circulation when he took office. When more were printed, these bills known as "red backs" because of their color, began to decrease in value. At first the Texas currency brought 37.5¢ per American dollar on the international exchange market. However, by November, 1840, as the credit of Texas began to sag, the red back dropped in value to 16.6¢; their worth was eventually to go as low as 12¢.[4]

During this time the meager revenues of Texas could not keep pace with the financial demands that faced the nation. In the first three years of its national existence, the tax structure of Texas had produced a total of $260,780. In the year 1837, under Houston, expenditures soared to $945,961. The following year, governmental costs leveled off at $841,401. However, in 1839, expenses soared to $1,504,173 largely because of the army that was necessary to fight Lamar's Indian war. But the worst was yet to come: in 1840 expenses reached a high of $2,174,752 while the income for that year was only $453,235.[5]

Obviously Texas needed both cash and credit. The

source of that assistance could well be one of the powerful and wealthy nations of Europe. Aware that an independent Texas would have both political and financial benefits for them, both France and Great Britain were cautiously responsive to Texan overtures for recognition.

When Lamar assumed the presidency, Texas had been recognized by no nation other than the United States. There could be no hope of securing either a loan or any form of financial help unless there could be political recognition by several of the major European powers. Lamar, sensing the importance of such international acceptance, made this the focal point of his foreign policy.

A Texan agent was already in Europe: J. Pinckney Henderson had gone to London in the fall of 1837 on the authorization of the first Texas Congress. Soon after his arrival he had interviewed Lord Palmerston, the British foreign minister, who had expressed interest in Henderson's request for a formal treaty of recognition. However, two problems immediately surfaced. A schooner under the flag of His Britannic Majesty had been taken captive by a Texan ship in August, 1837. Only after the vessel had been released, and Texas had agreed to pay damages, could further consideration of the matter be taken up. The other problem was even more difficult: this was the question of the Texan attitude toward the institution of slavery. Palmerston made it clear that he would have to have absolute assurances that Texas would not engage in the slave trade before recognition could be considered. The Abolition Party in the English Parliament strongly opposed any concessions to Texas because of the slave issue. Henderson finally gave up his attempts to consummate a treaty with Britain and left London in April, 1838.

When Lamar became president, a new Texan agent was appointed to seek recognition for the Republic in the capitals of Europe working with Henderson in attempting what he had been unable to do. The new appointee was James Hamilton. Educated in New England as a lawyer, he had served at one time as governor of the state of South Carolina. He was a man of considerable ability and was possessed with much personal charm. Lamar had known him in earlier years, and Hamilton agreed to help Texas by acting as a foreign agent for the young nation at least in part because of his friendship for the second president. Probably no better representative could have been found for this important task than Hamilton; he had once negotiated a foreign loan for the state of South Carolina where he had been president and director of a bank. In the spring of 1839, he met with Lamar and the Congress, was commissioned to seek both Texan recognition and a loan, and was granted a ten percent commission of the funds that he might raise for his own personal expenses.[6]

Hamilton arrived in London in September 1839, and did succeed almost immediately in securing from the British government a treaty of "amity, commerce and navigation."[7] Although this simple agreement was far from the full recognition that he sought, as a skillful negotiator, he realized that it was an important first step. While waiting for a more favorable climate in the English capital, he crossed over to the continent and proceeded to secure both a treaty of trade and of recognition from the government of the Netherlands. By September 15, 1840, the formal agreement was completed in Holland, and Hamilton was officially presented to the king who signed the document.

In the meantime Henderson had been negotiating with the French for recognition. In the fall of 1839, a general treaty of recognition was signed in France, and Saligny was made chargé d'affaires with instructions to go to Texas and establish an embassy. This was clearly the first step toward possible financial assistance.

Saligny did go to Texas, sojourned only briefly in the capital city of Austin, withdrew to the coast, and finally made his unfavorable report on conditions in the frontier republic that had much to do with cooling down French ardor for economic involvement in the future of the Republic of Texas.[8]

Hamilton, after his successful conclusion of the Dutch treaty, went to work in nearby Belgium. Although it took somewhat longer to secure a treaty of recognition there, finally in the fall of 1840, the Belgian government officially recognized Texas.[9]

However, the long sought acceptance by Great Britain was yet to come. Hamilton turned his efforts in this direction. On November 13 he and Palmerston agreed to a recognition statement, and on the next day, an agreement was signed that bound Texas to assume a million pounds sterling of the Mexican debt if within six months Mexico had acknowledged Texas through British mediation.[10] This stipulation was the basis of the English help that Lamar's emissaries received in Mexico and came very close to bringing about an end to the hostilities with that country.

In January, 1841, the commercial treaty with Great Britain was ratified in Texas, but a portion of the agreement that had to do with the suppression of the slave trade was delayed en route and was not ratified until the next year. Hamilton knew that some reaction to this could well set in and he deliberately arranged for this delay.

He wrote to Lamar in a letter dated January 4, 1841: "I did not apprise you of the slave trade convention which I had to conclude with Lord Palmerston to ensure recognition, because I was fearful unattended by those explanations Mr. Burney might afford, it would be liable to misconstruction." [11] Ratification was not finally completed until May, 1842, but a consul general, Charles Elliot, was appointed for Texas in the final days of 1841.[12] However, Texas had become a recognized nation of the world: the United States, Belgium, the Netherlands, France and Great Britain officially had declared that the Republic was a free and independent state. This had been consummated under Lamar's leadership and had been accomplished largely through the efforts of his personal friend James Hamilton. This was certainly no small achievement.

A contemporary wrote these words about Lamar:

> No president ever appointed wiser plenipotentiaries than he did when he commissioned these elegant gentlemen and accomplished statesmen to represent the young Republic in

Europe. They effected the recognition of her independence in England, France, Belgium, Holland and made such treaties with these countries as secured for Texas a respectable station among the leading governments of the old world . . . it formed such commercial ties between Texas and these governments that it made the annexation of the Republic to the United States absolutely necessary for the preservation of that great confederacy.[13]

That statement was a fair assessment of the situation of the nation that now existed beyond the Sabine. No longer could it be looked upon as a nondescript collection of irresponsible rebels that had gathered together on a temporary basis in a little known part of the world. Texas was now a nation that had to be reckoned with either as in independent entity or as a potential part of the union of American states. More and more it appeared that Texas might become a continuing nation that could very well extend its power from the shores of the Gulf of Mexico all the way to the Pacific Ocean.

The young Republic was now a recognized nation — but she was still a very poor one. World recognition was necessary for her very existence; but now, if she was to continue as an independent state, there would have to be money with which to operate. Hamilton's long-range objective was that of securing a substantial loan from European bankers backed by one of the more powerful governments. Since French recognition had come first, he began to concentrate his efforts toward securing a loan for Texas in Paris.

Lamar received a letter in May 1841, requesting that a special session of Congress be called to consummate the arrangements for a loan that Hamilton was then almost certain of obtaining. His correspondent added: "Houston has already taken grounds against the loan, and has, I am informed, sworn it shall not come into the country." [14]

This statement from the former president was in reaction to an announcement that had reached Texas earlier that Lamar's agent had arranged a contract for a large sum from Lafitte and Company of France.[15] In April the *New Orleans Bee* stated that "New York papers of the 26th (February 1841) contain the important intelligence of Gen. Hamilton's having effected the negotiation of a loan for Texas in Paris." [16]

In July, the *Texas Sentinel*, published in Austin, quoted Hamilton as having declared on May 18, 1841, that "I have completed my contract with J. Lafitte and Co., for the Texian Loan to which he issued the enclosed prospectus and explanatory notice." This agreement would make available to Texas the sum of seven million dollars or 37 million francs which would be used to establish a national bank. The contract, however, further specified that 5,000,000 acres of Texas land would be mortgaged: half of the custom house duties of the nation and half of the price of the sale of land belonging to the national domain would be obligated for the retirement of the debt.[17]

However, after Hamilton had left France for England, French reaction against the agreement began to set in.[18] On the other hand, the portion of the contract that proposed to put Texas land on the line for credit caused considerable misgivings in the Republic. This was undoubtedly Houston's objection to the plan. In any case, the French government decided to withdraw its support of the loan. It is difficult to determine the extent to which Saligny's negative assessment of his sojourn in Texas actually effected the decision. Possibly the general international monetary situation was the leading factor in the French rejection of the loan — at that time even the best United States securities were selling far below their face value in Europe.[19] However, the affair of the pigs, insofar as it may have led some French officials to feel there was a general instability and potential lawlessness in Texas, was at least a contributing factor.

Hamilton immediately turned to the British for help. He had good contacts in London and he began to plague the British ministry for the initiation of serious negotiations for a similar loan. In October 1841, he received a definite refusal from the government of Great Britain based largely on the French decision not to advance money for Texas. He then went to Belgium, but when it was known in Europe that there was reluctance elsewhere to underwrite such a loan, the last possibility for adequate funding for the Republic of Texas ceased to exist.[20]

This meant that Lamar's government was now in serious difficulty. Much had been projected on the assumption that the loan would be consumated and that this would provide financial stability for the nation. James Webb wrote early in the year 1841 that the treasury was empty. His letter dated January 18 was in answer to one of the many requests for funds in which he summed up conditions that existed then and that continued to exist throughout the remainder of Lamar's term of office: "I would have sent . . . some money if I could have got any from the Treasury department, but as yet there is no appropriation for the new year and the old is entirely exhausted." [21]

Alden Jackson reported later in the year from Galveston that in New Orleans "Texas money [is] selling at 12 to 13¢." [22]

Not long before this George Teulon had stated in the *Austin City Gazette* that "Congress will soon convene, and the pay of its members will not purchase their food. The members cannot long live upon patriotism and many of them have nothing else but that and their pay to live upon." [23]

Late in 1841 Samuel Roberts wrote to Lamar lamenting the "exhaustion of the mail transportation appropriation." [24]

Lamar, himself, as late as 1846, had not received his full salary as president.[25] Apparently he did not take advantage of his position to secure any special preferment. All of the members of the government were to suffer serious personal privation.

The use of promissory notes came into common practice when the depressed treasury sought to meet its necessary obligations. John G. Chalmers, Secretary of the Treasury, attempted to continue to operate in the face of the financial crisis, but these notes were usable at about only one sixth of their face value.[26]

Both Houston and Anson Jones, Lamar's leading opponents at the time, made considerable capital of the administration's predicament. They charged that Lamar had been extravagant and promised to move Texas toward a policy of strict economy once they gained political power. However, the records indicate that neither of Lamar's two successors in office were able to overcome satisfactorily the financial problems of Texas. While the public debt had increased under Lamar from $1,886,425 to over $7,000,000, the increase continued until Texas had a debt that nearly reached $10,000,000 before annexation ended the life of the Republic.

Texas, however, was not alone in her financial problems. The worldwide panic begun in 1837 continued for a full five years, and by the early 1840s had gripped most of the nations of the international trading community. Lamar was blamed — with some justification — for his failure to solve Texas's fiscal difficulties; however, he was not the sole cause of the worldwide monetary depression!

One of his supporters reacted to the charges of Lamar's loose handling of funds with these words:

> I challenge the proofs of his extravagance as president. The records of the Treasury vindicate him fully from the charge ... in no year of his administration did the expenditures of the government exceed the appropriation made by Congress one cent.[27]

Lamar's administration had operated in its early years with what seemed to Houston and his sympathizers to be excessive expenditures of money. This was done in the conviction that Texas could and would redeem herself and pay off her debts as she became established as a nation. A foreign loan would hold things together until that time; but when the loan from abroad failed to materialize, the Republic was in serious difficulty.

Lamar's conviction that such a loan was both possible and workable was an honest one. This was a conviction that, except for the worldwide financial situation and possibly the pigs of Mr. Bullock, might have been realized.

[14]

Texans at Sea

Clean white sails on tall masts caught the early morning winds as the war schooner *San Jacinto* put out to sea. It was late July in 1840. The command to cast off had just been given, and soon the new canvass was responding to the tacking of the helmsman as the vessel made its way against the prevailing breeze of the Gulf Coast. The morning sunlight sparkled on the water as the ship cut sharply across the wave crests steadily widening the distance landward as she left behind the coast of Texas.

There was nothing unique about a sailing vessel clearing Galveston harbor — countless others had done the same since before the days of Jean Lafitte. But there was one unusual feature about this event. This was the fact that the *San Jacinto* was a warship of the Texas navy and flew the flag of the Republic of Texas. Two other naval vessels were preparing to sail, the *Austin* and the *San Bernard*; these quickly followed their sister ship to sea. Four days earlier the steamer *Zavala* had been dispatched with fleet supplies and a letter of introduction from

Federalist General Canales to General Anaya of Yucatan. The Texas navy was now on the high seas.

Plans for a seagoing force for the young Republic had been under consideration as early as November of 1836. Memucan Hunt had written Lamar shortly after he had been elected to the vice-presidency urging that arrangements for the development of a navy be initiated. The fact that Texas had a long coastline, and was most readily accessible to the rest of the world by sea, made such a proposal quite logical. Hunt discussed plans for the purchase of a ship in New York that would become the flagship of the Republic's naval force and stated that "arrangements were almost complete when I left New York for the purchase of a vessel of 22 guns."[1]

When Houston took office shortly after this letter was written, plans for an active Texas navy were severely retarded. The logical assumption that most of his contemporaries had made was that if Texas was to be an independent nation it should operate a navy, was not shared by the first president of the Republic. He did appoint a naval commissioner and the Texas Congress approved the plan to purchase ships, but little was done toward creating an effective seagoing force during Houston's term of office. Houston's approach to the government of the Republic as being that of no more than a caretaker pending annexation to the United States had much to do with his lack of interest in a navy. In addition, the first president of Texas had a background that was far from nautical: he could see little value in naval operations.

Immediately after his inauguration, Lamar began to promote the concept of a Texan navy. His policy of genuine Texan independence mandated such action. In a message to Congress, he stated his convictions about the importance of such a service:

> Should the blockade of the Mexican ports by the Navy of France be raised (and there is no assurance that it will not shortly be) the ships of war of our enemy would again appear on our coast and annoy commerce. The protection of our maritime frontier . . . is a public duty . . . this duty may effectively be accomplished by a naval force of small mag-

nitude though under the present conditions of our credit and finances not at a moderate expense.²

Congress endorsed the proposal and efforts were accelerated to secure ships. The *Zavala* was purchased from an Englishman named Holford; this was a 569-ton steamship-of-war that could provide dependable reinforcement and supplies for other vessels. In the meantime a Baltimore shipbuilder was contacted and plans were made for a 600-ton full-rigged corvette of twenty-two guns, two 400-ton brigs each mounting sixteen guns, and for three 170-ton schooners mounting eight or nine guns each.³ This would produce an effective fighting force that could hold its own against fairly substantial odds in a battle at sea provided adequate personnel could be found to man the Texan fleet. Eventually eight vessels — ranging from the 600-ton sloop-of-war *Austin*, that carried twenty-three officers and 151 men — to the tender *Louisville*, of only 95-tons — sailed under the Texas flag.⁴

Essential to the success of such an operation was the selection of an able naval commander. Lamar immediately looked to the American navy for the experienced leadership that would be essential to the task of building an effective seagoing force. He found such a person in Edwin Ward Moore, a twenty-nine-year-old lieutenant who was then serving aboard the U.S.S. *Boston* of the United States' Gulf Squadron.

Moore had entered the American navy as a midshipman at the age of fifteen. Ten years later he received the gold stripes of a lieutenant. He was a man who had the basic prerequisites for naval command and who undoubtedly would have reached a captaincy in the United States navy, and in time possibly an even higher rank. However, peacetime seagoing did not provide much opportunity for rapid advancement, and he was responsive to the proposal that he be named post captain in the Texas navy. When this position was offered to him by Lamar, he readily accepted.

Moore has been described as "genial, blue eyed, fair complexioned and with brown hair." ⁵ He had had fourteen years of experience as a seaman, and he could boast of an excellent record; he was certainly qualified for the important responsibility that would be placed on his shoulders. In addition he was a person of considerable initiative: he had a creative temperament, and had worked on inventions to improve the marine steam engine then in use.[6]

On November 18, 1839, Lamar sent to the Senate a carefully executed paper listing naval appointments. Post Captain Edwin W. Moore headed the list. In addition there were to be four commanders, twenty lieutenants, five surgeons, seven pursers, four sailing masters, forty-four midshipmen, a navy agent and store keeper.[7]

The navy was ready for sea duty by mid-year in 1840. The first cruise under Moore, who by now was being greeted by the title of Commodore in recognition of the fact that he had a seaworthy fleet under his command, took the flotilla into Mexican waters.

One of the developments Lamar's government had been watching closely was the discontent with the central leadership of Mexico that was being exhibited by the inhabitants of the peninsula of Yucatan. An outbreak of revolutionary fervor had occurred there as early as May, 1839, and by the spring of 1840, a separate state had been proclaimed that sought independence from Mexico City. Moore's first assignment was to sail to Yucatan and explore the possibility of cordial relations with the leadership of that province. On August 28, 1840, he was able to report to the secretary of the navy that Santiago Mendez, the governor-elect of Yucatan, "was anxious that the most friendly relations should be established at an early period" between Texas and the breakaway state.[8]

Moore then wrote to Lamar he was convinced that the navy under his command now put Texas in a position to "push them [the central Mexican government] for they never were so prostrate."[9]

In the meantime the commodore was well aware that a state of war still existed between Texas and Mexico. Enemy shipping were logical prizes under the circumstances, and when the fleet returned to Galveston, he had in tow a Mexican vessel that had been captured on the high seas.

Lamar received a report in November that Judge Shelby had duly condemned the captive ship as a prize of war, ordered it to be sold at public auction, and the funds made available to the government of the Republic for the continued support of the Navy. Lamar's correspondent, Thomas Green, suggested in this letter that there should be "more resolution of approbation to Commodore Moore for thus defending our National Honor." [10]

The fact that the new naval force had begun to find ways to pay for itself was not the only positive factor in its operation. The British were taking renewed interest in Texas because of the existence of Moore's fleet. Hamilton's successful negotiation of a treaty of recognition in London in late 1840 was undoubtedly aided by this fact.[11] France, too, had noted the Texan naval strength. The French Admiral Baudin reported favorably on a meeting with Moore and his men.[12] In any case the simple fact that the young nation had been able to send a fleet to sea certainly had a positive impact upon the efforts of the Republic's struggling diplomats abroad. Then, too, the navy's very existence proclaimed to the leaders of Mexico that Texas meant business about maintaining its independence and confronted them with the possibility of extensive depredations upon their seagoing commerce. It was no coincidence that serious consideration of a treaty with Texas came closer to reality in the months that followed than at any other time in the history of the Republic. The government in Mexico City knew that an invasion by Texas into the heartland of Mexico was unlikely, but they were well aware that their ports and seacoast were open targets for Texan naval operations. Commodore Moore's force on the high seas certainly strengthened the hands of those who were working on the complicated problems of recognition and treaty completions both in Europe and Mexico.

For a time after its return to Galveston, the Texan fleet had to content itself with surveying the coast and doing routine patrol duty. This survey work was important, however, and Moore was able to produce charts of the Texas coast that were later published by the British Admiralty and were eagerly sought by all ship masters bound for the shores of the Republic.[13]

Earlier in the year, a letter had reported misconduct of Texan naval officers in New Orleans.[14] A statement of this same period indicated some discontent among the personnel of the navy over the "irregularity as to their pay."[15] These problems continued to beset the Texas seagoing force: lack of adequate financial backing and morale injured in part by the unwillingness of some to accept the necessity and the importance of the navy.

Interestingly enough, one piece of correspondence during this time indicated that the navy's strongest foe was on the verge of relenting in his opposition, and stated that Sam Houston was about to be converted to the usefulness of the navy. They quoted the crusty old hero of San Jacinto as saying that he "did not know that the Navy was so well fitted for service."[16] Apparently this was no more than a passing comment, for there is every indication that Houston continued his efforts to scuttle the entire operation and remained a staunch foe of Lamar's navy.

The opportunity for the greatest period of usefulness for Commodore Moore's fleet began in 1841 when the Yucatan revolt reached a new level. In June the separatist movement on the peninsula became a full-scale revolution: the leaders of Yucatan declared complete independence from Mexico. On June 29 Webb wrote to Lamar: "Let Texas enter into arrangements at once with Yucatan . . . and each party mutually recognize the Independence of the other."[17]

Lamar responded at once to this suggestion and his secretary replied to Webb that "the President . . . considers the questions involved of such magnitude as to determine him to go at once in person to Galveston."[18]

A letter was carefully prepared by Lamar addressed to the governor of Yucatan under the date of July 20, 1841. It was accompanied by the instruction that it should be published "if in his opinion compatible with the public interest."

In this statement he declared: "It has been my earnest desire to establish with the States of Yucatan and Tobasco and such others as may throw off the yoke of Central despotism in Mexico, relations of amity and friendship." [19]

Yucatan immediately responded by sending a commissioner, Martin Francisco Peraza, to treat with Texas. He arrived in Austin on September 11 to confer with Lamar, and an agreement was soon reached whereby his state was to pay the sum of $8000 to Texas to get the Texan fleet ready for sea and then continue to pay an additional $8000 a month as long as the fleet was needed. In addition the Texans were to take captive whatever Mexican ships they could capture with the prerogative of having these adjudicated in Texan ports with the prize money to be divided equally between the two states.[20] It was a rather generous arrangement and one that made Lamar's navy practical in terms of the Republic's economic situation. Texas at the time had three ships that were available for sea duty, and a group of seamen who were ready and anxious for action led by a very energetic commander. The funds agreed upon were ample to keep the navy at sea, provide regular wages for its personnel and make of this operation the only financially soluble department of the government.

Moore went to work in the fall of 1841 and got his ships fitted out for sea duty. He sailed on December 13 from Galveston for Mexican waters. In early January he arrived off Sisal. The Revolution had begun to become somewhat less active by this time, and a partial agreement between the two warring parties was in process. However, in spite of this, the Yucatan state honored its agreement with Lamar, and continued to make its monthly payments through March 1842. At that time Moore was notified that his services as head of a rented navy were no longer needed and he sailed back to Galveston arriving at his home port on May 1.

In the meantime Sam Houston had become president of the Republic. Never quite understanding or fully able to accept the importance of naval operations, he and his supporters had opposed the Texan navy from the outset. Immediately after his inauguration as president for his second term in late 1841, Houston had instructed the secretary of the war and navy, George W. Hockley, to order Commodore Moore and his fleet to "return forthwith to the port of Galveston and there wait further orders." [21] Moore, however, probably anticipating this action, was by then already at sea; there was no recall of a fleet in that day on the high seas once it was beyond the reach of land-based instructions.

When Moore did return home, he was not without support: even though he found himself commander of a naval force under a president who strongly opposed his operations, there was wide popular backing for the navy. Many Texans considered Moore's fleet the Republic's first line of defense. When Houston's followers tried to scuttle the navy in the Congress, they were unsuccessful. The commitee on naval affairs, although chaired by Oliver Jones, a Houston man who was opposed to the navy, finally reported out in favor of the Texan fleet, and a bill passed the Congress continuing that branch of the service.

Moore then began a personal campaign to gain both popular and financial support for the navy. The first he was able to achieve without much difficulty; the second was a near impossibility in debt-ridden Texas.

News in Texas about the treatment of Texans captured from the Sante Fe Expedition put Houston in a peculiar position: he had to take some action against the nation that had so severely used citizens of the Republic. He did the only thing he could and acted with some inconsistency: he declared a navy blockade of the Mexican coast from Tabasco to the Rio Grande. He had no other effective military force. Moore assumed that he was to carry out this instruction and proceeded to New Orleans to outfit his fleet. This he did, but Texan funds were not available to pay the costs of the repair and provisioning; for a time it looked as though the navy of Texas would be defeated by its own mortgage. The clamor for action against Mexico had died down in Texas by this time, and Houston was able to see that no funds whatsoever were made available to Moore. However, the resourceful commodore was not ready to give up his ships. The State of Yucatan again needed help, and agreed to pay to get Moore's fleet out of hock in return for his services as a fighting force off their coasts. The debt was paid by the representatives of Yucatan, and once more the navy of Texas put to sea. This was to be its last voyage but it was prepared to give a good account of itself in this final effort upon the high seas. This it did. While in Mexican waters, Moore's flotilla engaged a superior Mexican fleet off of Campeche and claimed a victory over his opponents. Although neither side won by a clear decision, the Texans did make a good showing and chased their opponents from the scene of the conflict.[22] Moore, with two sailing vessels, the *Austin* and the *Wharton*, successfully outmaneuvered the Mexican steamships, *Guadalupe* and *Montezuma*. Over 150 casualties were reported aboard the two heavily armed steamers, while the Texans only lost a total of five men.[23]

In the meantime Houston took action that was nothing short of paranoia: he declared Moore and his men pirates. Since they had not sailed under his express orders, he contended that he was justified in outlawing the commodore and all of his men. News of this action by the president of the Republic finally reached Moore, and he decided to sail for home to do battle with the more serious of his enemies. On July 14, 1843, his ships reached the navy yard at Galveston, and with that landing the history of the Texas navy came to a close.[24]

Moore then went to work to clear his own name and save the honor of the men who had sailed with him. He immediately demanded trial. At last he was given a court-martial in the latter part of the year 1844 and was finally acquitted of all charges other than that of insubordination for which no penalty was given to him. His ships he had so proudly commanded were left to rot in Galveston.

There can be little question that the navy of Texas played a substantial part in aiding Texas in her efforts to remain a free state. Both the French and the British were impressed with the fact that the Republic, under Lamar, had been able to put a fleet to sea. Although Houston's financial policies and his irascibility brought an end to its effectiveness, and the hope of annexation finally ended its necessity, Lamar's navy, even though its history was a short one, played an important role in the life of the young nation. For at least a brief time, the Lone Star flag flew on the high seas. It was a whimsical moment of glory, but one that Texas's second president could justly claim as his own.

[15]

Wagons Westward

A heavily loaded wagon train began to move slowly through the spring grass of central Texas now bleached yellow by the sunlight of the summer which comes early in that land. The creaking of the vehicles blended with animal sounds and the oaths of drivers as the entourage started northwestward. This was the Texan Santa Fe Expedition: it was mid-June of the year 1841.

There was excitement in the air as the two hundred and seventy plus volunteers took to the trail. The men had assembled on a grass-covered creek bank not far from the recently proclaimed capital of the Republic. There they made final preparations for the journey that was to take them over some of the most arid portions of Texas into New Mexico.

Just before the command had been given to move out, Mirabeau Lamar had spoken to the assemblage in what a contemporary called a "neat and appropriate address" in which he had reminded them of the great service that they were about to perform for Texas by opening a trade route to New Mexico. He then wished them good luck.[1] Well he might do so for they were going to need more than good fortune to counteract what lay ahead of them.

But on that June morning there was little thought among the travelers other than enthusiastic optimism. They were confident that their mission could be accomplished, and although little was known about the country over which they were to travel, they were full of the excitement of exploring the unexplored.

For a time Lamar, on horseback, accompanied the expedition as it slowly wound its way along hillsides and around rocky ravines. At noon he stopped with the men and cooked his own meal, and that night he slept on the ground, causing one admirer to comment: "There was a specimen of Republican simplicity." [2]

The next morning the president of the Republic returned to Austin to continue the affairs of state leaving the command in the hands of his friend Hugh McLeod. Three commissioners accompanied the expedition carrying an official communication from Lamar addressed to the people of Santa Fe. [3]

More than a year before Lamar had written a letter to the inhabitants of northern New Mexico addressing them as "fellow citizens of the Texas Republic." [4] The assumption expressed that those to whom he wrote were a part of Texas was based on more than wishful thinking. Santa Fe was far removed both geographically and politically from the center of power in Mexico. There was very little to link them to what was then the very unstable government in Mexico City other than the tie of a conquest that had occurred some three centuries before. Although they had been brought under Spanish influence by the conquistadors, during the years that followed, their relationship to the Republic of Mexico and with Spanish authority had become extremely tenuous. Certainly by Lamar's time, there was a real question as to whether or not the central government in Mexico had any working relationship with the inhabitants of the area. During the days of the Republic of Texas there was strong evidence that Mexico had given up any form of substantial political control over the

Santa Fe area. In addition there were indications that many in that land looked very favorably upon becoming a part of the new nation of Texas and were anxious for a close relationship with the Republic. Historically control from Mexico City had often proved to be oppressive. The capital of Mexico was far away from Santa Fe and little was known or understood about the needs of the New Mexicans. Austin was much closer. Texas had a seacoast with which trade relations could be developed. In any case there seemed to be a serious disintegration of central authority in Mexico with both Yucatan and Laredo having declared themselves to be separate political entities. Lamar could logically assume that in dispatching the expedition to Santa Fe he was dealing with a self-determinate people.

Although Lamar has been accused of seeking to enlarge the Republic by an act of military conquest in promoting the expedition, there is certainly no evidence of anything of this sort in his papers. His approach was that of seeking to woo the residents of New Mexico into a workable relationship with the Republic of Texas — assuming that they were no longer a part of Mexico.

His convictions were based on the fact that soon after he had become president, a rebellion had taken place in Santa Fe in January 1838, in which the people of northern New Mexico had renounced the authority of the central Mexican government.[5] He believed that he was dealing with a land-locked Yucatan. Because of this he began to urge that a massive trading expedition be sent westward under the official sanction of the government of Texas.

A letter in the Lamar Papers that was written on July 23, 1841, after the Expedition was on its way, attests to the reasonableness of this approach. Addressed to the president and signed by Thomas Blackrode, this document stated:

> I received a letter a few days ago from Wm. G. Dryden. He was in Santa Fe when he wrote. He stated he had written to you, but requested me to write to you, as you might not get his letter, and inform you that all was right in Santa Fe; he

said he had conversed with the Governor of Santa Fe and that he as well as the people were willing that Texas might establish her law and hold her government over that country. To use his words, 'all is right then for a project of that kind.' [6]

Lamar, in a message to Congress in November 1839, had urged that trade be established with the people of Santa Fe.[7] From the beginning, and throughout the planning of the expedition, there seemed to be no serious opposition to the concept. Both houses of the Texas Congress passed bills supporting such a proposal during the following year. The Senate's legislation authorized the use of the army for the undertaking, and the House approved a plan for the journey based on the enlistment of volunteers. The Congress then adjourned without actually working out a compromise bill, and made no definite plans for any form of an appropriation to pay necessary expenses. Lamar had been out of the capital at the time that the congressional session had ended. He had gone to New Orleans for medical treatment, and when he returned to Texas in February 1841, having found that both houses had passed a bill favorable to his proposal, he began to make plans to get the endeavor under way. He apparently was little concerned that no final bill had been passed, and at the time no one else seemed to take note of the fact since the differences between the two bills were relatively minor. There was no viable military establishment in Texas at the time, and Lamar proceeded to call for volunteers as the House version of the enactment had proposed. Possibly he believed that in this action he was fulfilling the stipulations of both houses of the Congress.

There was an enthusiastic and immediate response to his request for volunteers for the expedition. Apparently there was wide acceptance of the plan, and soon goods and wagons were assembled, along with a sizable company of adventurers. Considerable interest in the project existed beyond the borders of Texas and several journalists from abroad joined the westward bound travelers. Realizing that the journey had to be made during the summer months, final plans were completed quickly. It was at this point that an American agent in Texas reported to Daniel Webster, who was then secretary of state for the United States, on the progress of the undertaking:

> An expedition of 250 men, under the control of three commissioners, left Austin, on the 6th instant for Santa Fe. The object of the Republic is to open a trade with the people for that country, and induce them if possible, to become an integral part of Texas.[8]

This was perhaps as succinct a statement as any of the purpose of the endeavor.

As the wagons were rolling westward, Lamar in an address delivered in Houston, made reference to the reasons why he had such high hopes for the entourage "now on its route." He spoke of Texas as "our still infant Republic ... without a dollar in the treasury ... our credit ... still sinking." He believed that trade with the New Mexicans could solve the financial problems of the nation.[9]

Santa Fe had for centuries been a center of trade. Wagon trains from northern Mexico had met caravans from Saint Louis to exchange millions of dollars worth of goods each year. If a workable trade route could be established from the northern Rio Grande city that could bring some of that trade into Texas and supply not only the frontier settlements but establish a route to Galveston and the sea, it would mean a steady flow of commercial wealth into the Republic. It was an exciting possibility and one that was generally felt to hold real potential for the depressed financial condition of the nation. James Webb wrote to Lamar as the plans for the project took final form: "You are popular even in Houston: The Santa Fe expedition seems to meet with general favor all through the country."[10] Lamar was not alone in assuming that such a trade route would be a tremendous boon to the future prospects of the Republic of Texas.

There was but one serious fallacy in this assumption: this was the simple geography of western Texas. Lamar's planners believed that the trip was only a little over five hundred miles in distance. The route that was actually taken, because of the terrain and the unique ground cover of much of the country, was nearly 1300 miles. In addition there was little water to be found most of the year along the route that McLeod's caravan was to traverse. Heavy cross timbers greatly impeded the movement of the wagons of the expedition on part of the journey; at other points where there was no greenery, there was also no water. The simple fact was that there was no easy and practical wagon route from Austin to Santa Fe over the upward sloping and difficult terrain of the country. Although men had traversed these great expanses since the days of Coronado, there was still relatively little known about the area, and conceptions of both distances and geography were extremely vague. Even the best contemporary maps provided no accurate information. Arrowhead's map, published in 1841, shows scant knowledge of West Texas.

The expedition was well chronicled. Among those who accompanied McLeod's command was George W. Kendall, a writer for the New Orleans *Picayune*. He had been an early promoter of the attempt to establish a trade route to the west; he had stated in a mid-1840 article in the Louisiana journal that "our Texan neighbors have been talking lately about making a dash into the Santa Fe trade." He had further commented: "It will not do for them to waste much time in debating the matter if they wish to secure this branch of the trade."[11]

Lamar invited him to accompany the expedition knowing of his interest in the project.[12] His narrative became the most widely read account of the journey and was eventually to go through seven editions in the dozen years that followed.[13]

Another chronicler of the journey was an Englishman by the name of Thomas Falconer, who was a welcome guest among the adventurers. He had been a jurist and an editor; his many talents qualified him both as a man of science and a man of letters. He kept a diary from August 31, 1841, through October 9, 1841: this and his notes on the expedition have provided additional details about the trip.[14]

However, the only complete diary of the adventure was

one kept by Peter Gallagher giving a day-by-day account of the journey including estimates of distances traveled.[15] It is this record that is the basic source of information about the actual progress of the caravan.

The entourage moved slowly through the brush country of central Texas, and five days after its start, the travelers were barely fifty miles northeast of Austin.[16] In the days that followed, the journeyers were sometimes able to move no more than three miles during a full daylight period, and on other days the heavily loaded wagons advanced from twelve to fourteen miles. The vehicles were not adapted to rapid movement. Sometimes paths had to be cut by hand through the tangled undergrowth before any substantial progress could be realized. Since seeking water sources was essential, the trail had to be blazed through valley areas where rugged and tangled undergrowth generally abounded. Wagon wheels were often snarled and both human and animal progress was impeded.

By July 9 the expedition had sighted Comanche Peaks, and two days later, Gallagher recorded that they had crossed the Brazos River five miles below the peaks.[17] On July 20, camp was made on the head of a ravine running into the west branch of the Trinity River.[18] Movement continued to be slow with the average advance reported between six and twelve miles each day. That some real internal problems were developing in the ranks of the party is indicated by a report written when the entourage had been underway for a month that a "council requested Gen. McLeod to resign." [19] However, in spite of this discontent with Lamar's appointee, he continued to direct the progress of the caravan and the cumbersome wagon train slowly pushed westward.

The fact that there were hostile Indians in the land through which they were traveling became apparent when, on August 1, buffalo were chased into the camp as an harassment tactic by the native inhabitants of the area.[20] Three days later camp was made near a Waco Indian village.[21] But the travelers continued westward, sometimes changing their direction of movement to the northwest, or as Gallagher put it "west by north." [22]

A scouting expedition was sent out during August to locate the Red River which was discovered some fifty miles north of the line of march.[23] The caravan was now moving up onto the high plains with its endless horizons stretching as far as the eye could see into monotonous evenness. For most of the adventurers it was a new world: a vast, unbelievable stretch of openness that continued on ahead until it blended with a sky dominated by the searing heat of the summer sun. The importance of water became more and more apparent in the journal entries written late in the month: during this time camp was made from time to time at such locations as "fresh water lake" or "small water hole." [24] More rapid progress was evidenced during this part of the journey since the wagons were able to travel sometimes as much as sixteen miles a day. However, the location of water sources now became a major limitation to the caravan's movement as the West Texas sun began to bring its full force to bear upon the expedition: the wagons could only move as far as the next watering spot, and then wait until another could be discovered.

On August 30, a water search party was surprised by a band of Indians who apparently considered the usurpation of the scant supply of that commodity a serious trespass upon their rights. Five members of the expedition were killed by the indignant natives. The line of travel was then changed to take the caravan into Palo Duro Canyon where water was known to exist.[25] It was now apparent that the entourage was facing a serious crisis. They were on the high plains; water supplies were extremely short, and there were hostile Indians in the area who were prepared to fight to maintain their possession of the meager sources of water that existed in this semi-desert land.

Situated in their camp in the deep recesses of Palo Duro, a canyon that dramatically bisects the flatness of the plains country, some course of action had to be established. On August 31, a party of one hundred men was sent ahead under the command of Colonel Cooke with instructions to determine conditions, head across the arid *Llano*, and report back as to what route should be taken with the slower moving and heavily loaded wagons.[26] There was also the assumption that this advance party would be able to bring back help from the authorities in New Mexico, who were eagerly awaiting their arrival and would undoubtedly welcome them.

Then the fickleness of the West Texas climate became apparent: having sweltered under the heat of a summer sun for weeks, the men of the expedition experienced the phenomenon of a sudden Texas norther that swept down upon them with bone chilling air penetrating deep into the narrow walls of the canyon at the unusually early date of September 1. One of the chroniclers recorded this event with some amazement.[27]

Two days later the main body moved up river only to have the Indians, who by now were watching every move, force a cattle stampede resulting in the loss of eighty-seven valuable animals.[28] Tragedy seemed to be striking on every side as though the very walls of their canyon haven were closing in on them: a Major B.B. Sturgis died of what Gallagher called "consumption" on September 11, and on the next day, two men were killed by Indians. The chronicler recorded under the date of September 13 what must have been something of an understatement: "the men were dissatisfied." [29]

It was at this point that a Mexican arrived in camp with the message reported to be from Cooke's advance party urging the caravan to continue its journey westward. Once more the wagons began to move: they reached the head of Palo Duro on September 19, and the next day, slowly worked their way up a four hundred foot incline to what Gallagher called the "grand prairie." [30] Now on level ground rapid movement was possible: during the later part of the month, the expedition was able to cover 125 miles in six days. On September 28, the party made its descent from the high flatness of the *Llano Estacado*. Three days later they found water, and then continued in a generally westward direction through broken country to the *Laguna Colorado*, which they reached on October 4.[31]

There the final chapter in the tragic drama of the Santa Fe Expedition began. Near starvation from lack of food, harassed by hostile Indians, and uncertain about essential water supplied in a strange country that had proved to be very different from any terrain with which they were familiar, they were suddenly confronted by an armed party of Mexicans. The initial meeting seemed friendly: however, the Texans were immediately informed that they would have to give up their arms in exchange for food and a guarantee of freedom. A council of officers was called. It was obvious that they could not retreat over the impossible terrain through which they had just traveled. Weakened by lack of food and the hardships of the trail, they were in no condition to fight. They formally agreed to surrender their arms on the conditions that had been offered to them. Well aware of the quantity of goods on board the wagons and their worth, and seeing no other course, the decision was made to capitulate. Apparently they expected their armed hosts to live up to the agreement that had been reached.[32]

Once surrender was complete, the captors of the Texans took quick action to make the expedition as potentially harmless as possible. The officers and leaders of the party were sent on ahead to San Miguel, military headquarters for the territory that now was clearly under the control of the central government of Mexico. Whatever inclinations of separatism that may have existed in New Mexico earlier had by this time been effectively neutralized. A military authority was in firm control of the land and the Texans suddenly realized they were prisoners of war.

Gallagher, who had gone on ahead of the main party with the officers, reported that on October 12 they were told that they were to be sent immediately to Mexico City. Four days later they left on that long and difficult journey traveling by forced marches southward to Paso del Norte and then on to Chihuahua and Zacatecas. It was a brutal trail they traversed; little mercy was shown as the once proud Texans struggled simply to remain alive. Some died enroute: others were near death from maltreatment when they reached the population centers of Mexico. Some sympathetic aliens in Zacatecas took pity on the prisoners and hired two wagons for those who were too sick to continue their journey on foot. This act of compassion saved some lives. By December 9, the bedraggled unfortunates had reached San Luis Potosi. In February, after having experienced the most extreme of prison conditions in San Christopher and Puebla, at times being penned up with so many fellow prisoners that there was no room in which to lie down, Gallagher arrived in Perote Prison. There he and many of the other captives remained incarcerated for months. He was finally released in May, but many of his comrades were less fortunate: some had died on the long journey southward into Mexico and others expired while in prison.[33] In all it was a tragic conclusion to what had begun as an exciting adventure.

Back in Austin, lack of any intelligence of the progress of the Texan expedition by the early fall of 1841 began to raise feelings of apprehension. Rumors of disaster started to filter back to Texas in the closing days of Lamar's administration. There was even talk of impeachment of the president as the possibility of the imprisonment of expedition members became more and more apparent. However, there is no evidence that the House of Representatives in which such an action would have had to be initiated ever gave serious consideration to such an arraignment.[34] The rumors came more rapidly as time went by, and by the beginning of 1842, it was generally known that the entire entourage had been captured and that the survivors were prisoners. Anson Jones, who had just become secretary of state under Sam Houston's presidency wrote these words on January 3, 1842:

> The Santa Fe expedition has failed and all the poor fellows engaged in it have either perished or been led into hopeless Mexican captivity ... It has thrown a perceptible gloom over our city for several days past. How strange are the changes & vicissitudes of a few months or days. I now occupy the room a short time since used by H. McLeod, the Commander of that illstarred and foolish enterprise. It is

now the office of the Secretary of State. In this room the expedition was principally planned ... Now ask for all that crowd of fools and knaves & flatterers of power who basked in the smiles of executive influence — & where are they! Gone and scattered forever — some are dead, others doomed to hopeless misery ... in the Mines of Mexico, the rest powerless weak — accused & despised & wishing themselves with the others ...[35]

The details of capitulation of the Texans and the march into Mexico were soon available in Texas through a letter written by Senor Manuel Alvarez, United States Consul at Santa Fe. A wave of anger swept through the Republic. Congress reacted immediately by ordering that the boundaries of the Republic of Texas be moved westward to the Pacific Ocean and southward to the Tropic of Cancer. It was a futile gesture of retaliation that obviously could not be substantiated in any practical way. It was simply one of those parliamentary acts that such bodies perform when no action is possible. President Houston banded it a "legislative jest" and immediately vetoed it. Congress responded by overriding the veto and then adjourned.[36]

After the first wave of anger had swept the young nation, the public began to look about for someone upon whom to vent its anger. The new administration led by Houston had had little to do with the promotion of the undertaking, but by February the onus of failure was even falling upon them.[37] However, it was Mirabeau Lamar who logically enough was to receive the heaviest burden of the blame for the tragedy.

On January 26, 1842, *The Weekly Texian* printed a letter signed with the single initial "A" that made the proposal that Lamar be swapped to Mexico for the Santa Fe expedition hostages.[38] Houston commented that Lamar would probably duel with the author if he could identify him.[39]

Lamar did make an effort to determine who had written the anonymous piece although there is no evidence that he proposed to revive the outlawed code of honor.[40] He wrote James Webb in February asking that he seek an answer from the new secretary of state regarding rumors that the letter had

been "penned by one of the members of the Executive Cabinet
... Anson Jones." [41] Lamar described the article as one that
"after much personal abuse, proposes that I should be delivered up to the vengeance of Mexico for the redemption of the unfortunate Santa Fe prisoners." [42]

James Mayfield wrote Lamar in March stating he believed Jones was the author,[43] but the secretary of state made a denial of any involvement in the matter.[44] Apparently the ex-president decided to follow the advice of James Webb, who wrote him on March 3 advising that he should overlook the letter for "to pursue such game is hardly worth the candle." [45]

However, although Jones may not have composed the virulent letter that appeared in print, his personal feelings about the entire matter were not far from the sentiments the anonymous publication had expressed. He repeatedly not only blamed Lamar for the entire tragedy, but charged that he had acted without proper legal authorization. The fact that there was some variance in the language of the two bills which had passed the respective houses of Congress became a point of contention for Lamar's detractors. On one occasion Jones called the dispatching of the expedition a "despotic exercise of executive power, which no monarch would have dared venture upon in these times." He further described the expedition as a "chase of silly hopes and fears, begun in folly, closed in tears." [46]

Houston concurred in this belief and sought to take political advantage of the tragedy by repeatedly charging that Lamar had called for volunteers for the expedition without full legislative consent. "Had I sent and received commissioners ... and permitted them to be present at the outset of the ill fated Santa Fe expedition, and never laid these communications before the Congress," he declared in a speech in 1845, "I might have been charged with faithlessness to my office." [47]

These were statements of men in office who wanted to make it abundantly clear that they would accept no blame for a tragedy that had been planned by their predecessor. The fact that they held positions of leadership when the full extent of the disaster became generally known, and were powerless at the time to take any effective action, made it imperative that the entire responsibility be firmly fixed upon the former administration. They, of course, chose to ignore the fact that there had been almost universal acceptance of the concept of such an expedition at the outset; it was only after the complete failure of the endeavor was apparent that there was a general denunciation of the plan. Most modern writers have accepted uncritically the postmortem judgment of Lamar's political opponents in declaring the expedition a "fiasco," [48] "ill-judged aggression," [49] or a "wild goose chase," [50] that was entirely a deluded dream of the second president.[51]

One contemporary, however, defended the effort in the belief that it did alarm Mexico to the extent that the central government of that nation was compelled to strengthen its defenses on her northern frontier and the "settlements of Texas . . . were left entirely undisturbed" for the remaining years of the existence of the Republic.[52]

Certainly one positive gain that resulted from the Santa Fe tragedy was that reports of the expedition were widely read in the United States: this brought the question of Texas again before the American public and was an important factor in renewing interest in the annexation of the Republic. In addition, this conclusively ended any hope that remained among the inhabitants of the young nation that they could continue indefinitely as an independent state without eventual merger with the mother country. It was in essence the end of the policy of Texan independence.

For Mirabeau Lamar, it meant that his administration was to terminate with the dark cloud of dismal failure hanging over it. Whatever else he had succeeded in doing was now forgotten. The success of the Texas navy, the political progress that had been apparent in gaining recognition from major European nations, the building of a permanent capital city, and the efforts toward establishment of a responsible government at home were completely overlooked. All of this was to be negated by the tragedy of Santa Fe: the second president was to leave office with this black mark scratched across his record. He would forever after be remembered as the one who had dispatched men to death and captivity: from this onus his leadership would never completely recover.

[16]

The Impossible Dream

As the wheels of the Santa Fe bound wagons began to roll, Mirabeau Lamar turned his horse to the southeast to begin his trip back to Austin. He had shared camp that night with members of the expedition on the banks of a creek some dozen miles up trail. As the command to break camp was given on that second morning of the journey, he bade farewell to Hugh McLeod, waved to others, and made his way up the brush-covered hillside as he headed back toward the capital city of the Republic.

The caravan represented the last major effort that the second president would make as a part of his policy of Texan separatism: he had high hopes for the venture. But the slow trip over the rolling hills of the area doubtless gave him ample time to consider the other undertakings of his administration. In the Gulf of Mexico, Texas could boast a small, but effective navy. In the distant capitals of Europe, emissaries of the young nation were at work seeking to build financial stability based on the foundation that already granted treaties of recognition provided. Far to the south, in Mexico, efforts were underway which still held some hope for bringing about an official conclusion to the hostilities continuing to exist with that nation.

In his two and a half years in office, Lamar had sought to accomplish much — perhaps too much. But then, time was short. If Texas was to take its place securely among the recognized states of the world, much had to be done rapidly. The official recognition achieved abroad was only a first step: he knew very well that if the Republic was to survive, it would have to build solidly from within. The United States had rejected annexation, and Texas, at least for the foreseeable future, had to stand firmly upon her own strength. He believed that she could. His administrative policies were directed toward the goal of developing the frontier Republic into a self-sufficient nation that would and could stand alone. Texas was not to be merely an interlude between revolution and annexation. He saw his responsibility to the rapidly growing nation as far more than simply leading a caretaker government that would soon surrender its leadership to a larger and more powerful nation. He and those who worked with him in this period conceived of a Texas which had a right to exist as a separate and independent state. Much of what Lamar sought to do would have made little sense if his purpose had been simply that of breaking from Mexico in order to bring new territory into the union of the United States. Most of the criticism of his administration has been based on the completely non-historical concept that the leaders of the Republic were simply caretakers and no more. Lamar had no such thought: for him and for those who shared his leadership of the Republic, Texas *was* — and was to continue.

If the dream of independence was to be achieved, if a truly neoclassical democracy was to flourish surrounded by the forces of tyranny and darkness, then Lamar believed public school education must be available to all. It was a part of his own educational background that intellectual enlightenment was a foundation stone of a democratic society. If the citizens of a republic were to govern themselves effectively, then general education was essential in the structure of their governance.

One of the charges that had been brought against the government of Mexico by the signers of the Texas Declaration of Independence had been the fact that the rulers of the frontier colony had failed to make any effort to establish public education.¹ When the Constitution of 1836 was adopted, its framers went even a step further: they declared that "a general system of education was to be provided by Congress as soon as circumstances would permit."²

However, nothing was done to move toward this ideal that had been so dramatically proclaimed by the early architects of the Texas Republic until Lamar came to office. Perhaps even during the earliest days of the national existence of Texas there was a division between those who saw in the ideal of Texan democracy an opportunity for new directions and those who saw in the birth of the Republic nothing more than a caretaker situation.

But Lamar did not intend to promote caretakerism. In his message to Congress in December 1838, he stressed his deep concern for establishing "a comprehensive and well regulated system of mental and moral culture." It was in this statement that Lamar's most often quoted words occurred: "A cultivated mind is the guardian genius of democracy." He then went on to make this declaration:

> Our young Republic has been formed by a Spartan spirit. Let it progress and ripen into Roman firmness, and Athenian gracefulness and wisdom . . . Let me therefore urge it upon you, gentlemen, not to postpone the matter too long. The present is a propitious moment to lay the foundation of a great and moral and intellectual edifice, which will in after ages be hailed as the chief ornament and blessing of Texas. A suitable appropriation of lands to the purpose of general education, can be made at this time without inconvenience to the government of the people.³

Congress had responded to the president's challenge by appointing a committee which was ready to report as early as January 4, 1839. John A. Wharton had been chairman of the committee, but when he became ill, the Reverend W.Y. Allen helped prepare the report before the death of Wharton. The committee urged Congress to "make ... ample provision for education as the only safe ground of hope for the permanent prosperity of the Republic." They declared that plans should be formulated for a "system of general education" establishing "primary schools and colleges where every class can alike receive the benefits and blessings of education." They noted that emigration into Texas was beginning as great numbers came to Texas not only from the United States, but from England, Ireland, Scotland, and Germany. Among these would be many uneducated people who must be given the opportunity for learning if they were to become "competent to self-government." [4]

A bill was passed by Congress on January 26 and was immediately signed into law by Lamar: it provided that each county in the nation was to set apart three leagues of land in tracts of not less than 160 acres; if good land was not available in the county, they must survey and pay for land elsewhere. This land was to produce the income for establishing a vast system of public schools. In addition the president was to have surveyed fifty leagues of land for the founding of two colleges or universities. It was further provided that none of this land could be disposed of except by lease and that no such arrangement was to be allowed for longer than three years.[5]

An amendatory act was passed on February 5, 1840: this provided for school commissioners; another league of land was added to the original three that was to be dedicated to the cause of education. It was further stipulated that the commissioners were to organize school districts and establish schools where population warranted it.[6] Never before had a nation made such vigorous efforts to establish public schooling at the first initiation of its existence. It was a high and noble ideal, but by making use of the one commodity that Texas did possess in abundance, it was an extremely practical undertaking. In reality this laid the basis for public education in Texas and has had a long lasting impact upon the state which sprang from the Republic. For all of this Lamar was largely responsible; his idealism became a workable and practical reality.

The papers of the second president indicate that during the summer that the Santa Fe Caravan was rolling westward to its tragic rendezvous, that Lamar, then in the final months of his presidency, spent considerable time personally seeking to see that some substantial progress be made toward carrying out the stipulations of the public school bill that had been passed at the beginning of his term of office. Surveys of "Colleges and University Lands" were recorded in Fannin, Robinson, and Nacogdoches counties totaling fifty leagues of land. The education bill had placed this responsibility on the chief executive of the nation, and Lamar met this requirement, carefully listing his action in his personal records.[7]

In addition, county school lands were recorded in Gonzales, Harris, and Fayette counties; "Coshattie and Alabama Indian lands" were also designated to be set aside to provide adequate schools for those near them.[8]

These were but meager beginnings, but they were beginnings. The land thus stipulated for public education under Lamar's administration provided a strong base for the later development of schools when Texas became a part of the union of American states. After annexation, these endowments of real estate made it possible for the early development of a system of public education that was well on its way before the Civil War broke out; post-war advances in Texas were possible at an early time because of these initial beginnings.[9]

A number of educational institutions actually came into being during Lamar's term of office. A public school was established in Houston soon after he took the oath of office in that city. Academies were set up in such places as Galveston, Matagorda, Velasco, Quintana, Brazoria, Richmond, Gonzales, Columbia, Washington, Independence, Austin, Caldwell, Clarksville, DeKalb, San Augustine, Nacogdoches, Huntsville, Corpus Christi, and probably elsewhere.[10] His encouragement to the cause of education had much to do with the growing interest in schooling that was rapidly developing in Texas.

Lamar's correspondence indicates that he was involved in a "project of the Galveston University" which opened its doors in 1840[11] under the leadership of the Reverend W.L. McCalls, a Presbyterian minister, and continued to operate until 1844 with an annual enrollment of nearly one hundred students.[12]

A badly faded manuscript letter was preserved in the president's papers which was from Daniel Baker and dealt with a land endowment for a professorship at Austin College, one of the few institutions of higher learning that survived those early years.[13]

A number of other schools were established in Texas that had no direct relationship to Lamar: however, his interest in education was an obvious stimulus to the establishment of these intstitutions. Typical of the correspondence that has been preserved indicating this relationship is a letter addressed to Lamar before he became president of the Republic in which the writer, R.W. Chapman, asked the then vice-president to assist him in plans for a school "because I hear . . . that you . . . are a scholar and still devoted to letters, possessing learning, you can not fail to be a patron of schools." [14]

That he was generally considered to be a promoter of education is apparent from the fact that in December 1839, he was notified that he had been elected an honorary member of the Chosophic Society of the College of New Jersey,[15] and in July 1842, was made a member of the Phi Gamma Society of Emory College.[16] Whatever else his detractors might have said concerning the leadership of the second president of the Republic, there is certainly no doubt that he justly deserved the place given to him by many historians as the "father of education in Texas." [17]

His interest in the establishment of institutions of learning was related to his conviction that Texas could and should stand alone as an independent nation. This was no dreamy sort of scholasticism. This was a practical conviction that a free and separate state must have schools for the educating of its citizens and the training of its leadership. This was simply a part of Lamar's philosophy of Texan self-sufficiency: there must be adequate schooling available within the bounds of the Republic and those institutions should be able to provide the best possible education for the future leaders of Texas.

Another area of concern for Lamar was that of establishing the boundaries of Texas. If the Republic was destined to be a separate political entity, it must have as a nation a well-defined border. For some time there had been much uncertainty about the exact location of the boundary between the United States and the young nation that existed somewhere west of Louisiana and the Gulf Coast.

Soon after the second president assumed power, a commission began work on this question charged with determining the territorial limits of the two countries; this group had met initially in August 1839, in New Orleans. They assembled later in the year at Green's Bluff on the Sabine River, but no decisions were made. It was in 1841, apparently largely at Lamar's insistence, that the discussions were renewed and agreement was finally reached "about the first of July 1841:" the border of Texas would be established along the Sabine River and then run due north to the Red River.[18]

Related to this issue was the nagging question of annexation to the mother country. Controversy had continued around the presidential appointment of the envoy to the United States. When Lamar had come to office, Anson Jones was in Washington. He immediately dispatched Moses Austin Bryan, a nephew of the impresario, to assist Jones in his post. Two months later he appointed a member of his cabinet, Richard G. Dunlap, to succeed Jones, an action that Houston's appointee took as a personal affront.[19] He later sent one of his strongest men, Barnard Bee to Washington, and when Bee's work was questioned, Lamar vigorously defended the appointment.[20] The importance of this post had much to do with the attitude of Texas toward the question of annexation. When Lamar came to the presidency, there had been a wide spread reaction among Texans to the fact that the United States had turned down the proposal to establish the former

Mexican colony as a state of the Union. Lamar's feelings on the subject apparently were much deeper than that of the general public reaction to the rejection of Texas by the Van Buren administration. His inaugural address of 1838 had indicated a strong desire to see Texas remain a separate nation.

Lamar had declared:—

> If . . . the amalgamation shall ever hereafter take place, I shall feel that the blood of our martyred heroes had been shed in vain — that we had riven the chains of Mexican despotism only to fetter our country with indissoluble bonds, and that a young republic just rising into high distinction among the nations of the earth had been swallowed up and lost, like a proud bark in a devouring vortex.[21]

Very likely Mirabeau Lamar's own background that basically distrusted a federal union of states had much to do with his thinking, but this was a philosophy shared by many in Texas. In any case he was determined that the Republic would be represented in Washington by those who were in agreement with him on this all-important subject.

Lamar not only saw Texas as an independent nation free of both Mexico and the United States, but he saw his country as one that would have the same potential for westward expansion as did the federal union of states. A letter from A.S. Wright dated May 4, 1841, mentioned the possibility of the acquisition of California by Texas from the Russians who according to the writer "were anxious to sell." [22] This single piece of correspondence clearly illustrates that he could look westward and that he did envision the possibility of a Texas that would someday stretch to the shores of the Pacific.

On occasion he stated that he wanted Texas to remain free in order to develop her "internal resources [as] a great agricultural community with an open commerce with all the world." [23]

Since Texas was envisioned as an agricultural nation, the question of black slavery frequently surfaced in Lamar's correspondence. His cousin, John T. Lamar, had written in June 1839, objecting to the fact that Texas prohibited the slave trade and stated that without "slave labor . . . she cannot in a century rise in wealth and importance."[24]

Lamar's own attitude agreed to the prohibition of the slave trade, but he certainly believed what he wrote to Lord John Russell, while president, that "all persons of color who are slaves for life previous to their emigration to Texas . . . shall remain in the like state of servitude providing the said slaves shall be *bona fide* property of the persons so holding said slaves."[25]

It seems reasonable to believe Lamar's initial rejection of the annexation of Texas to the United States was related to his attitude toward slavery. However, there was much more involved in his concepts than this: his was a type of idealism that accepted slavery as a fact of life and yet believed in personal freedom and self-determination. He simply saw no conflict in these two conceptions. This was an approach that is difficult to grasp in the twentieth century; however, it was at that time highly comprehensible to those of Lamar's heritage.

When it was finally agreed that Texas could join the Union as a slave-holding state, he had no quarrel with the proposal; and even went so far as to denounce Sam Houston publicly for what he declared to be his torturous and elaborate perfidy in slowing the annexation process.[26]

During his three years in office he worked continually for a separate and independent Texas. This was the basis of much of his policy both at home and abroad. He sincerely believed Texas could stand on its own and exist as a separate and independent nation. However, the failure of the Texan loan and the eventual tragedy that resulted from the expedition to Santa Fe made it clear that continued independence was impractical: it had been no more than an impossible dream.

[17]

The Winter Chill

    Dry leaves suddenly began to swirl outside of Lamar's log cabin office. A sudden gust of wind had swept into Austin from the north: it brought with it the freshness of the open plains. The same norther that had amazed the chroniclers of the Santa Fe Expedition on the first of September would likely have reached as far as central Texas by the second day of the month. It would have resulted in no real temperature change in that mild climate so early in the season, but there would have been a noticeable wind shift: a gusting of stubble and debris in the streets and alleyways, and for those who were preceptive, there would have been the faint hint of the winter chill that was yet to come. The sky would no longer have reflected its summertime blueness in the waters of the Colorado; instead there would have been a fleecy overcast that would have presaged the early arrival of fall.
    Lamar may well have noticed the change of wind direction. If he had, he possibly wondered about the progress of the expedition that he had dispatched at the beginning of the summer. No word whatsoever had been heard from Hugh

McLeod and his command. If the distance had been no greater than the president's planners had assumed, there would have been ample time for the caravan to make its way to Santa Fe, and by then, some word could have been sent back to Texas.

As September wore on, others began to wonder about the fate of the Texans who had left Austin with such confidence in June. But the month passed and there was still no report on the travelers.

By mid-October there were those who were speaking openly about the likelihood of disaster and there were an increasing number of rumors of tragedy: by then it was obvious that something had gone wrong.

However, not only was the second president destined to end his three years of administration with this dark cloud hanging over him, but his entire last year in office had been one of growing frustration as one project after another ran into difficulty. He had been forced to go before the Congress on November 1, 1840, to admit the failure of one of the essential parts of his presidential program. In that statement he had reported that "Various circumstances have combined to impair the prospect of effecting a foreign loan." [1] He dealt at length with the difficult financial condition that the nation faced and declared that "rigid economy should be presumed in all departments of public business." [2] After that there would be little hope for the success of any of his proposals for Texas.

It was at the same time that he reported that "in relation to our position with Mexico I have nothing encouraging or satisfactory to communicate . . . our agent . . . has been received and accredited so far as to be allowed to submit the propositions he was authorized to lay before that government." [3] However, there was no actual progress to be reported toward a peaceful settlement with Mexico.

Lamar declared that "toward the United States we continue the same satisfactory relations . . ." [4] At that particular time, however, he noted that "the running and making of the boundary line between the United States and this Country has not yet been completed." [5]

All in all the tone and mood of his address was so contrary to the usually enthusiastic confidence that Lamar generally exhibited in his public deliverances, that were it not preserved in his papers in his own handwriting, one would be tempted to doubt its authenticity.[6]

He concluded the speech with a statement that he placed his confidence in Almighty God and upon "His benevolence" for which "we have reasons above all people to be satisfied with our condition." [7]

Lamar was keenly aware that he had been losing his popularity. Memucan Hunt had written him to this effect earlier from New Orleans: "Almost every one coming from Texas says so," he had stated.[8] James Love wrote in a similar vein from Houston,[9] and Lewis M.H. Washington informed Lamar in September 1840, that while in Nashville he heard criticisms of his administration.[10]

No national poll was necessary to confirm these observations. The constant attacks upon Lamar's leadership by Houston and his supporters and the continuing financial crisis added to the inevitable frustration which must have been his during his final months in office. During this time almost every administration project seemed to bog down in the face of the complexities confronting the newborn Republic that Lamar led.

Perhaps it was because of these factors, or possibly it was simply the lack of physical stamina that had always plagued him that caused his health to break. Shortly after the new Congress had begun its session, Lamar asked for a leave of absence. He requested permission to leave Texas and go to New Orleans for treatment for his illness. His friend Hugh McLeod wrote a letter of introduction to a Dr. John Baldwin in the Louisiana city,[11] and the president set out for that metropolis.

It is impossible to determine exactly what the nature of Lamar's difficulty may have been. Apparently it was something other than the malarial condition which had overcome him on his first trip to Texas. In any case, Congress granted him a leave of absence and he sought medical help in the United States.

In New Orleans he was treated for what he later described as a sickness that had caused him to be "almost wasted to the grave." [12]

He was still seriously ill in mid-January. James Webb wrote to him on January 18, 1841, stating the fact that he regretted "to learn your health is not much improved." [13]

It was during his illness that Lamar wrote two of his more somber poems: "Grieve Not for Me" and "Soldiers of the Cross." [14] The very titles of these two pieces are indicative of the contents that are demonstrative of both physical and emotional depression.

By February of 1841, he had begun to recover and before the end of the month, he made the journey back to Texas, and resumed his position as president of the Republic. In early March he received a letter offering congratulations "upon your recovery from your late serious illness and your resumption of the official duties of the high station." [15] This was signed by twenty-one persons, and contained an invitation to a public dinner in his honor.

This he declined because of "my inability at present to meet my fellow citizens . . . at the festive board." [16]

During his absence from office, Vice-president Burnet had assumed the functions of an acting president. The fact that Anson Jones was chosen as temporary chairman of the Senate over Harvey Kendrick, a supporter of Lamar's policies, is indicative of the fact that the Fifth Congress contained a strong contingent of Houston's followers.[17] When Acting President Burnet nominated William Memefee for the position of secretary of the treasury, Congress refused to confirm the appointment. Burnet finally got John G. Chalmers approved for this position, a post that probably by this time had little meaning, for the Texan treasury was more theory than fact. He did secure the confirmations of Thomas William Ward as commissioner of the General Land Office and Branch T. Archer as secretary of war.[18] By the time that Lamar was able to take up the full duties of office again, Congress had adjourned. Whatever influence his personal pres-

The Winter Chill

ence may have been able to exert upon that body was lost during this last and crucial year of his term of office as president of the Republic.

It was shortly after his return to Texas that he received word of tragedy in his own family: his brother Jefferson J. Lamar had died early in the year.[19] The fact doubtless added to the burdens that faced him.

But Lamar did take up the reigns of leadership once more: apparently he was determined to make some positive strides toward his policy goals during the remaining months left to him as president. A diplomatic dispatch was received in April by James Mayfield, United States Secretary of State in Washington, D.C., declaring there was news of "the re-establishment of Gen. Lamar's health and that he had resumed the duties of President of Texas." [20]

During the weeks that followed he was busy overseeing the planning of the Santa Fe Expedition and dispatching that entourage to the west. He completed such important, but unfinished details as that of seeing that the university lands were properly surveyed and set aside for future higher education in Texas. During these months the Texas–United States boundary settlement was made final.

But the tragedy of Santa Fe was to override whatever else he may have been able to do. Thomas Green, writing in the waning days of the Republic, praised Lamar as a man of "general chivalry of character" and defended his administration with these words: "He built the navy, and maintained the mastery of the Gulf; he beat back the Indians and extended the frontier." [21] Green lamented, however, that Lamar's administration "closed with much complaint of him as the cause of the then individual and national suffering." [22]

Houston, who was now preparing his campaign for a return to office, played upon the situation. Lamar could not succeed himself, but he did endorse his vice-president, Burnet, as his successor in office. Houston's adherents felt compelled to discredit Lamar as a part of the strategy of electing their candidate.

Almost from the beginning of their relationship, Mirabeau Lamar and Sam Houston had been at odds. From the time that they had disagreed over the disposition of Santa Anna, the two men had become increasingly polarized in their thinking toward each other. Although no formal party structures actually developed during the brief history of the Republic of Texas, definite political affiliations did form around the personalities and the policies of the first two presidents of the nation.

Sam Houston represented the traditional frontiersman. He was the rugged individualist who was action oriented and was generally disdainful of social convention. He was an admirer of Andrew Jackson and to some extent brought Jacksonian thinking to the Texas political scene. He was strongly convinced that the United States was destined to be a single united nation stretching from the Atlantic to the Pacific and saw Texas as a means of westward American expansion. He was consistently suspicious of any form of foreign entanglement or involvement with European cultural norms.

Mirabeau Lamar was all that Houston was not. He was from the cultured upper middle class which had increasingly provided leadership in the southern United States. He shared the views of the plantation owner, was agrarian in his outlook, fearful of the growing industrial power of the northeastern United States and benevolent toward both European culture and trade.

In a speech Lamar made in Alabama before coming to Texas, he had denounced Andrew Jackson, whom he compared with Nero as "a reprobate, as a military man, a murderer . . . a public functionary, the alternate flatterer and base betrayer of all principles and all parties." [23]

It was inevitable that Houston, the protegé of Andrew Jackson, would soon find himself at odds with Lamar. He had begun his vitriolic denunciations of his successor soon after Lamar came to office; the first president had declared in 1839 that "without some change in affairs, the Government must cease." [24]

When Lamar had a hand in the action that Houston considered the unthinkable (the removal of the capital to a site other than the city that had been named in honor of the first president), Houston fumed "I might have been happy in ignorance at home had I known the full extent of Lamar's stupidity." [25]

On another occasion, he declared that the second president was one who "ought not to presume too far upon the forbearance of an injured and oppressed people." [26]

Houston's objections to Lamar's leadership were many: basic to his criticism was the fact that he believed that his opponent was too extravagant and was bankrupting Texas.[27] He complained when he took office for the second time that "we are not only without money, but without credit . . . without honor." [28] The fact that Houston had ended his first term of office as president with a very sizable debt and with no plan to settle Texas's financial difficulties was conveniently overlooked. Lamar's proposal to solve the nation's money problems with a loan from abroad only heightened the conflict between the two men.

It was Anson Jones, who accurately summed up the first president's reactions to Lamar in a statement that the latter wrote in which he declared that Houston's "only intent" was that of making "Lamar's administration as odious as possible . . . He is willing the government should be a failure in order that he may have it to say there is no one but 'Old Sam' that the people can depend upon and that he is the only man that can successfully administer the Govt. of Texas." [29]

In the early months of the second president's term of office, Jones, who had just been relieved by Lamar of the important post of Texan minister to the United States, became a bitter foe of the former Georgian. Still smarting under what he considered to be Lamar's rejection of his talents, he joined Houston in denouncing Lamar by declaring: "He is a very weak man and governed by petty passions . . . obstinacy he possesses, and what his friends call honesty though it is a very equivocal kind . . . I will hold no other office until a change, and a radical one, is produced." [30]

Later in the year he fumed: "The administration is operating like certain fevers upon the constitution bringing the patient to the extremest point of exhaustion possible." [31]

On January 1, 1840, he declared. "Lamar is certainly no statesman and he and his friends are ruining the country and going to the Devil as fast as Gen. Houston can possibly wish — this he sees and chuckles at . . . He is skillful to destroy his enemy." [32]

Jones served as a senator in the Fifth Congress, and when four dollars were added to his pay, he reported in 1841 that he bought a nine hundred dollar carriage and then added with a note of sarcasm: "Not so fine as His Excellency's dazzling equipage, but better adapted to the rough and muddy roads between Travis County and Brazoria." [33]

Another congressman, Oliver Jones, had complained that Lamar ran his office in a slipshod manner and that he could never find him at home.[34]

However, in spite of the severe attacks upon him by his enemies, Lamar enjoyed a marked resurgence of popularity in 1841. The success of the navy and the widespread interest in the expedition to Santa Fe probably account for this renewal of confidence in his leadership.

In April 1841, a communication to the president from Galveston stated: "It gives me pleasure to say that a great change in public feeling is evidently going on in your favor." [35]

Shortly after this James H. Staff wrote to Lamar that "I am particularly gratified to witness the evidences of the daily increasing confidence in your administration which are every where evidenced." [36]

On August 8, Edward Hall reported from New Orleans that he had talked to "stubborn supporters of Sam Houston" who objected to "your Santa Fe expedition." He then added, "If the Santa Fe expedition succeeds it will immortalize you." [37]

The outcome of that endeavor was certainly destined to be a major factor in public acceptance or rejection of the policies of the second president. It was during the summer of 1841 while the wagon wheels carried McLeod's command closer to a tragic fate that the youthful Republic girded for its third presidential election.

Houston was determined to gain reelection to the office that he had previously held. Since he could not, under the constitution of the Republic, succeed himself immediately, he sought to do the next best thing: succeed his successor.

That he would be successful in his reelection attempt was almost certain simply because there was a severe dearth of possible candidates to challenge the popularity of the hero of San Jacinto. Thomas Jefferson Rusk was a potential candidate, but he refused to consider nomination. Henry Smith and Anson Jones were possibilities, but they would not consider running against Houston. David G. Burnet, the second vice-president, was the only willing opponent of Houston. The administration backed his candidacy, but there is no evidence that Lamar gave him strong personal support. He and the vice-president had been somewhat at odds in the last year of their term; however, when Burnet did agree to run, he was able to garner the backing of Lamar's friends. At one point, soon after his return to Texas following his illness in New Orleans, Lamar was said to have rejected Burnet and even endorsed Houston's candidacy. But if this were true, it was only a passing doubt about his subordinate's qualifications.[38]

As Lamar's vice-president, Burnet represented a potential continuation of Lamar's policies and general outlook. However, he was not a man of commanding personal presence: he was certainly no match for the flamboyant Old Sam who had the ability to magnetize his devotees, turn a phrase in a public debate with amazing agility, and always knew the proper moment for a dramatic appearance or a forceful utterance.

As election day approached, one more factor worked against Burnet: no positive news of the Santa Fe travelers' situation had arrived, and this very fact indicating some sort of disaster definitely darkened Burnet's election chances.

However, he did receive considerable support from a variety of sources. Dr. Francis Moore, Jr., editor of the *Telegraph*, the most widely read and probably the best-edited paper in Texas, backed Burnet's candidacy. There were others who had strongly supported Lamar who girded themselves for battle definitely preferring the colorless vice-president over the flamboyant hero.

Edward Fontaine wrote Lamar in late summer that "Burnet will get a better vote in Washington county than his friends anticipate, and Old Sam has declined in popularity." The fact that Houston's inability to handle liquor was widely known convinced some that his sober and deeply religious opponent had a chance of becoming the third president of Texas. "I think," Fontaine continued, "the people are becoming more and more afraid of trusting the righting of the Ship of State into the hands of a hero who can't stand upright himself." [39]

But Houston's tremendous popularity could not be denied. He was the classic hero: forceful, dramatic, shaped in the epic mold. Burnet was certainly a contrast to Old Sam: pious, sober, humorless. He even lacked Lamar's oratorical ability and was at best a mediocre candidate. Even H.P. Brewster, editor of the Brazos *Courier*, who was considered a strong Lamar backer, had endorsed Houston for a second term as president of the Republic simply because he was convinced that Burnet had little to offer Texas.[40]

William Sandusky wrote from Galveston where he was staying with Gail Borden: "Houston will get a large majority of the votes in this section of the country . . . Burnet stands no chance to be elected."[41]

The campaign became an increasingly bitter one. Burnet developed a passionate hatred for Houston: when the first president began to use his familiar weapon of ridicule and referred to his opponent as a "hog thief," Burnet exploded. He challenged Houston to a duel, an act that would have excluded him from holding public office under Texas law had the challenge been taken seriously. Houston passed off the invitation to fight lightly saying that Burnet would have to get in line as there were at least two dozen ahead of him.[42]

The Winter Chill

Electioneering became excitingly vigorous. The masses of new immigrants who were steadily entering Texas found the political give and take a fascinating diversion from the monotony of the simple life of the Republic. There were few other amusements and they delighted in the acrimonious efforts of both sides; they did not agree with the editor of the Houston *Morning Star* who wearily complained just before the nation was to go to the polls: "We should be heartily glad when this political canvas is over." [43]

When election day did come, the inevitable occurred: Houston won by a comfortable majority of 7915 to 3619 over his less colorful opponent. The vice-presidency went to Edward Burleson, the hero who had led the volunteer army of Texas to victory in the battle of San Antonio: he was able to easily defeat Memucan Hunt, who had once served as Lamar's secretary of the navy, 6144 to 4366.

These results were interpreted by the Houston party as a rejection of Lamar and his policies. In a sense this was the case; but far more, it was a simple affirmation of Houston's great popularity. He and his running mate, Burleson, were representative of the folk-hero frontiersmanship of Texas. This fact in itself had a wide appeal for a nation seeking to find its own identify as a part of the frontier. Given the situation that existed in the Republic and the participating personalities, it is something of a wonder that Burnet was able to garner as much support as he did.

Shortly after the election was over, Lamar received notice of a public meeting scheduled for October 5, 1841, in Nacogdoches, that proposed to offer a tribute of respect to the president elect, but that had been called for the specific purpose of challenging Sam Houston for "having on divers occasions and at divers places denounced the citizens of this county." The gathering sought a public apology from the newly elected chief executive. Appended to the notice was an invitation to Lamar to a public dinner in his honor to be held at a time convenient for him.[44] Repudiated or not by the electorate as a whole, Lamar still had his supporters and friends.

He was present on December 13 in Austin when the new leaders of the Republic were to be sworn in. He accompanied Houston and Burleson into the enclosure at the rear of the rustic capitol building escorted by committees representing the two houses of Congress. They were preceded by the Travis Guards who led the procession that was witnessed by a crowd that a contemporary estimated to be of "about a thousand citizens." [45]

Houston had appeared in a Washingtonian costume three years before for Lamar's inauguration. This time he chose to emphasize his allegiance to the cause of frugality by dressing down: he wore a hunting shirt, pantaloons and an old wide-brimmed fur hat. Once more he wanted to be a symbol: this time he was determined to portray the poverty he believed Lamar had brought to Texas. A witness later wrote: "I thought in this Gen. Houston demonstrated more vanity than if he had appeared in an ordinary suit." [46]

Lamar did wear an ordinary suit, and remembering Houston's lengthy speech three years earlier, declined to speak. Houston, however, took full advantage of the situation and did speak. In that oration he made it quite clear that his administration would take a far different course than Lamar's. One observer described his address as one in which "he dwelt too much and unbecomingly on the merits of his former services and administration." [47]

Immediately after the ceremonies were over, Houston recalled Lamar's agents abroad, dismissed Barnard Bee from his diplomatic post in Washington and replaced all in positions of responsibility with men of his own choosing. He even made plans to scuttle the navy as soon as public apathy permitted. He was anxious to make it very clear that the Republic would have a completely different foreign policy if his approach could be called a policy at all. At home the word would be "retrenchment" — this simply meant that in the name of economy there would be as little governmental process and as few services as possible. All salaries were drastically cut and many offices completely abolished.

For Lamar and for all who shared his aspirations and hopes for Texas, the winter chill had come.

[18]

The Lost Pines

    Lamar's capital city of Austin was situated on the edge of the Texas hill country: rugged outcroppings of native stone form hills that rise precipitously above the Colorado River. But only a few miles to the east, there is a dramatic difference in terrain. There, in the Bastrop area, the rise and fall of the land that surrounds the seaward bound stream is much more gentle. Its sandy soil had produced a sizable forest of pine trees. Because of the fact that such a sylvan growth is otherwise unknown in that part of Texas, this stand of timber has long been known as the Lost Pines.

    The journey from Austin back to his home near Richmond on the Brazos would have taken Mirabeau Lamar through that area. The towering pines with their evergreen hues, verdant even in December, would have been nostalgically reminiscent of both his Texas home to the east and his native Georgia. It could well have made him aware that he was leaving the exhilaration of political leadership of a nation for a far quieter life.

    The trip itself from the capital on the Colorado to the

Oak Grove on the Brazos was not a long one for a man who had frequently traversed the distances between the eastern United States and the frontier lands of the Republic: even by the circuitous routes of the time, it would have measured considerably less than 150 miles. But the distance from the rugged hill capital to Richmond was far greater than any that could be measured in geographical miles.

He was going back to establish a home in a place that he had built for that purpose, but in which he had never lived for more than a few weeks at a time. The last year of his term of office had been difficult in many ways. Not only had the problems of the executive position been considerable, but his health had broken. The illness that had taken him out of the Republic for medical help left him physically weak. He needed rest, a resurgence of strength and a renewal of spirit. He could not have been anything other than both physically and mentally exhausted. Although he firmly believed his policies had been wise ones and the future would vindicate his efforts as president of the youthful nation, he certainly was well aware that his leadership had been rejected by the people as a whole.

The forest of tall pines through which he would have passed near Bastrop following the inauguration of his arch enemy, Sam Houston, as his successor in office, would certainly have brought something of a balm to his troubled spirit.

When the trip was completed, Lamar was back in the small plantation home that Robert Handy had constructed for him early in his Texas political career. It was there that he began to put together the pieces of his former way of life. One task that attracted his attention was that of collecting and organizing his papers. His personal files show considerable effort during these days. Information on the Texas Revolution and its origins, the tragic Indian raid on Fort Parker, and various other portions of the brief history of Texas were carefully collected and arranged in order.[1]

But the life of the ex-president was not long to be one of peaceful serenity on the banks of the Brazos River. The aftermath of the tragedy of the Santa Fe Expedition had produced an anonymous letter denouncing Lamar[2] that had been printed in the *Weekly Texian*. His efforts to determine the authorship of this piece led him to Anson Jones, who replied curtly to Lamar's query on February 27:

> I have this moment received your note of the 25th Inst. in relation to the authorship of a certain anonymous article signed A which appeared in the "Weekly Texian" of the 26th Ultimo — I refer you [to] Gen. Hunt.[3]

This, of course, was a reference to Memucan Hunt, who, now, was at odds with the ex-president. Lamar soon decided to drop the affair of the acrimonious letter directed against him, but Hunt was not willing to let matters rest there.

In April, Hunt wrote Lamar accusing him of giving information for an article in the *Austin City Gazette* of July 28, 1841, which had been signed "Aristides."[4] Lamar at first pled ignorance of the nature of his offense, but later, when Hunt had given him explicit details, admitted partial responsibility in replies dated May 2 and May 4.[5]

He immediately received a formal challenge to combat from his petulant opponent calling upon him "to meet . . . at such time and place and armed with such weapons as their friends may agree upon to settle by single combat the quarrel existing between them."[6]

Lamar accepted the archaic challenge still protesting that he was "entirely unconscious of having ever afforded any wrongs to Gen'l Hunt."[7] However, seconds were duly appointed with Albert Sidney Johnston being named among those who would represent Lamar.[8]

However, on May 9, a paper was signed jointly by J.S. Mayfield in behalf of the former president, and by Charles Rossignol as a second for Hunt, agreeing that the dispute should be submitted to arbitration.[9]

The matter was concluded with a formal award signed by Johnston and other arbitrators declaring both Lamar and Hunt to be "brave and honorable men;" they declared that "after examining the correspondence between these gentlemen [we] have come to the conclusion, that there existed no original cause of controversy and less of a hostile meeting." The dispute was declared to have "grown out of a misconception of facts which would be very natural under the circumstances."[10] Mayfield and Rossignol then agreed to accept this award.[11] This was the closest that Lamar came to participating in an actual duel: he was still a child of the age that accepted this ancient code as a method for the solving of conflicts.

Later that year Lamar made a trip back to Georgia. He had long sought an opportunity to visit family and friends in his native state and to see his daughter, Rebecca. She had made a second trip to Texas to visit him during his term as president accompanied by her Aunt May Ann and her grandmother, Lamar's mother. While on that trip Lamar's mother was stricken in Houston with "congestive fever" and died. Rebecca also fell ill. However, she returned to Georgia: but she had inherited the frail constitution of her mother and she never completely recovered from her illness.[12] Lamar's trip east had as a primary purpose that of seeing her.

After spending the early part of 1843 with Rebecca and family connections in Georgia, and possibly settling matters in Georgia after his own mother's death, he returned to Texas. Edward Fontaine, who had been the ex-president's private secretary during his presidency, gave an account of an event that occurred soon after his arrival that not only indicates Lamar's whereabouts at the time, but something of his life-style. He called on Fontaine knowing that he had been ill, and urged him to get some fresh air as an aid to recovery; he then set out on a trip to nearby Washington County on horseback followed by Fontaine and his wife in a buggy. At one stop on the trip, Lamar arrived at a home en route and asked for a cup of coffee saying that he was an "old footman;" he was refused, but when Fontaine arrived a few minutes later, he informed the housewife that she had turned away the ex-president. Fontaine concluded the account of the incident by saying that he went on his way leaving the housewife "half dead with mortification."[13]

During the late spring and the summer of 1843, Lamar was at his best: apparently both his health and his spirits had revived. Perhaps rest had helped restore his vigor; possibly Houston's troubles as his successor in office gave the second president some encouragement. He traveled widely about the Republic accepting invitations to dinners that allowed him the opportunity of exercising his oratorical gifts. He had received an open invitation from the citizens of Bastrop to a "dinner and ball . . . at such time as may suit your convenience . . ." [14] He was in Galveston in May,[15] and in June he was invited to a "public Barbecue at the City of Austin." He was congratulated in this invitation on the "restoration to health and your return to this country." [16]

On one occasion he was the guest of honor at a public meal in La Grange, where he was welcomed by a cannon salute. He was later introduced in a highly laudatory manner whereupon he delivered a speech defending the various acts of his administration, and then proceeded to attack the shortcomings of Houston's leadership. Although an effective public speaker, one listener recorded that after this particular piece of oratory, the call for "three cheers for General Lamar" brought no response; he attributed this to either "the suffocating heat of the weather or [some] other cause." [17] Apparently Houston's popularity continued to be greater than Lamar's.

It was soon after this that tragedy of a personal nature again struck the former Georgian. Thomas Lamar wrote from Macon on August 2, 1843, these words: "Rebecca Ann has been taken from us — she is no longer of earth." [18] She had died at the age of sixteen on July 29. Her obituary appeared in the *Georgia Telegraph* soon after the letter had been penned.[19]

Lamar reacted to the tragic information by giving vent to his grief in writing one of his more melancholic pieces of poetry. In "On the Death of My Daughter," he declared:

> The morning star that fades from sight,
> Still beams upon the mind;
> So doth her beauty leave the light,
> Of memory behind.

> Though lost to earth — too early gone —
>   By others seen no more,
> She is to me still shining on,
>   And brighter than before.[20]

He could not forget that last meeting when he had visited with the frail girl who was so reminiscent of her long dead mother, Tabitha:

> The smile she wore when last we met
>   The tear she shed in parting . . .
> That smile and tear and parting kiss,
>   Oh, how can I forget.[21]

Almost immediately after receiving news of Rebecca's death, Lamar made plans for a trip back to the United States. A letter penned in November 1843, by Edward Fontaine was addressed to him in Macon, Georgia, with instructions to "forward this to him wherever he may be." This epistle went to Galveston and then to Washington. In this he spoke of having "heard of your overwhelming affliction." He urged Lamar to "pray fervently that you may be enabled to bear your irreparable loss." [22]

Lamar's journey eastward included a stopover in Mobile.[23] There he visited a woman who had been a childhood friend of his sister, Mary Ann, Octavia Walton, now Mrs. Henry S. LeVert. It was in her drawing room that he met Richard Henry Wilde, writer of "My Life Is Like a Summer Rose," and A.B. Meek, who was then writing *Songs and Poems of the South*, which he dedicated to Lamar.[24]

In Georgia he visited the grave of Rebecca, and spent some time with relatives and friends in the area.[25]

By the beginning of the following year, 1845, he was in New York.[26] There he was accepted as a celebrity in a country in which there was increasing interest in the possibility of annexing Texas. A New York publication hailed him a "a romantic specimen of southern chivalry . . ." [27]

A seven stanza poem idealizing him, entitled "To General Mirabeau B. Lamar," was written by Caroline Sawyer during this period. This manuscript he preserved among his papers.[28]

Late in February he was in Washington. There he was accorded the courtesy of a seat in the Senate.[29] He made a favorable impression on the society of the city: Cora Montgomery, writing in the *United States Magazine and Democratic Review*, declared him to be "remarkably gentle and affectionate in his manners, habitually self controlled." [30] One can easily detect in this description some surprise among the inhabitants of the United States' capital drawing rooms that a man who had lived in Texas could act in a gentlemanly fashion!

Lamar's attitude toward the question of Texas annexation to the American union had altered by this time. He was convinced that the reasons for separatism that he had once espoused were no longer valid. He was not only willing to see the Republic absorbed into the Union, but he was by now an enthusiastic supporter of annexation. During his sojourn he served as something of an unofficial emissary for the cause of entrance of Texas into the American federation.[31]

By April he had returned to Macon, where he was invited to the twentieth anniversary of the founding of the Macon Volunteers.[32] He stayed there for the remainder of the summer living in a boarding house. The proprietors of that institution had a daughter named Cassandra Flint, with whom the lonely ex-president became infatuated. Although the possibility of indiscretion can readily be assumed in the circumstances of the affair, the exact nature of this romance is difficult to ascertain: in any case it was to Cassandra that he wrote one of his more romantic poems entitled "My Gem of Delight." In this he declared:

> O bright is the maiden who wakens my sighs,
> No planet can equal the light of her eyes . . .
> O, thou art — my Cassa — that maiden so bright.[33]

The relationship was serious enough that he included these lines in his ode to Cassandra:

> Then fly with me, Cassa, — there's bliss in the flight,
> And glory shall circle my Gem of Delight.[34]

A tradition existed in the Flint family that Lamar once offered Cassandra an engagement ring, which she refused since she considered the gossip that spoke of the difference in their social positions a valid impediment to a continuing relationship. There is nothing to indicate Lamar's serious intentions other than his fanciful ode. For him this was probably no more than a romantic interlude: he was a lonely man and a very human one! He returned to Texas soon after this, leaving the starry-eyed Cassa with nothing but the momento of a poem sung in later years to the tune of "Flow Gently Sweet Afton." [35]

There was ample reason for him to be back in the Republic. Events were now moving rapidly toward annexation. Although Lamar had been gone from the frontier nation for sometime, he had not been completely out of contact with affairs there. Houston's popularity had declined during his second term: his confident assertion that he could easily right the affairs of the nation had resulted in little other than rhetoric. In a frontier society where personal independence was valued above all else, anyone in a position of authority might soon come to be resented. Something of the same distrust that had made Lamar's term as president a difficult one had become an onus for his successor in office.[36]

Lamar had been mentioned as a possible candidate in the election of 1844. Houston could not run again: it was conceivable that Lamar might return to Texas and make another try at the office he had once held. James Webb had written to Lamar some time prior to the election that "Houston is tottering on his throne." He spoke in that letter of "those who oppose his high-handed lawlessness."[37]

There is no indication, however, that Lamar gave serious consideration to seeking office in the election of 1844. At that time he was in Georgia, where he was still grieving over the grave of Rebecca and receiving the consolation of friends. A Houston editor stated that although he had been urged to run for president again, he had declined because of the "recent domestic affliction which he had sustained . . . he was determined to revisit the scene of his childhood . . . and if possible soothe the afflictions that now press heavily on a wounded spirit." [38]

However, he was not totally disinterested in the affairs of the Republic during this time. He wrote to James Webb urging him to consider running for the presidency of Texas: he decided against doing so, and Lamar later wrote to James Polk recommending Webb for the position of a United States District Judge.[39] Lamar then backed General Ed Burleson, who had by this time, lost favor with Sam Houston.[40]

Anson Jones won the election in a close contest during which Burleson felt called upon to deny that he was controlled by men who had dominated Lamar's administration.[41] Shortly after Jones took office, his secretary of state, Ashbell Smith, negotiated a treaty with Mexico that would have recognized the independence of Texas. However, the agreement included a clause that provided that Texas would never become a part of the United States. The government of Mexico immediately ratified this pact forcing Texas to decide for or against the arrangement.

On March 1, 1845, the Congress in Washington followed the recommendation of President Taylor by adopting a joint resolution for the annexation of Texas as a part of the United States. The Texas Senate rejected the proposal for a treaty with Mexico because of its limiting provision. This left the door open for the Republic to become a state. President Jones called for a convention which met in Austin on July 4 and then proceeded to approve the plan for annexation to the American union almost unanimously. A constitution was drafted in October, and on December 29, 1845, the Congress of the United States accepted this document making Texas a state. This ended the life of the Republic and brought closer the fact of the inevitability of war with Mexico.

Lamar was in Texas in November 1845.[42] His name had been mentioned as a possible candidate for the office of United States senator. However, he declined consideration of such an office, and Houston and Rusk were elected to represent the new state when annexation was consummated.[43]

Late in the year he visited Galveston where he indulged his love of the theater by attending the presentation of a troupe of players who were then in the island city. One of the actors, Harry Watkins, was one of Lamar's favorites. He, Lamar, and a Captain Lewis, editor of the *Galveston News*, dined together on several occasions after performances.[44] Lewis asked Lamar to write a "New Year's Address to the Patrons" for his paper: however, no copy of this edition is extant.[45] Watkins, after leaving Galveston, later said of Lamar, "A more loveable man never lived." [46]

The ex-president's correspondence indicates that he was in Austin during the months of February and March, 1846.[47] It was during this time, on February 16, amid the booming of cannon, the flag of the Republic with its single star was lowered in a public ceremony in front of the rustic capitol building, and the Stars and Stripes were unfurled. Anson Jones solemnly declared on the occasion: "The final act in this great drama is now performed: the Republic of Texas is no more." [48]

Lamar was undoubtedly present for this event. He had long enough been among the Lost Pines; he was now ready to become involved in the affairs of his adopted Texas even as war clouds hovered on the horizon.

[19]

Laredo's Blooming Plain

It is a unique land that stretches northward from the Rio Grande to the Nueces River: its endless uniformity has about it something of the appearance of the open sea as it rises and falls in the sunlight as far as the eye can see. It is a country of gently rolling hills covered by mesquite, cactus plants and the low-lying brush able to survive the semi-desert climatic conditions of the region. Much of it is sparsely settled ranch country; in Lamar's time it was a lonely wilderness. It is capable of producing life-sustaining vegetation only where irrigation is possible. The broad waters of the Rio Grande are a source most of the year for luxuriant plant life in the near tropical valley of the river. But to the north, there stretches a land of vast distances and endless nothingness.

During the days of the Republic, the question of whether or not this was Texas or Mexico had not been settled. Both claimed the territory. However, at the time, Mexico claimed all of Texas and the particular portion of the Republic which lay south of the Nueces River was of little concern to most Texans. When annexation made Texas an integral part of the

United States of America, this boundary issue suddenly became a matter of considerable importance. When discussions between the government of Mexico and Washington began to give way to the likelihood of armed conflict, General Zachary Taylor, who had been stationed on the Nueces since the summer of 1845, moved his regular army detachment to the mouth of the Rio Grande. There he established himself in a position where he could easily blockade the Mexican town of Matamoros. President Polk's administration hesitated to take a decisive action until some incident should occur that would give moral sanction to this military position. On April 25, 1846, the Mexicans obliged by crossing the Rio Grande and raiding the northern bank, land claimed by Texas that was now considered a part of the United States. Several of the men in Taylor's command were killed. As soon as news of this event was known in Washington, Polk asked Congress for a declaration of war against Mexico. This occurred on May 11. America was ready to go to war to establish the boundary of Texas at the Rio Grande and to affirm the right of the Republic to join the union.

Volunteers quickly inundated the area where Taylor was camped. Texans were especially ready to respond. J. Pinckney Henderson, recently elected governor of the new state, took a leave of absence from his executive position to lead Texas troops with the rank of major general. Lamar joined him as a member of his command staff, as the Texas Mounted Volunteers became a part of Taylor's army that had now moved across the river into what was clearly Mexican territory establishing by this action a firm hold on the city of Matamoros and the mouth of the Rio Grande.

George Kendall, the New Orleans *Picayune* reporter who had accompanied the Santa Fe Expedition, had survived his ordeal, and was on hand when the Texans joined the United States forces preparing for the further invasion of Mexico. In his correspondence describing the military operations that were then underway, he spoke of "convivial occasions" when he joined Lamar, Henderson, and Edward Burleson "to drink

Laredo's Blooming Plain

warm champaign together out of a tin cup."[1] Apparently the early days of the war were jovial times as a near holiday atmosphere existed in the army of General Zachary Taylor.

One document is extant in Lamar's personal papers, however, of a deeply serious nature and was written in his own hand during this period. In this he made a vigorous protest against the martial law that had been imposed on the City of Matamoros during the early summer of 1846. He called for "respect . . . to civil as well as military rights." He lamented that "at present the sword is predominant in Matamoros . . ." He urged that "in carrying liberty to Mexico, let us not walk over the liberties of our own countrymen. 'O it is excellent to have a giant's strength, but it is tyrannous to use it like a giant.' "[2] This was certainly the reaction of an idealist, but one who sought conscientiously to be consistent in the application of his principles.

The American forces soon moved inland to take up positions near the Mexican provincial capital of Monterrey. Considerable efforts were being made to defend the city against the intruders from the north, but their endeavors were not sufficient to stem the tide of invasion. Taylor's regulars, along with his large force of volunteers that included the Texans under Henderson, were now well established in northern Mexico and prepared to do battle for the city.

One fascinating piece of poetic expression came from Lamar's pen during this period that again gives considerable insight into the person and character of the man himself. Having met a young lady who lived in the area named Carmelita, he composed this ode to her.

> I soon shall seek the battle-field,
> Where Freedom's flag is waving —
> My Texas comrades by my side,
> All perils madly braving;
> I only grieve to think each blow
> That vengeance bids the steel bestow,
> Must make thee mine eternal foe,
> O Donna Carmelita.[3]

The excitement of impending battle seemed to bring out the poetic strain in his nature. A similar piece was written "To a Mexican Girl;" this was addressed to Donna Maria Innocente, daughter of Don Rafael Lopez de Aropoza.[4] Lamar, the soldier, believing firmly in the cause for which he was about to risk his life, was still a romantic and a perceiver of beauty. He exhibited a delightful empathy with the Spanish-speaking people with whom he came in contact. He believed firmly that he was fighting for a principle, the cause of freedom and liberty. He believed somehow that by carrying the war to Mexico, he was helping to extend that principle to the people against whom he fought. Naive or not, he certainly had no thought of seeking to demean a nation or subjugate a people.

When the three-day battle for Monterrey began, Lamar was attached to the Second Regiment of the Texas Mounted Volunteers with the rank of captain. He led a contingent of this force into battle and acquitted himself well enough under fire that his superior, Colonel George Wood, reported that he had displayed "lofty courage." [5] The muster roll of his company indicates that at the time he was commander of a sixty-seven-man unit.[6]

However, when the battle was over, the decision was made to send Lamar and his company back north to secure a rear position. He was to be stationed at Laredo some 150 miles to the north. He himself felt that this would deny him the opportunity for further battle experience on what all believed would be the southward march to Mexico City, and that some unjust political maneuvering had taken place to give him what he considered an unimportant post. However, he was aware that he was a soldier under orders, and in the late autumn of 1846, he journeyed north to take command of the frontier post on the banks of the Rio Grande.[7]

Another poetical outburst from his pen had at some time prior to this declared:

> O'er loved Laredo's blooming plains,
>   I soon shall wander free,
> And I shall hear the Bravo roll
>   In music to the sea.[8]

He arrived in Laredo in November 1846, and found nothing blooming there over which to wax eloquent in verse: his subsequent correspondence indicates that he experienced very little satisfaction in his sojourn on the plains above the Bravo.

He sent his commanding officer, General Taylor, a report in December on his arrival at his post on November 8, commenting that he found the local inhabitants friendly as he took up quarters in one of the buildings surrounding the plaza not far from the northern bank of the river. He described Laredo as "little more than a heap of ruins" in which "there is scarcely a comfortable house." And, "The desolation was the effect of the most unprecedented rains which fell in 1842 from which it has never recovered." He reported that the city was divided into two distinct villages on opposite sides of the Rio Grande, "both however bearing the common name of Laredo and governed by the same local authorities." In addition to heavy rains, the area had suffered from Indian ravages that had, according to Lamar's account, cost seven hundred lives in the last twenty years out of a population of "some nineteen hundred souls." He described the land surrounding the twin towns as "uninhabited except when corn is cultivated on 25 or 30 rancheros scattered for 30 miles up the river." [9]

He had only been in the area a few days when a band of Comanches captured a Mexican boy. Lamar organized a party of his men to track them. After following the trail for some fifty miles, he and his men forced the Indians to release the boy who was then able to return home safely. [10]

As military commandant of the area, the ex-president immediately took a firm hold on the local political situation: only a few days after his arrival, he addressed a letter to Don Andres Martiñes, Alcalde of Laredo, in which he requested full cooperation and required that all strangers arriving in the town report to him because of the "state of public affairs." [11] The Alcalde responded by assuring the company commander of his good intentions, and readily agreed to assist Lamar in his task. [12]

Among his concerns were the health conditions in the city. What seemed to him to be considerable uncleanness existed, and in reporting to his army superiors, he expressed fear that an epidemic could sweep Laredo. However, he stated: "The town . . . has the reputation of healthfulness." [13] At least the usual dry Laredo dust, though unpleasant to a Georgian, did not breed the mosquitoes which brought death in that day to less arid climates.

His desire to be back with the main force of American troops in Mexico soon came to conflict with a sense of the importance of his immediate mission. Correspondence reaching him in December could only further his appetite for participation in the military push that he believed would take place south of Monterrey.

A letter from H.P. Bee commented on Lamar's arrival in Laredo and stated: "I presume you are out of the world." He then went on to tell how Mexico was arming for the conflict that was to come.[14] E. H. Winfield wrote at about the same time from Camargo that "there is talk in town this morning that San Anna [sic] is en route for Monterrey with twenty thousand men to retake the town." [15]

However, when Lamar heard of the possibility of moving the Laredo garrison as a total unit to Camargo, a base camp behind Taylor's lines in Mexico, he objected in a letter to Major George McCall because of "the importance of guarding of the Steamer *Major Brown* and the preservation of its contents." [16]

The small river ship was at the time anchored against the north bank of the Rio Grande at Laredo as a military supply vessel supporting the operations in Mexico. Lamar was given assurances from the headquarters of the Second Division on November 22, that the guarding of the ship was an important task and that a continuing provision for its security would be provided by the army.[17] He believed his company's presence at its post was necessary, but he, himself, longed for an opportunity for more active participation in the war to the south.

Lamar's desire to administer his post with military exactness is apparent in the documents which have been preserved from this period. Early in his stay in Laredo he dismissed four privates for drunkenness.[18] The lack of further reference to this crime indicates that he may have become more lax in dealing with this problem as time went by. Possibly indulgence in the distillates attainable in the area was one of the few recreations available to his men. He himself drank on social occasions, but he took a stern view of the excessive use of alcohol. At one point he complained that the authorities of Texas "have not taken steps toward extending the laws of the state over this portion of its territory."[19] He was determined to do all possible to bring law and order to the area.

In December, he came into open conflict with a subordinate, a Lieutenant T.M. Likin, who was his garrison quartermaster. A lengthy series of documents, over a hundred pages of manuscript material, bear detailed testimony to the fact that Lamar considered Likin to be both incompetent and dishonest. In late December he accepted his resignation, but permitted Likin to appeal his case to higher military authority. Two specific charges were brought by the captain of the garrison against his lieutenant: "gambling time after time,"[20] and the fact that Likin had "purchased bad beef."[21] However, Lamar's charges did not hold up in the face of appeal, for Likin was eventually cleared and allowed to collect his own personal expenses. Lamar agreed to "a speedy adjustment of his accounts on terms the most liberal which the law will allow."[22] Later, he wrote to Likin: "I have in my possession a body of testimony . . . which . . . cannot fail to overwhelm you with shame."[23] Apparently the mass of material that today is a part of the Lamar Papers was the evidence he carefully preserved to substantiate his case against his former subordinate.

However, exercising administrative responsibility on the bluffs of the Rio Grande was certainly not his idea of military service. By the end of 1846, Lamar began a barrage of letters asking for a transfer to a more active assignment. He wrote directly to Taylor[24] on December 24, and on the same date he prepared a letter to James Pinckney Henderson, who was now back in Austin, asking that he use his influence to make it possible for him to join "the main army. It will not suit me so well to remain at Laredo in idleness," he declared, "whilst the tide of battle is rolling in another direction." [25] Obviously Lamar's dislike of Laredo and his inability to see anything attractive on the plain above the Rio Grande spoke less of the dismalness of the south Texas town and more of the impatience of the company commander to be a part of the dramatic actions of the war taking place far to the south.

In February he received some encouragement in response to his pleas for active service when a letter from W.W.S. Bliss, writing in behalf of Taylor from the "Headquarters Army of Occupation," told Lamar to "hold yourself ready to join him [Taylor] say by the 1st or 5th of April . . ." [26]

On March 1, he received a similar letter from Colonel Samuel R. Curtis from Camargo indicating that Lamar would probably be permitted to soon "unite with a larger force." [27] Lamar immediately asked permission to increase the size of his unit.[28] However, April came and went and Lamar was still in Laredo. He continued to send requests "to be led at once to the seat of the war." [29]

Bliss answered one of Lamar's petitions on July 23 in behalf of General Taylor stating that "in case he makes a forward movement, he desires to employ your services and those of your company . . ." [30]

However, it was not Taylor's army that would make the decisive maneuvers of the war. On June 26, Lamar received a report that General Scott was at Puebla "expecting soon to move to the capital." [31] In September he heard of the "battle of Mexico" in which American forces "took all the outworks . . . but did not enter the city . . . [of Mexico] . . . Our loss 1000 killed and wounded —Mexican supposed to be 6000 . . ." [32] Another account reached Lamar at about the same time stating that "our troops gained a signal victory over the Mexicans on the 20th of August . . . carrying and destroying some of the enemy's works near Chapultepic [sic] . . ." [33]

In September Lamar reorganized his company, accepted applications from additional men to partially replace some who had been allowed to transfer out,[34] and reported on October 19, 1847, to Henderson in Austin that he had a company "at this point, well mounted armed and equipped . . . [of] forty men . . . I should like to have it increased to one hundred . . ." He gave as a reason for enlarging his force: "The Country abounds in robbers . . . with three hundred men I feel pretty confident that I could put down these guerrilla parties and maintain tranquility."[35]

Taylor's headquarters had sent Lamar a dispatch, dated September 23, renewing his order to command a company under the authority of the Governor of Texas to be stationed at Laredo with the full support of army ordinance and quartermaster stores.[36]

By the end of the year, Lamar was complimented on having filled his company's muster roll to a total of "90 men . . . all well mounted." H. P. Bee described it as "the best looking and best conditioned corps I have seen in the volunteer service."[37]

However, the ex-president of a nation, in spite of his desire to see more active service, was destined to remain as a frontier garrison commander for the duration of the war. Two tasks faced him in his administrative capacity at the post on the border: one was that of pacifying the local population who had an inherent loyalty to Mexico, and the other was that of protecting the area from hostile Indian raids.

In a letter to Governor Henderson, dated September 6, 1847, Lamar commented on the need of maintaining a strong military force at Laredo because of the "growing discontent of the population, the impunity with which robberies and other acts of hostility have lately been committed."[38]

Other correspondence of the same period indicated threats of either guerrilla action against Lamar's company or possible Indian raids in the area.[39]

During the summer, he had sought to bring some semblance of democratic government to the Rio Grande community by ordering and supervising an election that would establish a county government for the Texas portion of the Laredo area.

On July 14 Henderson wrote from Austin concerning the importance of organizing the counties on the border; he urged that elections be held as soon as possible.[40]

But Lamar was one day ahead of the governor. On July 13, the polls had been open in the border town: two justices of the peace, Augustin Soto and L. T. Tucker, were chosen for office, and Thomas Flores was named as county commissioner.[41] The order for the election had been published under the garrison captain's instructions on the third of July.[42] However, only forty inhabitants bothered to register.[43] Lamar had declared just before initiating this experiment in the democratic process that he was then "arranging the extension of the jurisdiction of Texas over this part of her territory and shall hold an election in a few days." However, he lamented, "the people are far from being reconciled to the change, and probably very few will appear at the polls." [44]

In October, Lamar acting as military commandant, agreed to a communication with Andres Martiñes to forget the "wheel tax" that had been imposed on traffic in Laredo "because the custom no longer exists in other parts of the country." [45]

However, the conduct of the affairs of Laredo was far from being enough to continue to challenge a man who had once led a nation. The election in Laredo was part of an effort to establish a system of counties throughout the south Texas area: the immediate result was the organization of San Patricio and Nueces Counties which constituted a political unit entitled to representation in the state legislature.

Governor Henderson wrote on August 17 telling the ex-president that "I hear it rumored . . . that you would be a candidate for the Legislature. I hope it may be so." [46] H. L. Kinney had written from Corpus Christi indicating that he would do everything to aid Lamar "in a political way." He invited the potential office holder to visit his city, some 150 miles from

Laredo strategically located at the opposite end of the district.[47]

Lamar announced his candidacy in September. A friend living in the southern corner of the newly created congressional district, R. Garland, wrote telling him that he had seen a statement in print declaring Lamar's intention of seeking the newly created office of state representative for the two southern most counties of the state. He included these reassuring words: "It will give me much pleasure to give you my little support . . . I have conversed with a number of persons . . . and find a general disposition to support you."[48]

The importance of the organization of the county systems in the area was stated in Garland's letter: "The absorbing question all along the Rio Grande is the creation of two or three new counties on the river from the mouth to Laredo or some point above. It is expected you will favor . . . such a measure — it is a *sine qua non* with all of us."[49]

The election was held in November. Lamar's contacts in the area, and the fact that his name was generally known, gave him an easy victory over his single opponent: he received a total of 521 votes to only 59 for H.L. Long. J. Benton Johnson, Chief Justice, certified the results and wrote to Lamar: "You will therefore proceed to the next meeting of the Legislature."[50]

Lamar was in Austin when the Texas House of Representatives convened. An effort by his friends to have him elected as speaker of the House failed, but he was named as chairman of the committee on state affairs. The only action as legislator that he preserved in his personal papers was one in which his committee recommended that a judgment of $20,000 against Gail Borden be dropped.[51] It was a brief session, and by February 1848, Lamar was back in Laredo.[52]

During the spring he continued to administer his post on the border. Veatch wrote, in late February, "I was pleased to hear you had retained your command as there is some prospect of active service in the way of Indian warfare this spring."[53]

In March his company was asked to guarantee protection for a family that was traveling northward to San Antonio "through the dangerous part."[54]

However, no spring raids by roving Indians were recorded. Lamar, nonetheless, still felt that he was fighting a battle with local attitudes: in a letter dated April 8, he accused a José Ramon of seeking to establish Mexican authority over Webb County, that had now been organized as a separate political entity.[55] Ramon replied in Spanish indicating that the American occupation of Laredo had not been beneficial to the area.[56] The post captain responded in boldly written English in his own hand demanding that Ramon "submit your communications to my inspection." He accused him again of seeking "to establish the Mexican laws in the County of Webb."[57]

Not all of his relations with the non-English-speaking people at this time were hostile: in May he received a beautifully written invitation in Spanish from the inhabitants of Santa Rosa, Mexico, to go there in person to attend a ball.[58]

However, on June 17, 1848, the company commander acknowledged an order announcing the definite settlement of peace and ordered the mustering out of his remaining garrison. In this response he urged that troops be retained at Laredo to protect the area against hostile Indian raids.[59]

But Lamar was ready to leave Laredo.

[20]

In Search of a Home

The waters of the Rio Grande flow relentlessly past the buff colored hills of Laredo. It is a stream that is capable of reflecting the varied hues of the vast lands through which it flows: in times of upstream turbulence, it can become vigorously chocolate; when there have been months of little rainfall, it can retreat pliantly within the recesses of its banks and move quietly toward the sea. Although it is a mighty river for a relatively arid area, it differs from the great effluences of the eastern United States: it never gains the calm, self-sufficient serenity of the Mississippi or the Alabama or the Savannah.

For over two years, Lamar's activities had centered around the Rio Grande, and for most of the nineteen months that preceded his mustering out from the army, he had lived on its banks. Perhaps the relentlessness of the Bravo had effected his spirit. His correspondence in this period clearly indicated a strong desire to return to a quieter land; to more familiar scenes among family and friends of earlier years. The excitement of the Mexican War was over. His responsibilities as a frontier cavalry post commander were at an end. The

Texas Republic was no more; in its place was a state that had now become an integral part of the United States of America. Lamar began to look to the east, doubtless in search of a home for his spirit in the midst of the restless loneliness that he now knew.

He was in Austin in late 1848. In November of that year he received a formal invitation to a ball in the Texas capital for the "officers of the United States Army now in the city." [1] Apparently he was still considered as a part of that elite group, although he had been mustered out of the service prior to that time.

In December he received some casual correspondence from John Veatch concerning a scheme for the manufacture of gum arabic from the mesquite trees that were plentiful in Texas.[2] Perhaps like so many others, these early Texans were seeking some means of making good use of the native shrub that grows abundantly in the state.

In early January, 1849, Lamar was in Galveston. On the fifth day of that month, he wrote to Henderson concerning a land grant in which he had an interest. However, he was ready to leave Texas, and he stated to the governor: "I can remain no longer and must therefore request you to send your replies to my letters to me at Macon, Georgia, to the care of Dr. Thos. Lamar, my brother." [3]

Lamar went to Georgia and spent only a brief time in Macon. A letter dated March 26, from Lamar to Henderson was written from "Washington City." [4] Apparently he visited the nation's capital in the spring, and in the early summer, he made his way back to Macon.[5]

At this time he wrote to Fontaine that he was prepared to abandon his own claim to the land grant that he had hoped to make his own.[6] All of his earlier efforts at land speculation had been unsuccessful. Apparently this one was as well.

But Lamar's consuming interest always seemed to center upon the political issues of the time. The nation was becoming more and more immeshed in the concerns that revolved around the compromise that Henry Clay would introduce to

In Search of a Home

Congress early in the year 1850. Once again the issue of slavery was threatening to divide the nation. The south was well aware that the Missouri Compromise of thirty years earlier had placed her in a difficult position as more states were ready to be carved out of the territories that had been agreed upon as non-slave lands.

Clay's proposal would admit California as a free state, organize New Mexico and Utah without mention of slavery, abolish the domestic slave trade in the District of Columbia, and adjust the boundary between Texas and New Mexico.

Lamar spent the early part of 1850 in the vicinity of Mobile, in the home of a friend, R.H. Slough, who lived near the Alabama city.[7] During this time "the great Southern question" was a subject of frequent "conversations in the street." Lamar was urged to speak at a public meeting on the issue in Mobile, where "the many friends you have here would welcome you to the city and appreciate your views." [8]

His attitude at this time is apparent in a letter written soon afterwards by Lamar that was addressed to friends in Macon where he had been asked to speak at a similar meeting opposing Clay's compromise. He declined the invitation to make the address, but he agreed with his southern friends in general opposition to the plan: however, his strongest objection had to do with his unwillingness to see New Mexico separated from Texas.

"It fell to my lot while President of that Republic to become intimately connected with her claim to the Santa Fe Country," he declared, and then added this statement:

> The right of Texas to all the territory west to the Rio Grande was considered as indisputable as her right to any other portion of her possessions. During my administration I dispatched an army to Santa Fe to enforce our jurisdiction . . .[9]

However, he agreed with his correspondents in Georgia in opposing the proposal that would be adopted before the year was out. He sympathized with them in seeking "the best means of securing the rights of the south and preserving the

Union."[10] However, he strongly opposed those who saw in the admission of Texas to the union a possible means of providing additional slave states by carving up the territory of Texas in order to maintain the balance of power between north and south in the United States Senate. In this Lamar had become more of a Texan than he was a southerner. It is interesting that he concluded his statements in this document with a bit of a Lamarian flare by declaring his objection to "all compromises except the compromises of the Constitution . . . [which] when formed . . . was based on a series of compromises."[11] Lamar was certainly a southerner in his outlook and had he lived to see the nation divided by war, he would have cast his lot with the Confederacy; however, he was never a radical in regard to the issues that would bring about the tragedy of 1861.

But at this time the ex-president had other concerns than those that were related to the great political issues of the time: he was still in search of a home.

It was late in the year 1850 that Lamar's wanderings took him to the city of New Orleans: he was on his way back to Texas, but he lingered in the Crescent City for a time before continuing on to his small plantation on the Brazos. On this occasion he was a guest in the home of Mrs. John Settle, one of the several friends he had made in the city over the years. During his stopover, there was another visitor in the Settle home: the attractive twenty-three-year-old Henrietta Moffitt of Galveston. Lamar had known her family for a number of years. He had made a point of seeking to hear her Methodist minister father, John Newland Moffitt, on his first visit to New Orleans some sixteen years earlier.[12] Moffitt was pastor of the church that Lamar had visited at the time, but had not been in the pulpit on that particular Sunday. Noted for his oratory and his unusual gifts as a preacher and evangelist, he often spoke to houses so full of persons clamoring to hear him, that on occasion he had been forced to enter the place of meeting through a window. He had died in 1850 leaving three daughters: Eliza, and two twins, Matilda and Henrietta. The last two had been born in Tennessee in 1827, had lived for a time in Louisiana before moving to Galveston: they were both famed for their beauty. Henrietta at the time was engaged to marry a Galveston gentleman, but the circumstances of her visit to New Orleans were destined to change her life.[13]

The lonely Lamar quickly gave up his plans for an early return to Texas as it became apparent that he was captivated by Henrietta's charms. In the brief courtship that followed, he gave vent to poetical expression as he wrote these words to her:

> O Lady, if the stars so bright,
> > Were diamond worlds bequeathed to me
> I would resign them all this night
> > To frame one song befitting thee,
> For thou art dearer to my heart
> > Than all the gems of earth and sky.
>
> Wher'er I wander sad and long
> > I will thine angel-image bear
> Upon my heart as on a stone
> > In deathless beauty sculptured there.[14]

But the poet was through with solitary wandering. The New Orleans courtship was a rapid one that resulted in Henrietta's breaking of her engagement to her Galveston fiancé, and her agreement to marry Lamar.

The wedding took place in February, 1851.[15] Immediately afterward the two set out on a honeymoon trip to Georgia. They visited in Columbus and in Fairfield, and then spent most of the remainder of the year 1851 in Macon.[16]

A whimsical bit of verse was produced by Lamar soon after the marriage in which he declared to his bride, who by then could not have been more than twenty-four:

> > O is it not a pity . . .
> > That I am now, of fifty-three . . .
> > Upon the shady side?[17]

But shady side or not, Lamar's delight in his young bride, less than half his age, was unbounded. He had at last found a home for his wandering heart. The marriage was readily consummated, and a daughter, Loretto Evaline, named after two of the bridegroom's sisters, was born to the couple in early 1852. The extended visits with the numerous Lamar relatives continued as Lamar began putting some of his poems together for future publication.[18]

Travel was difficult in those days, and plans to return to Texas were delayed until after pregnancy, and the new-born child was old enough to make the trip without difficulty.

In 1852, the three Lamars finally made their way westward with the intention of taking up residence on the small Richmond plantation and making that a permanent home. However, when they did arrive there, things were in bad repair as a result of years of neglect. Henrietta still had relatives in Galveston: this fact and the condition of the property led Lamar to begin a search for a more comfortable house, looking at locations closer to the city where his young wife had lived much of her life. On one such trip the depth of his tenderness was apparent when he wrote home:

> I love you more than language can express . . . and feel that your presence is all that I want . . . Since we parted I have been going night and day in search of a home, and shall still persevere until I gain one . . . Kiss the little one.[19]

Another letter of about the same period declared "I think I will never leave home again without you . . ."[20]

However, the search for a more adequate place nearer Galveston did not produce results; or probably there was nothing suitable that could be afforded on Lamar's uncertain income. Instead, he finally secured additional acreage from Mrs. Jane Long, in whose home the couple boarded for a time, and then proceeded to renovate the Richmond house. For a time the Longs and the Lamars shared the enlarged plantation dwelling. However, this did not work out as evidenced by a letter from Lamar January, 1855: "I never will again . . . subject you to such difficulties as must inevitably arise from having two families of equal authority in the same house," he wrote Henrietta. "Our experience on that point suffices for the balance of my life." [21]

The double family living arrangement had been necessitated in part by financial considerations. Lamar had stated in a letter to a friend in 1854 something of his continuing monetary problems: "For many months I have had a use for five or six dollars which I am not able to raise except by the slow process of selling a little butter which my wife saves from a few cows." [22]

But in spite of his financial difficulties, Lamar's generous spirit had led him to give regular donations to a young boy that he addressed only as "Juan," who had lived in Laredo during the days of his military service there. Six letters are preserved among Lamar's papers written to Juan during 1852 in which he enclosed money and lent regular encouragement to the young man who was then in New York seeking to advance his education.[23] During Lamar's wedding tour, he had sent $30.00 a month to Henrietta's sister Eliza, in Galveston.[24] Undoubtedly this spirit of ready generosity was a contributing factor to Lamar's continual financial difficulties.

However, Lamar finally negotiated a substantial loan from his cousin, Gazaway, with which he paid for the improvement to the house and the enlargement of the farmlands.[25] This gave him some temporary relief from the pressure of his financial problems.

Correspondence during this period indicates his continuing interest in the Spanish speaking people. He had received a letter in March 1851, asking for his personal participation in a Cuban revolution that was being promoted by Ambrosio José Gonzales. The writer assured Lamar that he planned to invade Cuba with two steamers, a small army, and "10 pieces of brass artillery." He hoped "for the redemption of the hundreds of thousands of Cubans who labor under Spanish tyranny." He declared to Lamar that if he would but join the movement, he would become known as "la Liberte de deux peuples," a sort of a latter-day Lafayette, and that Cubans would be "grateful in contradistinction to their proceders in annexation." [26]

However, Lamar was not ready to engage in such an enterprise: he replied that it was "entirely out of my power to cooperate with you in your noble endeavors," and he asked that he "communicate to the incorruptible old veteran and patriot Genl. Lopez . . . [my hope that he] may be as triumphant as his heart can desire." [27]

He later wrote to Lopez in Spanish discouraging the enterprise, believing that a small party of Americans could not bring about such a revolution unless the Cuban people as a whole initiated the revolt.[28]

He had no intention of leaving the peacefulness of the Brazos River plantation for such an endeavor. Henrietta tended the flowers near the house, and on occasion, made the table in the dining room fragrant with the blooms from her garden. The fresh smell of the fields mingled with the breezes that played through the pleasant Oak Grove: this was a time of idyllic existence. Lamar's search for a home and family was complete.

The year 1853 found him busily engaged in one of his favorite undertakings: that of the collection of historical materials concerning the development of Texas. A nine-page manuscript in Lamar's hand is headed "Notes taken from Colonel James Morgan, New Washington, 27 April, 1853"; this document recorded recollections of pre-Republic days in Texas.[29] A similar paper has been preserved, also written by Lamar, entitled "Information derived from Joe Kuykendall;" this is a record of the history of migrations of Anglo-settlers to the region.[30] This material is indicative of a serious effort of Lamar as a historian to preserve information concerning the development of Texas and much of his extensive collection of papers was aimed at this end. His historical method included both the collection of significant documentary materials and the gathering and the recording of oral history.

An interesting description of him is extant dating from this period of his life. Judge A.W. Terrell wrote these words about his appearance in 1853:

Long jet black hair . . . tinged with gray . . . He was of dark complexion and about five feet, ten inches tall with broad shoulders, deep chest, and symmetrical limbs. From under his high forehead, blue eyes looked out in calm repose, while his clearcut, handsome features bespoke of an iron resolution.[31]

This description not only indicates that Terrell was a friend and an admirer, but that Lamar, at least in this period, was a contented man. He certainly had every reason to be: he was enthusiastically happy with his young wife and his domestic situation; the home in which he had spent but little time previously had now taken on a warmth that added to his contentment. His correspondence during this period indicated a sense of moral integrity and confidence about what he had sought to accomplish feeling that whatever his distractors might say about his political career that history would certainly exonerate his efforts. Perhaps he felt that his own collection of historical materials would have much to do with speeding the day when the wisdom of his leadership of Texas would be more readily recognized.

He spent these days in a variety of activities. He corresponded with friends advising them on moral issues urging the highest possible standards of personal conduct.[32] He became active in the affairs of the Southern Commercial Convention, an organization that had as its aim the strengthening of the economic position of the southern states, and that sought to support whatever political measures appeared to promote the interests of the South. In January 1855, he presided over that body's fifth gathering in New Orleans, and closed the session with a flowery farewell address thanking the members for "the high honor" of being president.[33]

He wrote home to Henrietta telling about his term as the presiding officer of the convention, and then added: "Tell our pretty angel that I will bring her a rocking chair." [34]

Between such activities as those of leading a semi-political gathering in New Orleans and managing the enlarged plantation in Richmond, Lamar was busy preparing his volume of poems for publication. For years he had been writing verses, that to some degree, emulated the style of the eighteenth century English romantic poets. Born in the very year that Wordsworth's *Lyrical Ballads* had appeared, he had been strongly influenced by this type of literary expression.[35]

Collecting what he considered to be the best of his own poems, and adding some verses from other sources, he was prepared to see his work through the press. This required a journey to New York, where his volume was published on October 4, 1857, under the title, *Verse Memorials*. The W.P. Fetridge Company were the printers for the work that consisted of a total of 224 pages. An impressive engraving of Lamar by J. Sartain is opposite the title page showing him with folded arms, dark, flowing hair, a thick nose and penetrating eyes.

The book was dedicated to Mrs. William Cazneau, the former Cora Montgomery, whom he declared to be the "wife of one of my best and long cherished friends." [36]

He immediately wrote to her sending a copy of his collection enclosing a clipping reviewing the work that stated

> the poems in the volume chiefly relate to the affections and are characterized with a tender regard for woman and her many virtues. Many of the poems breathe a true poetic spirit, though some fall short of the conception of true inspiration.[37]

A letter from Sue Capers to Lamar thanked him for including her verses in the work;[38] these were two poems written by her addressed to Lamar himself.[39] Another, by A.B. Meek, "To Mrs. Henrietta Lamar," was in the volume.[40] The remainder of the book, however, was Lamar's own.

Both his style and his content were highly romantic, given to moments of ecstatic imagery. He wrote of

> ... Texan shades,
> Fair land of flowers and
>   blooming maids

or of

> The velvet green
> Beneath the moon's inviting sheen.[41]

One would find it difficult to accept most of his work as valid poetical expression in the modern understanding of this art form. At best his was the poetry of fanciful escape that may have played some function for an age that found delight in literary materials that had little relationship to the realities of life in what was still a frontier nation.

One theme that was constantly recurrent in his writings was that of the beauty and virtue of womanhood; his glorification of feminity took form in such verses as "Carmelita," [42] "Isabele" [43] or the "Village Coquette" [44] or when he spoke of

> . . . beautiful Irene . . . Sweet mistress
> of the tuneful art.[45]

A correlative motif, that of romantic love, was set forth in such works as "The Ruling Passion," [46] and "No Girl Can Win My Stubborn Breast." [47]

One poem, however, did have definite political overtones. This was entitled "Arms for the Southern Land," [48] and gave expression to the rising martial spirit evident in the south that would lead to the tragic events of the 1860s. There is little biographical material in the volume other than that related to the deaths of his first wife and his daughter. Taken as a whole, *Verse Memorials* can hardly be considered as having any lasting literary merit. However, it did make of Lamar a published poet. This was a goal toward which he had been working for some time; here was the fulfilling of a long-standing ambition.[49] It was his own conviction that his volume had made available poems "rescued from the turmoils of a life that permitted little leisure for literary recreation." [50]

Perhaps his own was the best evaluation of his poetry: this was nothing more than literary recreation.

One piece of verse had described his "Home on the Brazos." [51] It was there that he returned after completing the work of seeing his publication through the press. However, his stay there was not to be a long one. During the months that he had been preparing *Verse Memorials* for the printers, he had been actively seeking political appointment. His efforts at authorship, although emotionally fulfilling, did not result in financial gain: his economic situation was still precarious. He was heavily in debt and money was desperately needed both for his family and to maintain the Richmond home.

Thomas Rusk had been writing to influential contacts in March 1857, that "Genl. Lamar is an applicant for appointment of resident minister to some of the European or South American republics or would accept the governorship of a territory." [52] President Buchanan received a letter dated March 8 endorsing Lamar for such an appointment.[53]

He was now looking beyond the Brazos for a practical means of maintaining the home that he had found.

[21]

Minister in Residence

A small sailing vessel slowly made its way up the placid waters of the San Juan River. The northern bank of the heavily foliaged stream was Nicaragua; to the south lay Costa Rica, then on hostile terms with her neighbor. On board, Lamar, as the newly appointed resident minister of the United States, was able to get fleeting glimpses of the two countries where he would live for the next eighteen months as he peered through the jungle-like growth along the stream. He was on the last leg of his journey to the capital city of Nicaragua, Managua, where he would soon take up his official duties.

An ominous puff of white smoke suddenly appeared over the ragged battlements of a riverside fortress known as Castillo Viejo. The sound of cannon fire echoed across the water making it apparent that the ambassador's ship was either under fire or was vigorously being commanded to put into shore.

The helmsman brought the vessel alongside the river dock. The report that had reverberated across the waterway had been no more than the discharge of a signal cartridge, but the sight of guns pointed toward the ship, and excited conversations along the riverbank, made it clear that an explosive situation existed. Lamar went ashore and had an opportunity to exercise his talent for diplomacy even before he had been formally presented to the government to which he had been assigned. He was told that an American named Dunn had nearly killed a native boy: this had caused the inhabitants of the area to riot, necessitating the calling out of the local militia. As the official representative of the government of the United States, Lamar was expected to settle the problem and make restitution.

When tempers had calmed a bit, the newly appointed ambassador was able to get at some of the facts of the situation: Dunn had struck the boy with a barrel he was unloading. However, this, he claimed, had been an accident. The alerted military had arrested the American, whose life was in jeopardy. Lamar was able to talk with those on both sides of the dispute. The injured youth, by this time, had recovered sufficiently to be willing to accept financial recompense for his indignity consisting of a total of two dollars which the Minister Resident presented to him in the name of the United States of America. Dunn was finally released and peace was restored to the Rio San Juan.[1]

However, the incident was not an isolated one: it was indicative of the deep feelings of resentment that existed toward citizens of the United States. This event was more than symbolic of the problems that confronted the new ambassador, for he was about to enter into a situation in which persons from north of the Rio Grande were generally distrusted.

Lamar boarded his ship and proceeded without further incident to the capital city of Managua. There he disembarked and prepared to present himself to the government of General Tomas Martinez, who had recently become president of the nation, a position he held more by virtue of the effectiveness of the bayonets of the army he controlled than by any form of popular support.[2]

For sometime prior to his appointment to ambassadorial

status, Lamar had sought a diplomatic post. As early as 1853, his arch enemy Sam Houston had quipped: "I will not be surprised to see Lamar come into favor and get a good appointment from Pierce. It would not be worse than the appointment of Gadsden to Mexico." [3]

But it was not until Buchanan's administration that serious consideration was given to granting Lamar such a position.

In July 1857, he heard indirectly through an article in a Washington paper that he had been appointed as Minister to Argentina. He was in Macon, Georgia, at the time, and he immediately wrote to Howell Cobb in Washington for details of the assignment.[4] A few days later he received official notification from Lew Cass, Secretary of State, declaring that he had been named "Minister Resident . . . to the Argentine Confederation." [5] Further instructions from Cass stated that the new appointee would be expected to "repair to your post as speedily as is consistent with the proper arrangement of your private affairs." [6] His salary of $10,000 a year, a handsome sum for that day, would begin when he left his home enroute to his legation.[7]

Lamar readily accepted the appointment.[8] His first action in preparation for his foreign assignment was to send a letter to Cousin Gazaway in which he declared "I am extremely desirous to accept." He stated that he felt it necessary first to "make some arrangements with my creditors among whom you are the most considerable." [9]

Lamar returned to his home in Texas after receiving news of his appointment where he received a letter from James Hamilton who wrote to him about the possibility of arranging an advance on his salary to help ease the financial problems that still plagued him.[10]

While in Richmond he also received a note from Burnet, who wished him well as he prepared to leave for overseas service stating that he regretted he could not visit with him as "an old friend who it is more than probable I shall never see again in this changing world." [11]

Soon after this he set out for Washington, accompanied by Henrietta, who considered for a time the possibility of going with him on his overseas mission. After arriving at the national capital, he received a letter from Hamilton referring to an unsuccessful effort to induce Charles Lamar to advance money for Lamar's immediate expenses and an outfit worthy of his new post.[12]

However, shortly after that, Gazaway wrote stating that he could "go ahead and arrange my debt by the payment to me as you proposed of $1000 annually from your salary."[13] The generous financial arrangements of his appointment would make it possible to begin to absolve some of his debts.

Henrietta suffered a severe attack of bronchitis while in Washington, and possibly for this reason, and partly for financial considerations, gave up the trip with her husband to return to Richmond [Texas] and manage the plantation.[14]

Lamar remained in Washington throughout the fall awaiting a final determination of his diplomatic post.[15] That he was an enthusiastic supporter of the administration is indicated in a statement declaring his "determination to accept the appointment recently tendered me" as proof of his high regard for Buchanan whom he considered to be "the most enlightened reliable and safest statesman now in the United States."[16]

By late fall the assignment had been changed from Argentina to Nicaragua. In light of the rapidly developing interest in Europe in a possible commercial route across Central America connecting the Atlantic and Pacific oceans, a diplomat was immediately needed there. Apparently it was felt that Lamar's talents could be of greater use in that situation: the assignment of an ambassador with a fairly prominent name to Nicaragua would in itself help ease a difficult situation. On December 23, 1857, Lewis Cass countersigned a commission to the ex-president of Texas as minister to Nicaragua and presented him with a memorandum that his salary of $10,000 a year would commence on that date.[17]

In early January, 1858, Lamar was in New York preparing to sail for Central America.[18] On January 18, he arrived on board the *Susquehanna* off the coast of Nicaragua at San Juan del Norte.[19] Within the month he was at the lakeside capital.

The bitter feeling toward the United States that had been evident in the riot on the river dock had resulted in part from an invasion of the country by a band of filibusters led by an American named Walker. A reign of terror had followed while he and his undisciplined force had controlled the nation with a high hand for nearly two years prior to Lamar's arrival. One report which the new ambassador collected stated that during Walker's months of misrule, he had shot "without any proofs of trial" all who opposed him and had nearly wrecked the economy of the nation by appropriating to his own use whatever he could find of commercial value.[20] He was overthrown on May 1, 1857, but no stable government immediately followed his expulsion. The United States at first failed to recognize the new leadership of the country; however, American concern over the European interest in Nicaragua as a possible route across the isthmus, finally led to recognition of the presidency of General Tomas Martinez. Yrissari, who was then serving as minister to several of the Central American republics, had been appointed as interim ambassador until a resident minister would reach the country. Yrissari had negotiated a treaty to gain permission for the American Atlantic and Pacific Ship company to operate in the Lake of Nicaragua and to conduct an overland transit across the Isthmus. Lamar now had the task of seeking ratification for that treaty in the face of the bitter hostility toward the United States that still existed in the country. The assignment was one of gigantesque proportions.

Lamar immediately presented himself to the government led by Martinez, and on February 8, was cordially received.[21] Cass had given him direct instructions to "convert" the Nicaraguans to the treaty that was then under consideration.[22]

He went to work on this assignment without delay, suggesting to Martinez's representatives that a transit route would be opened with or without their consent.[23] This line of reasoning seemed to make some impression on government leadership in the light of American power and influence. However, in March, Monsieur Felix Belly of France, arrived in Managua prepared to present the French case for a treaty between Nicaragua and the nation he represented. Lamar was aware that he had to move rapidly. Two weeks after Belly's arrival he reported to Cass with some jubilation that the treaty between the United States and Nicaragua had been ratified by a single vote.[24] But the treaty had yet to be signed by the president. In the meantime, Belly undertook to urge rejection of all American proposals as the efforts of the United States minister languished on the desk of the Nicaraguan president.[25]

Between diplomatic efforts, Lamar began to take note of the country in which he found himself. He penned his observations of Niccaragua as a land inhabited by some "250,000 souls" consisting of two classes: one was the "pure indians" and the other was the "mixed race" in which "negro blood predominates." He described the "moral and political condition of the country" as "horrible" and the government as "a military despotism" supported by no regular income except "contributions levied at the discretion of the authorities." In addition to this, he believed the church to be "oppressive and corrupt" and he decried the fact that there was "no freedom of speech" in the country.[26]

However, there was much about the area that did intrigue him. In April he petitioned the municipality of Granada, a community immediately south of Managua, for permission to purchase land on the lake front.[27]

Lamar was received socially by the ruling class of Nicaragua as is apparent from the fact that he not only was entertained on several occasions by both the president's family in circumstances other than necessary official functions, but also by other members of the nation's aristocracy. He even exercised his poetical skills to advantage by charming the daughter of President Martinez with a poem written in her honor entitled "The Belle of Nindiri." [28] Nindiri was the Martinez family home, some eleven miles from Managua, in which Lamar visited on occasion. His last known poetic effort was one that he called "The Daughter of Mendoza," written in behalf of the offspring of José Mendoza of Pueblo Nuevo, head of another prominent Nicaraguan family.[29] He sent a copy of this to Señorita Mendoza with a note signed "Amigo" in which he apologized for composing in English regretting "Siento no haber podido escribirlas en el idioma de U." [30]

Although he spoke passable Spanish, and was able to correspond in the language, he was probably not highly fluent in the idiom of the people. Nonetheless he apparently did have excellent personal relations with many Nicaraguans particularly those in places of influence: he was certainly able to move easily in the circles of Central American aristocracy.[31]

J.M. Cazneau wrote to Lamar in early April from Washington that "all your friends in and out of authority are delighted with the impression you are making on the people of Nicaragua." [32]

In spite of his seeming early success with the treaty, Lamar was aware that the French agent, Belly, was making considerable progress toward annulling his efforts. He wrote to Cass in May indicating that he was aware of the considerable opposition to the unsigned treaty.[33]

In the meantime he received word that the United States had ratified the pact.[34] While his major assignment continued to be that of securing a Nicaraguan response to his action, and, at the same time, discouraging the completion of a French treaty, he carried on the normal duties of a consular official. Various claims against Nicaragua are in his papers[35] in which Americans sought redress from acts of alleged oppression or injustice.

On May 28 he reported to Washington that he was seeking to protect the persons and interests of his fellow countrymen.[36] This task in itself was a considerable one. On one occasion he interceded with the president in behalf of an American named Calaudio Cueblo, who was under sentence of banishment.[37] He had other requests for similar efforts that apparently he sought to fulfill as best he could.[38]

However, his major concern remained that of securing Nicaraguan acceptance of an American treaty. By July his correspondence indicated a deep mood of discouragement: rumors had reached him that the French agreement was assured. In addition to this, he had made little progress in gaining any commitment for redress of claims that he had filed against Nicaragua for reparation for the loss of American life. At one point he even discussed with his superiors in Washington the possibility of sending "a war vessel on this coast. . . . Without it, it is idle to think of bringing this government to any terms." [39] However, the use of gunboat-diplomacy was rejected, and Lamar continued his efforts at peaceful persuasion. He carefully kept a record of congressmen who were favoring ratification of the French Belly contract: one extant document, apparently in Lamar's hand, shows four "for Belly" and four others in "opposition" with cryptic marks besides the names of most of the others.[40]

He continued to argue against the French proposal with President Martinez declaring that not one "intelligent native . . . seriously believes that the contemplated canal is a practicable enterprise." [41] "Mr. Belly should first be required to execute the work before granting the ratification." [42] "Even if it were practicable, it would only be effected by expenditures altogether too enormous for the present demands of commerce." [43]

In the meantime the Nicaraguan government was hesitant to openly reject the American proposal. Martinez and his ministers discussed with Lamar a modification of the originally planned treaty that would include in its provisions one matter that was of considerable importance to Central American thinking: that the United States guarantee there would be no future filibustering activities. Such surety for neutrality would carry with it the agreement of never "employing any force." [44] This would mean that if any American trade route were established across the isthmus that there could be no military protection for the trans-oceanic commerce other than that provided by Nicaragua. Lamar simply communicated this proposal to Cass.

The discouragement of his assignment was apparent in a letter penned to Henrietta in October, 1858, in which he declared that he missed her very much and vowed he was only forcing himself to stay in order that he be able to provide adequately for her.[45]

Since the Belly contract involved a French agreement with both Nicaragua and Costa Rica to the south, Lamar received instructions to go to the neighboring state with the status of United States ambassador and do what he could to prevent acceptance of the French proposal there.

In early August he wrote the local newspaper in Leon, where he had been living, thanking his neighbors for their hospitality to him,[46] and then he requested passage for Costa Rica.[47] A boundary dispute between the two nations caused him some difficulty in reaching his destination, but he was at last able to make his way southward to the Costa Rican capital, San José. He filed his August report to Cass from Managua, but by September 10 he was in the neighboring nation.[48]

An interesting arrangement had been made by Washington in assigning Lamar as minister resident of both countries. He no longer would receive his salary of $10,000 as envoy extraordinary, but would, instead, receive $7500 as minister resident of Nicaragua and an additional $3750 for the same position in relation to Costa Rica.[49] In any case the financial remuneration resulted in a situation that caused the double minister to reply to Washington: "I am extremely content with the change."[50]

Leadership of the government of Costa Rica was in the hands of an aristocratic gentleman named Juan Rafael Mora, who was described by Dr. Marquis Hines, U.S. Consul at San Jose, as a leader possessed with "wisdom and moderation" in whom he had "great confidence."[51]

President Mora immediately received Lamar: in October he invited him to visit at his hacienda outside the city,[52] and later in the month, issued him a special invitation to a banquet.[53] Obviously Lamar was able to relate to a man of this type, and he had some opportunity to urge upon him acceptance of American policy. A written statement in Spanish is extant in Lamar's hand headed "Confidential. Señor Presidente." In this he summarized in writing what he had urged upon the president in person. He assured him that American policy meant "no intervention en los asuntos y negocioses de Centro-America." [54] He sought to defend American concern over the Belly contract, and he gave an explanation of the Monroe Doctrine. He declared with something of a Lamarian flourish that he favored "el orden, la ley y la justice." [55]

On November 12, 1858, Lamar wrote to Mora about his plans to return to Nicaragua,[56] and shortly after that penned another strong plea to him as president of his nation to reject ratification of the Belly contract.[57]

However, Consul Hines sent Lamar a dispatch on December 18, stating that the French pact had just been ratified and that President Mora had told him he would write Lamar. "Perhaps," he added, "he will make some explanations.' [58]

In late November, Lamar sailed from Punta Arenas for Nicaragua. When he finally reached his former residence in Leon, he wrote to Hines that his trunks were soaked in transit and that his papers were damaged even though he had paid "$30 in advance for transportation." He added: "I have been occupied several days in drying them." [59]

He once more took up his duties in Nicaragua. That he continued to have both a cordial and a warm relationship with President Martinez is indicated by the fact that he received an invitation to the baptism of the president's first son in January 1859.[60]

Martinez later commended Lamar's conduct, and stated that he took "satisfaction in attesting the zeal, energy, and good success with which he had applied himself." [61]

When Lamar considered purchasing property in Nicaragua,[62] Martinez wrote to him that "we still flatter ourselves with the hope that Nicaragua may yet count you among her citizens." [63]

In March, Lamar presented some 200 books to the public library in Managua. This likely was an act done in behalf of the United States government as an indication of good will, but the deed brought him generous praise from the recipients of the gift.[64]

Although Lamar seemed to be still enjoying a good relationship with citizens of the nation where he was serving as minister resident, his ambassadorship was under fire at home. In February 1859, J.M. Cazneau wrote to him from Washington enclosing clippings for and against him. He stated "a very bitter feeling [is] growing up throughout the country in consequence of the non-ratification of the treaty." [65]

One of the clippings that had been sent to Lamar was from the *New York Times* of February 9, 1859, that condemned "General Lamar's excesses in Nicaragua." This was based on reports from officers of the United States squadron in port at Leon who claimed to have seen Lamar "openly lying in a public warehouse without hat, coat, shoes or stockings." [66]

However, a Washington paper had defended this report as merely an attack from the "abolition press" that had censored him "for mingling too freely and cordially with the common people." This statement declared that he "is a person of simple manners and democratic habits." His editorial supporter declared that in spite of the difficulty of his assignment, he had "given general satisfaction to the governments to which he is accredited." [67]

Cazneau wrote Lamar declaring that Washington was giving no credence to the "vile attacks on you" by "the northern press." [68]

His major project, that of defeating the Belly contract while at the same time gaining some sort of acceptable American treaty with Nicaragua, was not beyond hope of success. Both Central American countries were deeply afraid of possible American intervention. In spite of Lamar's good personal relations with leaders in both countries, his influence was not sufficient to change public policy.

On April 29, 1859, he wrote to Cass in dismal discouragement that "The Belly contract . . . has been ratified by the Republic." This, he believed, was "no other . . . than . . . a conspiracy against the United States." [69]

However, Lamar did not give up completely in his efforts to salvage something from his diplomatic career. He had been negotiating with one of Martinez's ministers, Pedro Zeledon, for a treaty that would at least give the United States and Nicaragua some sort of a basis for international cooperation.[70] In order to do this a clause had to be inserted in the proposed terms of agreement that would guarantee non-intervention in the affairs of the Central American nation: any United States military presence in the country would be prohibited. When Lamar forwarded this proposal to Washington, Cass rejected it as totally inadmissible.[71]

This was Lamar's last serious effort at treaty negotiation, an area in which he had failed completely. In addition there was criticism at home of his work as a diplomat. His normal reaction to failure and criticism was poor health. Apparently during the early days of his diplomatic career, his very enthusiasm for a new task brought a resurgence of strength. But continued discouragement for him generally led to physical decline. Doubtless this was a genuine illness, but when his sensitive spirit met continual rebuffs, his physical health always seemed to suffer.

Consul Hines wrote Lamar in June regretting to hear that "you have been sick for several days." [72] Two other letters of this period made similar references to his poor health.[73]

Lamar was simply ready to go home. In August he wrote to Cass to this effect and he made mention of the difficulties of his mission, and stated that he had tried "to create confidence to allay their apprehensions." [74] He sent with this request an accounting of his expenses,[75] and a few days later wrote to the State Department what he declared to be his "last official communication" in which he apologized "for the undiplomatic style in which my letters from Nicaragua were sometimes written." He stated that he was "intent only upon placing before the department what I deemed the exact state of things." [76]

Expressions of appreciation of his stay in Nicaragua poured in as he prepared to sail for home. Pañfilo Osorno wrote in behalf of the City of Managua declaring the warm feelings the people had for him.[77] Other letters of farewell made it clear that this was more than a single opinion.[78]

But Lamar was ready to go home. His health was not good, and he had failed in his primary objective as a diplomat — at least in an official capacity. He reached Washington in September, reported briefly to the State Department, and then began the journey to Richmond and Henrietta. He was home at the Oak Grove by early October.[79]

Edward Fontaine wrote a few days later that he was "gratified to learn through the papers that you have returned safely to your home." [80]

Burnet wrote a similar note and regretted that "neuralgia in the back" would prevent him from visiting Lamar.[81]

To Loretto he had brought a monkey and a parrot from Nicaragua. However, an even greater gift to his family was the fact that the handsome salary he had received during his diplomatic career was enough to help alleviate some of the financial difficulties that had so long confronted him.

But he was at home: the family prepared for a festive Christmas in the plantation home amid the oaks. A holly wreath was hung on the door as a happy reminder of the season. Lamar relaxed in the winter sunshine of the moderate Texas climate.

On December 15 James Starr wrote to him sending congratulations on his homecoming.[82] Four days later, at ten o'clock in the morning, the ex-ambassador felt a sudden, severe pain. He grabbed his chest as he slumped to the floor. By the time his family could reach him, he had breathed his last, dead of an apparent heart attack. Lamar had lived just over sixty-one years.

Friends quickly gathered at the home of the stricken widow: someone hung a bow of black crepe on the wreath on the door of the house.[83]

The Galveston Weekly News of December 27 carried news of

the death and reported that the funeral had been held in Richmond. Other papers from Texas to Georgia picked up the story as friends far and near sent their condolences to the Oak Grove.[84]

Burial took place in a small cemetery near the house. When a permanent marker was later erected, it was made of Texas granite surrounded by a twelve-foot shaft of Italian marble. On the west side of the tomb there was chiseled a shield bearing the name *Lamar* encircled by a wreath; the other side was decorated with muzzles of two cannon, doubtless symbolizing the belief of family and friends that he had served his two countries both in peace and in war.[85]

At last Mirabeau Lamar was at home.

Epilogue

Summer thunderstorms often develop rapidly in Texas.

A sky that has been vividly blue all day except for occasional white clouds will suddenly darken: cumuli will form into towering nimbi that emit ominous rolls of thunder. But because of the aridness of some parts of the land, such storms do not always mean rain. There may be the rumbling echoes of thunder, but unless considerable moisture has been drawn up from the distant Gulf, no appreciable amount of life-giving precipitation will fall. In the semi-desert vastness of the land, there is often thunder but no rain.

There were those who thought of Mirabeau Lamar as just such a storm: reverberating noise but nothing more.

Was he, then, merely thunder beyond the Brazos?

Mirabeau Lamar certainly had a share in creating the noise of battle on the plain of San Jacinto. He had arrived as a permanent resident only days before that battle: this fact made it possible for him to be accused of being a late-coming glory seeker. In the days that followed, and during his term as vice-president under Sam Houston, he found himself increasing in opposition to the Father of Texas on many political issues. Those who considered Old Sam as a sojourner from the heights of Olympus were quick to reject the leadership of the squat son of a Georgia plantation owner. The two men differed vastly not only in their political philosophies but in personality and background.

Houston saw in Lamar everything that he personally disliked: he was not of the frontier, he was highly cultured and educated, and he was a southern aristocrat. He and his followers vigorously opposed all that Lamar did and stood for. The first president of the Republic considered his successor as a surplanter who would tarnish his own personal claim to glory and he did everything possible to discredit him. Contemporary documents make it clear that Houston's witty diatribes against Lamar and his negative assessment of the second president of Texas have had a strong impact on much of the modern writing of Texas history.

Was Lamar only an idle dreamer who was drunk with visions of grandeur, a complete incompetent whose every effort resulted in the disruption of Texas? Some modern historians have naively written him off as such.[1] Crusty old General Sam would have said so, and likely have put his thoughts in much stronger terms using expletives that could have had a little difficulty in finding their way into print even in this age of uncensored communication.

Was he merely the sound of thunder that might be heard on a Texas plain with reverberating noise and nothing more? Or was he more like the moisture that would follow the storm and bring life giving refreshment to a desert land?

To answer these questions, let us briefly review some of the facts concerning Lamar's accomplishments and failures.

As president of the embryonic Republic, he did have a consistent policy in spite of the claims of his enemies. This policy was based simply on the belief that Texas was destined to be an independent nation. At the time this was the only rea-

Epilogue

sonable course open to the successful revolutionists. The United States had rejected any consideration of annexation due to its own internal problems revolving around the delicate balance of power between slave-owning and free states. It did not appear that any likelihood of immediate change in this arrangement would take place. If Texas was to exist, it had to function completely on its own, and Lamar's efforts were based on this ideology. The foreign loan, the national bank, the elaborate efforts for European recognition were all aimed in this direction. Proposals for education, universities, and cultural development, as well as the new capital in the geographical center of the nation were a part of this concept. The development of a Texas navy, the Cherokee War, and the Santa Fe Expedition were further extensions of such policy.

To some degree these endeavors were successful. Recognition of Texas as a sovereign state was achieved by Lamar's emissaries during his administration. This was no small accomplishment: without this achievement, Texas could have never made a serious claim to nationhood and the revolutionists might well have been written off historically as nothing more than rebellious renegades.

Most of his proposals were logical emanations of his policy of Texas independency: the national bank and the foreign loan were reasonable propositions that came near fruition, and one, the quixotic Texas navy, had its own peculiar area of success.

His dream of an educational system for Texas that would provide learning and cultural advancement for all of its citizens was a noble one, and the setting aside of public land for the development of a school system was a practical step which did bear fruit in later years. Lamar is justly honored today in the Lone Star State as the "Father of Texas education."

The relocation of the capital at Austin was the act of his administration that was the most vigorously opposed by the Houstonian party of all he did: but even this has been approved by the test of time.

However, two tragic failures must be acknowledged. One

was Lamar's Indian policy that resulted in the inhuman expulsion of the Cherokees from the Republic. The only defense that can be made of Lamar in this action is that he echoed the contemporary thinking of the great mass of the Anglo-American settlers. Viewing this event from the distance of the years, however, one cannot help but wonder why Houston's proposals to allow these people to live peaceably within the bounds of Texas could not have been carried out. Such policy would have ultimately created far less difficulties for all parties concerned. Lamar was simply acting with the blindness that won the West, and that has left an indelible scar on the face of the American ideal of justice and human decency.

The other tragedy must be recounted in any consideration of the life of Mirabeau Lamar was that of the Santa Fe Expedition. Although the second president of Texas acted with the whole-hearted approval of the majority of his people, upon him must fall the onus of the dismal failure of this quasi-military invasion of a nearby territory. He can be defended only on the basis of his lack of information both about the people of New Mexico and of the geography of the land between Austin and Santa Fe. Even the best maps of the time were inaccurate in regard to the land that is today West Texas and eastern New Mexico. Very little was known about this great expanse of semi-desert country. Perhaps some smaller exploratory expeditions should have been attempted before a large scale trading entourage was sent into this vast unknown area. In any case, the expedition itself was a tragic failure and Lamar as the president of the nation responsible for the endeavor cannot be absolved from blame for the suffering and death which resulted from the catastrophe.

However, Lamar did accomplish much. He did put together a workable government that was the basis of what limited stability the youthful nation possessed. He was certainly an intelligent and capable administrator. These were qualities Houston had lacked completely: although the first president had been an effective and charismatic leader in the crisis of battle, he was lacking in the ability to work within the frame-

Epilogue

work of an ongoing governmental structure. Lamar's personal relations with most of his co-workers, his congress, the leading and intelligent men of the time were far better than those of his predecessor's. He was able to create some degree of nationhood out of the confusion that was Texas before his term of office. In most matters he acted diplomatically and wisely. His concepts of republican government were basically sound, and although he made mistakes of judgment, he was neither scoundrel nor imbecile. On the other hand, he was a responsible and able leader who for a brief time was Texas: the Republic could not have existed for its decade of life had there not been present some manifestation of the Lamarian approach.

Failure did dog much of his efforts. There was the failure of the foreign loan, the rejection at the polls of his would-be successor to office whom he had endorsed, and finally there was the fact of his unsuccessful diplomatic career in Central America. But even in these failures, one can clearly discern in Lamar a man of dedication and integrity. There were few of his contemporaries who did not at least acknowledge him to be a person motivated by high moral principle. Yet, in spite of his lack of political success, much of what he proposed, in time, did come to be a permanent part of Texas.

Was Mirabeau Lamar merely thunder that echoed up and down the canyons of the Brazos for a brief time or was he more?

He was more: he was the gentle rain that can follow the thunder, and is absorbed into the dusty soil in time to bring renewal and refreshment. He was one who made it possible for Texas to bloom in later years.

He was thunder for a time, but he was rain.

Endnotes

Chapter 1. BATTLE ON THE PLAIN

1. Philip Graham in his careful study of Lamar as a poet (*The Life and Poems of Mirabeau B. Lamar*, Chapel Hill: University of North Carolina Press, 1938) said of him that when he arrived in Texas, "in the eyes of Texan frontiersmen," he was "highly cultured" (p. 7). This work was published only in a limited edition.

2. Two biographies of Lamar have been available in general circulation: one was prepared by Herbert Gambrell, who cited this statement. (*Lamar: Troubador and Crusader*. Dallas: Southwest Press, 1934, pp. 21,22.) The other is the more recent brief life of Lamar in the Presidents and Governors of Texas Series edited by Dorman Winfrey and written by Stanley Siegel (*The Poet President of Texas*. Austin: Jenkins Publishing Company, The Pemberton Press, 1977).

3. Graham cited an unfavorable description of Lamar: he was "not handsome, below medium height, but stout and muscular" with hair that was "black and straight, face oval," (*op. cit.*, p. 9).

4. Dixon, Sam Houston, and Kemp, Louis Wiltz, — *The Heroes of San Jacinto* (Houston: The Anson Jones Press, 1932), p. 300.

5. "Letter from Alexander E. Patton to Mr. Kilgore," dated 25 March, 1836, cited by Gambrell, *op. cit.*, pp. 74, 75.

6. Lane in his autobiographical account says that when he was unhorsed, "Gen. Lamar rode up to succor me, shot the Mexican, and thinking I was dead, fell back with the command . . . twenty Mexicans were round me . . . Karns saw me . . . ordered his company to wheel and fire . . . which they did . . . an old man told me 'son, get up behind' . . . I did." (Walter P. Lane, *Adventures and Recollections*, News Messenger Publishing Company, Marshall, Texas, 1928, p. 13).

7. Some accounts of this action state that Lamar's act of daring was greeted by an involuntary shout of admiration from the Mexicans and that Lamar then took a moment to acknowledge this tribute with a bow. However, even if the shout of admiration was fact, one can hardly accept the courtly bow on the battlefield as other than imagination based upon the tendency of the time to add dramatic embellishment to actual events. Graham, (*oop. cit.*) discussed this legend and noted that it did appear in contemporary newspapers such as the *Galveston Weekly News* of December 27, 1859, *The Telegraph* (Houston) April 14, 1838, *The Colorado Tribune*, November 12, 1849, *The Texas Almanac*, 1858. However, each of these publications appeared after enough time had elapsed to allow a legend to grow. One student of the life of Lamar referred in an unpublished thesis to a tradition in the Lamar family that he received a wound in saving Lane's life. However, if such were the case, it must have been quite superficial (Ruth Reese, "Mirabeau B. Lamar: Father of Texas Education" (MS), p. 54).

8. The Lamar Papers (MS), Number 353.

9. Eugene C. Barker, "The San Jacinto Campaign," *Texas Historical Association Quarterly*, Volume IV, p. 353.

10. *Loc. cit.*

11. "Houston's Letter to Burnet" dated, April 25, 1836, cited in C. Newell's *History of the Revolution in Texas*, Appendix 8, pp. 213, 214.

12. Castenada, Carlos Eduardo. *The Mexican Side of the Texas Revolution*, (Dallas: The Turner Company, 1928) p. 77.

13. *Loc. cit.* An excellent modern account of the battle can be found in Frank X. Tolbert's *The Day of San Jacinto* (New York: McGraw-Hill, 1959).

14. An example of the acceptance of the Houstonian view of Lamar can be found in the preface of *The Autobiography of Sam Houston* (Norman: The University of Oklahoma Press, 1954). The editors, Donald Day and Harry Herbert Ullom, state that Lamar was "drunk with visions of grandeur and empire" and that in "three short years" as president he "made a shambles of the government." (p. xiii). C.R. Wharton in his *History of Texas* (Dallas: The Turner Company, 1935) described Lamar as "a poet and a dreamer with visions of empire." (p. 199) Even Stanley Siegel in his carefully documented short life of Lamar described him as being "hampered by a dreamy temperament and a vaulting ambition" (*The Poet President of Texas*, p. 103). These negative evaluations of Lamar are clearly based on Houstonian rhetoric produced by the crusty first president of the Republic in the heat of political conflict.

Chapter 2. FAIRFIELD

1. Philip Graham's study (*op. cit.*) of the early years of Lamar is enhanced by the fact that he had access to papers and letters in the possession of the Lamar family that have been unknown to many who have written in this field and who have depended largely on Texas sources. For this reason his study is the most thorough investigation of the pre-Texas years of Lamar that is available.

2. Graham traced the ancestry of John Lamar. In 1660 four Huguenot brothers settled in Maryland and Virginia. About a century later, John Lamar, the grandfather of Mirabeau's father, moved to Beach Island in the Savannah River. The grandson, born 1769, married a Rebecca Lamar, a first cousin, and established himself on a plantation in Jefferson County, Georgia (Graham, *op. cit.*, pp. 4ff).

3. Some lists of the brothers of Mirabeau include the name of Lavoisier Legrand. Graham (*op. cit.*, p. 5) is correct in concluding that this was a grandson of John Lamar who was also named by Zechariah. However, the uncle's heavy hand is not apparent in the names given to the five daughters who were born to the family: Louisa, Amelia, Mary Ann, Evangelina and Loretto Rebecca. Uncle Zechariah lived for a time with his brother's family but later married and gave his own children simple names: Mary and John. (Ruth Reese. "Mirabeau B. Lamar: Father of Texas Education," an unpublished MS in The University of Texas library, p. 12).

4. Graham, *op. cit.*, p. 6. Edward Fontaine "Biographical Sketch of General Mirabeau B. Lamar, Third President of the Republic of Texas," (MS).

5. A.K. Christian in his study of Lamar that appeared in two volumes

of the *Southwestern Historical Quarterly* concluded that he had the best schools offered in the area but that he never went to college (A.K. Christian, "Lamar," *Southwestern Historical Quarterly*, Volume 23, p. 154). A manuscript in the Lamar Papers in his own hand gives some interesting insight into the form that his early education took: in this he declared that [I] "... have made no small proficiency in the art of composition, being the son of a very wealthy farmer I would practice myself when young in writing papers" (The Lamar Papers, Number 55 (MS)).

6. Reese, *op. cit.*, pp. 31–37.
7. Gambrell, *op. cit.*, p. 24.
8. Lamar published *Verse Memorials* in New York in 1827 which was a collection of his poems prefaced by tributary poems by admirers (Mirabeau B. Lamar. *Verse Memorials*. New York: W.P. Fetridge and Company, 1857).
9. None of the papers in this series are in Lamar's handwriting, but several include notes written across them that appear to be his. The three mentioned above are unsigned and two have the notation: "I forgot who wrote the above." Another has the statement written in Lamar's hand: "The above is one of Alfred Iverson's compositions whilst at college." The word "college" here probably refers to Eatonton Academy (The Lamar Papers, (MSS) Numbers 12, 13, 14, and 28).
10. Lucius later became a respected jurist and the compiler of an important legal work, *The Laws of Georgia*. His son, born in 1825, took his father's name, and distinguished himself as a member of the legal profession. In 1873, the son was elected to the United States Congress, and in 1877, he became a senator; in 1888, he was named Associate Justice of the United States Supreme Court.
11. Graham, *op. cit.*, pp. 11, 19; A.K. Christian, *op. cit.*, Volume 23, p. 154.
12. Graham, *op. cit.*, pp. 107–109.
13. Lamar Papers, Number 34, (MS).
14. There is little doubt that "Mr. Lanthernbalvon" was Mirabeau Lamar although he stated in his prospectus that the proposed free style paper was to be "supported by several young men whose names it will be vain to inquire after" (Lamar Papers, Number 34, (MS)).
15. Lamar Papers, Numbers 43 and 44.
16. *Loc. cit.*
17. Lamar Papers, Number 50.
18. Graham, *op. cit.*, p. 14.
19. Gambrell, *op. cit.*, pp. 34–39.
20. Lamar Papers, (MS) number 69.
21. Lamar Papers, Number 91.
22. Cited by Gambrell, *op. cit.*, p. 40.
23. Lamar Papers, (MS) Number 104.
24. *Loc. cit.*
25. The states' rights theme is apparent in much of Lamar's work at this time. One lengthy document in his papers declared that "it is contended by the Union party that the General Government is not a confederation of the union of States, but that it is a government of the people in their aggregate capacity ... I am not that kind of union man who can take the

oath of alleigance to twenty three states and deny it to the one that I live in
... I am satisfied myself that many of the union leaders who contend for absolute dominion in the General Government, and unlimited submission in the states — that those who assert the right of the former to enforce her unconstitutional mandates by the bayonet, and deny to the latter all right of resistance and redress without incurring the crime and consequences of treason, have gone into these doctrines from some other consideration than a full conviction of their truth and soundness" (Lamar Papers, Number 177). Similar sentiments are stated in a twenty three page manuscript that Lamar prepared at about the same time for publication in the *Columbus Inquirer* (Lamar Papers, (MS) Number 180). A speech by Lamar is preserved from a later date that followed this same line of reasoning (Lamar Papers, Number 196).

Chapter 3. SOUL IN DESOLATION

1. Graham cited a legend concerning Lamar's courtship of Tabitha that attributed their first meeting to the year 1821 when she was only fourteen. He saw her again in 1824 and was so impressed with the fact that she had blossomed into womanhood, that he immediately proposed marriage; she at first refused but finally accepted. About the only solid fact about this courtship that is extant consists of a letter written by Mirabeau to Tabitha, dated December 3, 1825, from the executive office. In this he wrote: "I pray you to write if it be only three lines giving the state of your health." In less than a month they were to become husband and wife" (Graham, *op. cit.*, p. 12).

2. Graham stated that Lamar resigned as Troup's secretary in order to nurse Tabitha back to health (Graham, *op. cit.*, p. 21). However, it seems more likely that the wedding was timed to coincide with the conclusion of his official position on the governor's staff. A.K. Christian in his study of the early years of Lamar held this point of view (Christian, *op. cit.*, Volume 23, p. 155).

3. Graham gave the date of Rebecca's birth as November 7, 1827, which he stated was taken from the inscription in Rose Hill Cemetery, Macon, Georgia. (Graham, *op. cit.*, p. 21). Dixon and Kemp erroneously gave 1829 as the date of her birth and mentioned a son as being born to the couple in 1827. No other record of a male birth exists. Apparently, this too, was an error (Dixon and Kemp, *op. cit.*, p. 299).

4. Graham cited an interesting legend to the effect that Tabitha was badly injured in a carriage accident during her wedding trip and that Lamar had to sew up her wound, a deep facial cut, in an Indian hut. This was claimed as the reason for her poor health. However, the fact seems to be clear that her health was always delicate and that her early death was the result of tuberculosis (Graham, *op. cit.*, pp. 19, 20).

5. Barker, Eugene, "Mirabeau Buonaparte Lamar," *University of Texas Record*, Volume II, p. 148.

6. The Lamar Papers, Number 73.

7. *The Columbus Enquirer*, August 9, 1828, cited by Graham, *op. cit.*, pp. 21–25.

Endnotes

8. The Lamar Papers, Number 78.
9. The Lamar Papers, Number 79.
10. The Lamar Papers, Number 80.
11. John H. Martin, *Columbus, Georgia*, pp. 5–123, cited by Graham, *op. cit.*, pp. 21–25.
12. Graham established this date on the basis of information in the *Columbus Enquirer* and a scrapbook owned by Rebecca Curry, Tabitha's sister. Other authors have incorrectly given 1833 as the date of Tabitha's death. A fire destroyed the Muscogee County Records in 1839 obliterating official information. All facts point to the accuracy of the 1830 date. Graham, *op. cit.*, p. 25.
13. Martin, *op. cit.*, p. 26.
14. Lamar, M.B., *op. cit.*, p. 22.
15. Philip Graham, "Mirabeau Buonaparte Lamar's First Trip to Texas," *Southwest Review*, July 1939, Volume 21, Number 4, p. 375.
16. Lamar, M.B., *op. cit.*, p. 110. These lines are from "Monody, Written at Evening on the Banks of the Chattahoochee" and were first published in the *Columbus Enquirer* on November 7, 1834.
17. Gulick, et al., *The Papers of Mirabeau Buonaparte Lamar*, Volume I, pp. 149ff.
18. *Ibid.*
19. Graham cited a license issued to Lamar to practice law dated April, 1833, which is now in the possession of the Lamar family. He noted, however, that Lamar never actively engaged in legal practice. Graham, *op. cit.*, p. 27.
20. Graham, *op. cit.*, p. 28.
21. Graham cited letters in the possession of the Lamar family for dates of the deaths of Evalina and Mirabeau's father. *Ibid.*
22. Graham, *op. cit.*, p. 29.
23. Graham cited Lucian Lamar Knight's *Georgia and Gerogians*, Six Volumes, (Chicago, 1917) Volume II, p. 943 for information concerning Lucius' death and burial (Graham, *op. cit.*, p. 29).
24. Graham, "Mirabeau Buonaparte Lamar's First Trip to Texas," *Southwest Review*, Volume 21, Number 4, p. 370.

Chapter 4. LAND OF FRUITION

1. Philip Graham "Mirabeau Buonaparte Lamar's First Trip to Texas," *Southwest Review*, July 1939, Volume 21, Number 4, p. 371.
2. *Loc. cit.*
3. *Ibid.*, p. 370
4. *Loc. cit.*
5. *Ibid.*, p. 371.
6. *Ibid.*, p. 370.
7. Lamar Papers, Number 382 (MS).
8. Lamar Papers, Number 284.
9. *Loc. cit.*
10. Lamar Papers, Number 226.

11. Graham, *Southwest Review*, July 1939, Volume 21, Number 4, p. 372.
12. *Ibid.*, p. 374.
13. *Loc. cit.*
14. *Loc. cit.*
15. *Loc. cit.*
16. *Ibid.*, p. 375.
17. *Loc. cit.*
18. *Ibid.*, p. 376.
19. *Loc. cit.*
20. *Ibid.*, p. 377.
21. *Loc. cit.*
22. *Ibid.*, p. 378.
23. *Ibid.*, p. 381.
24. *Ibid.*, p. 382.
25. *Loc. cit.*
26. *Ibid.*, p. 383.
27. *Ibid.*, p. 384.
28. *Loc. cit.*
29. *Ibid.*, p. 386.
30. *Ibid.*, p. 387.
31. *Ibid.*, p. 389.
32. *Loc. cit.*
33. *Loc. cit.*
34. Graham cited the *Galveston News*, January 30, 1879, as recording this event (Graham, *The Life and Poems of Mirabeau Buonaparte Lamar*, p. 33).
35. H.P. Grambrell, *Anson Jones: The Last President of Texas* (Austin: The University of Texas Press, 1964), p. 54; Reese, *op. cit.*, p. 53.
36. Graham cited the *Texas Republican*, Brazoria, October 10 and 24, 1835 (Graham, *The Life and Poems of Mirabeau Buonaparte Lamar*, p. 34).
37. *Loc. cit.*
38. Dixon and Kemp, *op. cit.*, p. 299.
39. Lamar Papers, Number 288. Letter dated January 5, 1836, of John T. Lamar to Thomas Ward.
40. Lamar Papers, Number 351.
41. *Loc. cit.*
42. *Loc. cit.*
43. *Loc. cit.*
44. These lines are from "Give to the Poet His Well Earned Praise" written between July and October, 1835, during Lamar's first visit. This poem was first published in the *Texas Republican*, October 10, 1835 (Graham, *The Life and Poems of Mirabeau Buonaparte Lamar*, p. 193).

Chapter 5. THE NERO OF THE PRESENT DAY

1. Cited by Frank Tolbert, *The Day of San Jacinto* (New York: McGraw-Hill, 1959), p. 202.
2. *The Writings of Sam Houston* (edited by Amelia W. Williams and Eu-

Endnotes

gene C. Barker, Austin: The University of Texas Press, 1943), Volume I, p. 430.

3. The Lamar Papers, (MSS) Number 374.
4. The Lamar Papers, Number 362.
5. *Ibid.*
6. *Ibid.*
7. *Ibid.*
8. *Ibid.*
9. *Ibid.*
10. Burnet wrote Lamar on July 8 enclosing a copy of the secret treaty with Santa Anna indicating that Lamar may not have been fully privy to these discussions (The Lamar Papers, (MS), Number 403). Stanley Siegel in his study of Lamar (*The Poet President of Texas*), p. 22, indicated his belief that a reference in this agreement to the Rio Grande as a possible border for Texas was highly significant and would indicate Lamar's involvement in the treaty process. However, this is an assumption that is unrelated to fact. Lamar's chief interest at this time was simply the disposition of Santa Anna. His later willingness to recognize the Republic of the Rio Grande would bring into question any likelihood that he had an all consuming desire to place the southern border of Texas as far south as the Rio Grande, an area of Texas that at this time, he knew nothing about.
11. The Lamar Papers, Number 521.
12. A letter from Lamar to Burnet, written on July 17, 1836, mentions a move in the army to seize Santa Anna and kill him. Lamar declared that while he agreed that the Mexican should die, that it was his conviction that only the congress of the Republic of Texas could pass a death sentence and that such must not take place at the hands of a "rebellious mob of strangers." The Lamar Papers, (MS) Number 414.
13. Gambrell, *Lamar: Troubador and Crusader*, p. 140. Austin wrote Lamar on July 2, 1836 "asking . . . for a conference at Bell's regarding Santa Anna." (The Lamar Papers, (MS) Number 397) Another letter dated July 8 from Austin was addressed to Lamar in which he reiterated Santa Anna's desire to end the war (The Lamar Papers, Number 406).
14. Gambrell, *op. cit.*, p. 155.

Chapter 6.   GENERAL FOR A DAY

1. The Lamar Papers, (MS) Number 374.
2. The Lamar Papers, (MS) Number 381. A letter dated June 1836 from Benjamin F. Smith mentioned Lamar's proposed visit to the United States. The Lamar Papers, (MS) Number 383.
3. The Lamar Papers, Number 389.
4. Garrison, George P. Editor. *Diplomatic Correspondence of the Republic of Texas.* (Washington: Government Printing Office, 1908–1911), Volume I, p. 104.
5. The Lamar Papers, (MS) Number 400.
6. The Lamar Papers, Number 407.
7. The Lamar Papers, (MS) Number 410.
8. The Lamar Papers, (MS) Number 392.

9. The Lamar Papers, (MS) Number 393.
10. The Lamar Papers, (MS) Number 384.
11. The Lamar Papers, (MS) Number 386.
12. The Lamar Papers, (MS) Number 414.
13. William Campbell Brinkley, *The Texas Revolution* (Baton Route: The Louisiana State University Press, 1952), p. 115.
14. Gambrell, *op. cit.*, p. 129.
15. *The Writings of Sam Houston,* Volume VI, p. 458.
16. The Lamar Papers, Number 412.
17. The Lamar Papers, (MS) Number 414.
18. The Lamar Papers, (MS) Number 397.
19. The Lamar Papers, Number 368 and 369.
20. The Lamar Papers, (MS) Numbers 532 and 541.
21. The Lamar Papers, (MS) Numbers 545, 547, 649, 703 and countless others.
22. The Lamar Papers, Number 427.
23. The Lamar Papers, (MS) Number 409.
24. The Lamar Papers, (MS) Number 411.
25. Cited by Gambrell, *op. cit.*, pp. 130, 131.
26. The Lamar Papers, (MS) Number 445.
27. Brinkley, *op. cit.*, p. 115.
28. Houston received 5,119 votes as president; his only opponent after Henry Smith had withdrawn from the race was Austin, who received only 587 votes. The constitution of the Republic was ratified almost unanimously.

Chapter 7. GENEROUS INDULGENCE

1. The Lamar Papers, (MS) Number 466.
2. The Lamar Papers, (MS) Number 466.
3. The Lamar Papers, Number 478a. This document is a torn page from which much is missing consisting of a sheet from the *Telegraph and Texas Register*, printed in Columbia, November 9, 1836.
4. The Lamar Papers, (MS) Number 494. This letter was dated November 20, 1836.
5. The Lamar Papers, (MS) Number 499.
6. The Lamar Papers, (MS) Number 542.
7. *Ibid.*
8. The Lamar Papers, Numbers 550, 551, 552, 553, 554, 556, 67, 558, 560, 561, 562, 563, 566, 567, 569, 570, 571, 573, 574, 577, 578, 582, 583, 584, 585.
9. The Lamar Papers, Numbers 557, 566, 568, 575, 599.
10. The Lamar Papers, Number 566.
11. The Lamar Papers, Number 568.
12. Cited by Gambrell, *op. cit.*, p. 184.
13. The Lamar Papers, Number 569.
14. The Lamar Papers, Number 558.
15. The Lamar Papers, (MS) Number 598.
16. The Lamar Papers, Numbers 601, 606.

17. The Lamar Papers, Number 601.
18. Gambrell, *op. cit.*, p. 176.
19. The Lamar Papers, Number 615.
20. *Ibid.*

Chapter 8. OAK GROVE ON THE BRAZOS

1. The Lamar Papers, Number 677.
2. Cited by Graham, *op. cit.*, p. 49.
3. *Ibid.*, p. 65.
4. The Lamar Papers, Number 677.
5. The Lamar Papers, Number 605.
6. The Lamar Papers, Number 666.
7. Cited by Herbert Gambrell, *Anson Jones, The Last President of Texas*, (Austin: The University of Texas Press, 1934), pp. 112, 113.
8. Cited by Herbert Gambrell, *Lamar: Troubador and Crusader*, pp. 183, 184.
9. The Lamar Papers, Number 466.
10. The Lamar Papers, Number 661.
11. The Lamar Papers, Number 705.
12. The Lamar Papers, Number 804.
13. Cited by Graham, *op. cit.*, pp. 48–50.
14. The Lamar Papers, Number 799.
15. Cited by Graham, *op. cit.*, p. 50.
16. The Lamar Papers, p. 789.
17. The Lamar Papers, Number 623.
18. The Lamar Papers, Number 631. Lamar wrote to Rusk asking for a conference: "I have just received a letter [urging] me to become a candidate for the next presidency. As you have been spoken of for the same high office . . . I am anxious to see you before I give a final answer" (The Lamar Papers, Number 630). This letter bore the same date, December 7, as the letter to Everitt. Lamar was going to run regardless of Rusk's answer, but he wisely sought encouragement here before he publicly acknowledged his candidacy.
19. The Lamar Papers, Number 632.
20. The Lamar Papers, Number 646.
21. Cited by Gambrell, *op. cit.*, p. 181.
22. The Lamar Papers, Number 684.
23. The Lamar Papers, Number 694.
24. The Lamar Papers, Number 743.
25. The Lamar Papers, Number 755.
26. The Lamar Papers, Number 754.
27. The Lamar Papers, Number 742.
28. The Lamar Papers, Number 744.
29. Cited by Gambrell, *op. cit.* p. 186.
30. Christian, *op. cit.*, p. 170.
31. *Loc. cit.*
32. The Lamar Papers, Number 767.
33. The Lamar Papers, Numbers 799 and 800.
34. Christian, *op. cit.*, p. 170. Lamar was the first president of Texas to

hold a three-year term. The constitution of 1836 provided that the first president would serve only for two years and that all other chief executives would retain office for three years. No one could immediately succeed himself.
    35. The Lamar Papers, Number 832, 837, 844 and 860.
    36. The Lamar Papers, Number 830.
    37. The Lamar Papers, Number 867.

Chapter 9. THE SCROLL OF HISTORY

    1. Two documents in the Lamar Papers, Numbers 913 and 914, represent the bases of these two addresses. One is a printed series of six badly mutilated pages entitled: "The Inaugural Address of Mirabeau B. Lamar, President of the Republic of Texas to Both Houses of Congress." (The Lamar Papers, Number 913) The other is a manuscript of five pages in Lamar's hand that gives his reasons why he is opposed to annexation. *The Calendar of Lamar Papers* (p. 114) called this "notes for the inaugural address on the annexation of Texas" (The Lamar Papers, Number 914).
    2. The Lamar Papers, Number 913, p. 5.
    3. *Ibid.*, p. 9.
    4. *Loc. cit.*
    5. *Ibid.*, p. 11.
    6. Gambrell, *Anson Jones*, pp. 205, 206.
    7. W.R. Hogan, *The Texas Republic, A Social and Economic History* (Austin: The University of Texas Press, 1964), p. 62.
    8. The Lamar Papers, (MS) Number 1873.
    9. The Lamar Papers, (MS) Number 1087.
    10. Gambrell, *Anson Jones*, pp. 164, 165.
    11. The Lamar Papers, (MS) Number 1305.
    12. The Lamar Papers, (MS) Number 2075.
    13. Gambrell, *Anson Jones*, pp. 184, 185.

Chapter 10. THE SEAT OF EMPIRE

    1. The tradition of the buffalo hunt and Lamar's words on the site have been accepted by many historians. The tradition itself is based on statements made by Judge A.W. Terrell (cited by Seymour Connor, *Adventure in Glory*, Austin: Steck-Vaughn Co., 1965, pp. 100, 101). The hunt itself was almost certainly fact. Lamar's exact words have been called legend by some modern writers, but it was the type of legend that had behind it some element of substantial fact (Stanley Siegel, *op. cit.*, p. 97).
    2. O.M. Roberts, "The Capitals of Texas," *The Quarterly of the Texas State Historical Association*, Volume II, Number 2, pp. 117–123.
    3. The Lamar Papers, (MS) Number 1264.
    4. The Lamar Papers, (MS) Number 1294.
    5. The Lamar Papers, (MS) Number 1320.
    6. The Lamar Papers, (MS) Number 1363.
    7. The Lamar Papers, (MS) number 1368.
    8. Cited by Gambrell, *Anson Jones*, p. 175.
    9. The Lamar Papers, (MS) Number 1388.
    10. The Lamar Papers, Numbers 1404 and 1405.
    11. The Lamar Papers, Number 1413.

Endnotes *221*

12. Gambrell, *op. cit.*, p. 179.
13. P.E. Pearson, "Reminiscences of Judge Edwin Waller," *The Texas Historical Association Quarterly*, Volume IV, p. 47.
14. *Ibid.*, p. 48.
15. *Loc. cit.*
16. Cited by Gambrell, *op. cit.*, p. 180.
17. *Ibid.*, p. 175.
18. *Loc. cit.*
19. *Ibid.*, p. 181.
20. *Ibid.*, pp. 181, 182.
21. *Ibid.*, p. 192.
22. Connor, *op. cit.*, p. 117.
23. *Ibid.*, p. 118.
24. The Lamar Papers, (MS) Number 2151.

Chapter 11. THE FORKED TONGUE

1. Christian, *op. cit.*, p. 53.
2. *Ibid.*, pp. 53ff.
3. *Loc. cit.*
4. *Ibid.*, pp. 48, 49. Mary Whatley Clarke, *Chief Bowles and the Texas Cherokees* (Norman: University of Oklahoma Press, 1971), p. 86.
5. *Ibid.*, p. 52.
6. *Ibid.*, p. 69.
7. Several papers in the Lamar files indicate that Indian depredations were increasing in 1838: Lamar Papers 876, 878, 901, and 953.
8. The Lamar Papers, (MS) Numbers 995 and 1100.
9. "Letters of His Excellency the President to Col. Bowles and Others" (photostat in the Texas Archives), p. 3.
10. *Loc. cit.*
11. *Ibid.*, p. 5.
12. *Ibid.*, p. 7.
13. Christian, *op. cit.*, pp. 77, 78; Clarke, *op. cit.*, pp. 100 ff.
14. The Lamar Papers, Number 1362.
15. The Lamar Papers, Numbers 1372 and 1373 (MS).
16. Connor, *op. cit.*, p. 117.
17. *The Houston Morning Star* of March 21, 1840, reported "Indian murders" in Austin on March 13. Cited in *The Journal of Francis Sheridan*, edited by Willis Pratt (Austin: University of Texas Press), 1954, p. 71.
18. The Lamar Papers, (MS) Number 1855.
19. The Lamar Papers, (MSS) Numbers 1863 and 1874.
20. Connor, *op. cit.*, pp. 121ff.
21. The Lamar Papers, (MS) Number 1857.
22. The Lamar Papers, (MS) Number 1810.
23. Christian, *op. cit.*, pp. 210–216.

Chapter 12. THE RESTLESS GIANT

1. The Lamar Papers, Numbers 959, 984, and 1068.
2. Christian, *op. cit.*, p. 121.

3. The Lamar papers, Number 1079.
4. Christian, *op. cit.*, p. 121.
5. Garrison, *Texas Diplomatic Correspondence*, Volume II, p. 449.
6. *Ibid.*, p. 450.
7. *Ibid.*, p. 458.
8. *Ibid.*, p. 467.
9. The Lamar Papers, (MS) Number 1892.
10. Connor, *op. cit.*, p. 133.
11 Christian, *op. cit.*, p. 128.
12. *Ibid.*, p. 216.
13. *Ibid.*, p. 197; Connor, *op. cit.*, p. 121.
14. Connor, *op. cit.*, p. 120.
15. *Ibid.*, p. 121.
16. The Lamar Papers, (MS) Number 1703.
17. The Lamar Papers, (MS) Numbers 1746 and 1748.
18. Gambrell, *op. cit.*, p. 276
19. The Lamar Papers, (MS) Number 1851.
20. Gambrell, *op. cit.*, p. 199.
21. Connor, *op. cit.*, p. 144.
22. The Lamar Papers, (MS) Number 2016.
23. Connor, *op. cit.*, p. 160.

Chapter 13. THE AFFAIR OF THE PIGS

1. Cited by Connor, *op. cit.*, p. 150.
2. Christian, *op. cit.*, pp. 239–241.
3. The Lamar Papers, (MS) Number 1679.
4. Christian, *op. cit.*, p. 244.
5. Christian, *op. cit.*, p. 245. Christian lists the following Public Debt Table. (p.246):

1836	$1,250,000	1839	$3,855,900
1837	1,090,948	1840	6,241,409
1838	1,886,425	1841	7,446,740
		1846	9,949,007

While the largest increase was obviously under Lamar's administration, it is interesting to note that even the strong retrenchment measures of Houston did not completely solve Texas's debt problem.

6. Connor, *op. cit.*, p. 105. Hamilton, by 1850, had a bill of some $210,000 against Texas for his efforts in representing the Republic in unsuccessfully seeking the foreign loan. This money he had spent from his own funds and his inability to collect it caused him embarrassment. While on the way to seek an adjustment of the debt, his ship sank in the Gulf of Mexico. Connor says concerning him: "It is a reflection of the man's character that, when the ship was going down, he gave his life preserver to save a woman and child."
7. Christian, *op. cit.*, p. 228.
8. *Ibid.*, p. 234.
9. Connor, *op. cit.*, p. 131.
10. Christian, *op. cit.*, p. 229.

Endnotes

11. *Ibid.*, p. 230.
12. *Loc. cit.*
13. Edward Fontaine, "Biographical Sketch of M.B. Lamar" (MS), pp. 27, 28. Fontaine was Lamar's private secretary during 1841. He wrote these words in 1857.
14. The Lamar Papers, (MS) Number 2018.
15. *The Calendar of Lamar Papers*, p. 226.
16. The Lamar Papers, Number 1991.
17. The Lamar Papers, Number 2068.
18. *Loc. cit.*
19. Connor, *op. cit.*, p. 130.
20. *Ibid.*, p. 153.
21. The Lamar Papers, (MS) Number 1967.
22. The Lamar Papers, (MS) Number 2078.
23. Cited by Gambrell, *op. cit.*, p. 196.
24. The Lamar Papers, (MS) Number 2103.
25. The Lamar Papers, (MS) Number 2219.
26. Connor, *op. cit.*, p. 141.
27. Fontaine, *op. cit.*, p. 41.

Chapter 14. TEXANS AT SEA

1. The Lamar Papers, (MS) Number 484, p. 1.
2. Cited by J.D. Hill, *The Texas Navy* (Chicago: The University of Chicago Press, 1937), p. 107.
3. *Ibid.*, pp. 108, 109.
4. Tom Henderson Wells, *Commodore Moore and the Texas Navy* (Austin: The University of Texas Press, 1960), Appendix C.
5. Hill, *op. cit.*, p. 111. Wells' study of the life of Edwin Moore included a reproduction of a portrait of the Texan navy commander. Wells, *op. cit.*, opposite title page.
6. Hill, *op. cit.*, p. iii.
7. The Lamar Papers, (MS), Number 153.
8. Cited by Christian, *op. cit.*, p. 198.
9. Cited by Christian, *op. cit.*, p. 199.
10. The Lamar Papers, (MS), Number 1941.
11. Hill, in his study of the Texas Navy, declared that "to an appreciable degree it expedited British recognition of Texas which was the greatest achievement of Lamar's administration" Hill, *op. cit.*, p. 139.
12. *Ibid.*, p. 112.
13. Wells, *op. cit.*, p. 56.
14. The Lamar Papers, (MS) Number 1698.
15. W.W. Pratt, editor, *The Journal of Francis C. Sheridan* (Austin: The University of Texas Press, 1954), p. 78.
16. The Lamar Papers, (MS) Number 1741.
17. Cited by Christian, *op. cit.*, p. 200.
18. *Loc. cit.*
19. *Letter from the President of Texas to the Governor of Yucatan*, The Texas Archives.

20. Christian, *op, cit.*, p. 202.
21. Hill, *op. cit.*, p. 150.
22. *Ibid.*, p. 190.
23. Wells, op. cit., p. 153.
24. Hill, *op. cit.*, p. 191. Hill made this statement about Houston's betrayal of the Navy: [This] "was unbecoming to the Houston of mythology." *Ibid.*, p. 190.

Chapter 15.   WAGONS WESTWARD

1. George Kendall, *Narrative of the Texan Santa Fe Expedition* (New York: Harper and Brothers, 1844), I, p. 70.
2. Fayette Copeland, *Kendall of the Pycayune* (Norman: University of Oklahoma Press, 1943), p. 60.
3. Two MS copies of a "Carta Dirigida a 'l Pueblo de Santa Fe" are in the Lamar Papers. These are apparently copies of the document that was in the possession of the Santa Fe Commissioners. The Lamar Papers, (MS) Number 1972.
4. The Lamar Papers, Number 1773.
5. Christian, *op. cit.*, p. 89.
6. The Lamar Papers, (MS) Number 2070. Dryden's original letter written March 10, 1841, and stated that "every American more than two thirds of the Mexicans and all the Pueblo Indians . . . whenever they hear of your sending troops here has been rejoicing."
7. Cited by Christian, *op. cit.*, p. 111.
8. This letter, signed by George Flood, was dated June 22, 1841, from the legation of the United States in Galveston. June 6 is the earliest date given by contemporary accounts for the time of the expeditions's departure. Other records set the date some two weeks later. However, this seeming discrepancy can be explained by the fact that it probably took that much time to assemble and organize the wagon train for actual movement on the trail. "Correspondence and Reports of American Agents and Others in Texas, 1836–1845" (MS), cited by Horace Bailey Carroll, *The Texan Santa Fe Trail* (Canyon: Panhandle-Plains Historical Society, 1951), p. 9.
9. The Lamar Papers (MS) Number 1960. This MS is undated other than the reference to the fact that the Santa Fe Expedition was then underway.
10. The Lamar Papers, (MS) Number 1992.
11. Copeland, *op. cit.*, p. 47.
12. *Ibid.*, p. 58.
13. Kendall's *Narrative of the Texan Santa Fe Expedition* was published in two volumes in 1844 by Harpers in New York. Other editions followed, the last of which was dated 1856.
14. Thomas Falconer's *Letters and Notes on the Texas Santa Fe Expedition 1841-1842* (New York: Dauber and Price, 1930).
15. Carroll in his study (*op. cit.*) considered Gallagher's record as the best source of information about the details of the expedition. He noted that Gallagher's account was used by Stephen Holye, who produced the *Journal of the Santa Fe Expedition* while both were prisoners in Mexico (Carroll, *op. cit.*, p. 7). Other accounts in addition to Kendall's and Falconer's were the

orders written by Theodore Sovery, adjutant for the operation, and a diary kept by George W. Grover in his "Minutes of Adventure from June 1841." Carroll used all of these sources in his work.

16. Peter Gallagher, *The Santa Fe Expedition* (Dallas, 1935), p. 3.
17. *Ibid.*, p. 7.
18. *Ibid.*, p. 8.
19. *Ibid.*, p. 9.
20. *Ibid.*, p. 11.
21. *Ibid.*, p. 12.
22. *Ibid.*, p. 16.
23. *Ibid.*, p. 18.
24. *Ibid.*, pp. 21, 22.
25. *Ibid.*, p. 23.
26. *Ibid.*, p. 24.
27. *Ibid.*, p. 25.
28. *Ibid.*, pp. 26, 27.
29. *Ibid.*, p. 30.
30. *Ibid.*, p. 32.
31. *Ibid.*, p. 37.
32. *Ibid.*, p. 42.
33. *Ibid.*, pp. 43–54.
34. Gambrell, *op. cit.*, p. 228.
35. *Ibid.*, pp. 229, 230.
36. *Ibid.*, pp. 229, 230.
37. *Ibid.*, p. 239.
38. *Ibid.*, p. 230.
39. *Loc. cit.*
40. The Texas Congress passed a bill in 1840 that prohibited duelists from becoming office holders (Hogan, *op. cit.*, p. 284). Lamar was challenged to a duel by Memucan Hunt in 1842 after his term of office was over. He initially accepted the challenge, but allowed friends to work out the disagreement (The Lamar Papers, Numbers 2131, 2132, 2133, 2138, 2140, 2141, 2142, 2132 and 2144).
41. The Lamar Papers (MS), Number 2126.
42. The Lamar Papers (MS), Number 2126.
43. The Lamar Papers (MS), Number 2128.
44. The Lamar Papers (MS), Number 2127.
45. The Lamar Papers (MS), Number 2129.
46. Cited by Gambrell, *op. cit.*, p. 210.
47. Amelia Williams and Eugene Barker, editors, *The Writings of Sam Houston 1813–1863*, (Austin: The University of Texas Press, 1943), Volume II, p. 436.
48. Connor, *op. cit.*, p. 154.
49. William H. Brown, *The Glory Seekers* (Chicago: A.C. McClung and Company, 1906), pp. 298–337.
50. Gallagher, *op. cit.*, Introduction, pp. i, ii.
51. Siegel, (*op. cit.*, p. 108) in his study of Lamar, spoke of the Expedition as "conceived hastily and of questionable legality." In this he echoes the generally accepted view of the Lamar era in Texas history that accepts

without examination much of the rhetoric of the enemies of the second president.
52. Fontaine, *op. cit.*, p. 21.

Chapter 16. THE IMPOSSIBLE DREAM

1. Lewis Newton and Herbert Gambrell, *A social and Political History of Texas* (Dallas: The Turner Company, 1935), p. 214.
2. *Ibid.*, p. 177.
3. "Journal of the House of Representatives of the Republic of Texas: Third Congress," cited by Hogan, *op. cit.*, p. 138.
4. Gambrell, *op. cit.*, p. 236.
5. "Laws of the Republic of Texas, First Session, Third Congress," cited in *Southwestern Historical Quarterly*, Volume I, p. 100.
6. *Ibid.*, p. 99.
7. The Lamar Papers, (MS) Number 2095.
8. A letter dated September 20, 1841, from Thomas Ward accompanied the survey contained in the Lamar Paper, Number 2095, stating that these were done in compliance with the acts of January 26, 1839, and February, 1840. The Lamar Papers, (MS), Number 2096.
9. Gambrell and Newton, *op. cit.*, page 216, state: "The real importance of these educational acts of the Republic lies not in the fact that a system of public education was actually established, but in the fact that an endowment said to be greater than that provided by any other American state, was begun for the support of public education." One can not help but wonder at this point why the system of public education in Texas is not the best in the nation. However, it is significant that the beginnings were based upon a high degree of idealism and genuine interest in the fact of widespread educational opportunity: for this Lamar must be given much credit.
10. Hogan, *op. cit.*, p. 140.
11. The Lamar Papers, Number 1728.
12. Hogan, *op. cit.*, p. 149.
13. The Lamar Papers, (MS) Number 2494.
14. The Lamar Papers, Number 651.
15. The Lamar Papers, Number 1576.
16. The Lamar Papers, (MS) Number 2148.
17. William McCraw, *Professional Politicians* (Washington: The Imperial Press, 1940), p. 71.
18. The Lamar Papers, (MS) Number 2121.
19. Gambrell *op. cit.*, pp. 161–165.
20. The Lamar Papers, (MSS) Numbers 2098 and 2101.
21. The Lamar Papers, Number 361.
22. The Lamar Papers, (MS) Number 2015.
23. The Lamar Papers, Number 2200.
24. The Lamar Papers, (MS) Number 1331.
25. Garrison, *op. cit.*, Volume II, p. 904.
26. The Lamar Papers, Number 2200.

Chapter 17. THE WINTER CHILL

1. The Lamar Papers, (MS) Number 1932, p. 4.
2. *Ibid.*, p. 8.

Endnotes

3. *Ibid.*, p. 3.
4. *Ibid.*, p. 1.
5. *Ibid.*, p. 5.
6. *Loc. cit.*
7. *Loc. cit.*
8. Cited by Gambrell, *op. cit.*, p. 173.
9. The Lamar Papers, (MS) Number 1595.
10. The Lamar Papers, (MS) Number 1891.
11. The Lamar Papers, (MS) Number 1955.
12. The Lamar Papers, (MS) Number 1976.
13. The Lamar Papers, (MS) Number 1967.
14. Graham, *op. cit.*, pp. 208 and 211.
15. The Lamar Papers, (MS) Number 1974.
16. The Lamar Papers, (MS) Number 1976.
17. Gambrell, *op. cit.*, p. 198.
18. *Ibid.*, p. 200.
19. The Lamar Papers, (MS) Number 1965.
20. Garrison, *op. cit.*, Vol. 1, p. 489.
21. Thomas Green, *Journal of the Texas Expedition Against Mier* (Austin: The Steck Company, 1935). This is a facsimile reproduction of the original published in New York by Harper and Brothers in 1845, p. 19.
22. *Loc. cit.*
23. The Lamar Papers, Number 194.
24. Williams and Barker, *op. cit.*, Volume II, p. 322.
25. *Loc. cit.*
26. *Ibid.*, p. 366.
27. Donald Day and Harry Herbert Ullon, *op. cit.*, p. 184.
28. Cited by Connor, *op. cit.*, p. 166.
29. Cited by Gambrell, *op. cit.*, p. 203.
30. *Ibid.*, p. 163.
31. *Ibid.*, p. 176.
32. *Ibid.*, p. 203.
33. *Ibid.*, p. 201.
34. *Ibid.*, p. 188.
35. The Lamar Papers, (MS) Number 1996.
36. The Lamar Papers, (MS) Number 2022.
37. The Lamar Papers, (MS) Number 2077.
38. Gambrell, in his biography of Anson Jones, cited a Henry Milland who wrote on March 16, 1841, that Lamar had "declared himself in favor of Sam Houston for next president" (Gambrell, *op. cit.*, p. 207).
39. The Lamar Papers, (MS) Number 2071.
40. Gambrell, *op. cit.*, p. 205.
41. The Lamar Papers, (MS) Number 2039.
42. Connor, *op. cit.*, pp. 162, 163.
43. Cited by Gambrell, *op. cit.*, p. 211.
44. The Lamar Papers, (MS) Number 2105.
45. Gambrell, *op. cit.*, p. 215.
46. *Ibid.*, p. 216. This was a statement by Josiah Gregg cited by Gambrell.

13. The Lamar Papers, (MS) Number 2297.
14. The Lamar Papers, (MS) Number 2255.
15. The Lamar Papers, (MS) Number 2262.
16. The Lamar Papers, (MS) Number 2236.
17. The Lamar Papers, (MS) Number 2239.
18. The Lamar Papers, (MS) Number 2297.
19. The Lamar Papers, (MS) Number 2297.
20. The Lamar Papers, (MS) Number 2258.
21. The Lamar Papers, (MS) Number 2263.
22. The Lamar Papers, (MS) Number 2296.
23. The Lamar Papers, (MS) Number 2217.
24. The Lamar Papers, (MS) Number 2297.
25. The Lamar Papers, (MS) Number 2300.
26. The Lamar Papers, (MS) Number 2315.
27. The Lamar Papers, (MS) Number 2318.
28. The Lamar Papers, (MS) Number 2320.
29. The Lamar Papers, (MS) Number 2323.
30. The Lamar Papers, (MS) Number 2336.
31. The Lamar Papers, Number 2341.
32. The Lamar Papers, (MS) Number 2350.
33. The Lamar Papers, (MS) Number 2343.
34. The Lamar Papers, (MS) Number 2351.
35. The Lamar Papers, Number 2358.
36. The Lamar Papers, (MS) Number 2352.
37. The Lamar Papers, (MS) Number 2363.
38. The Lamar Papers, (MS) Number 2346.
39. The Lamar Papers, (MS) Numbers 2347 and 2348.
40. The Lamar Papers, (MS) Number 2338.
41. The Lamar Papers, (MS) Number 2337.
42. The Lamar Papers, (MS) Number 2334.
43. The Lamar Papers, (MS) Number 2337.
44. The Lamar Papers, (MS) Number 2336.
45. The Lamar Papers, (MS) Number 2359. This document, in Spanish, appears to be in Lamar's own hand, indicating the possibility that he had gathered a considerable knowledge of the language by this time. Here the tax was referred to as a "piso de los extrangeros quien vienen aca con carritos o mulos para traficar."
46. The Lamar Papers, (MS) Number 2342.
47. The Lamar Papers, (MS) Number 2340.
48. The Lamar Papers, (MS) Number 2354.
49. The Lamar Papers, (MS) Number 2354.
50. The Lamar Papers, (MS) Number 2361.
51. The Lamar Papers, (MS) Number 2365.
52. The Lamar Papers, (MS) Number 2377.
53. The Lamar Papers, (MS) Number 2377.
54. The Lamar Papers, (MS) Number 2381.
55. The Lamar Papers, (MS) Number 2382.
56. The Lamar Papers, (MS) Number 2383.
57. The Lamar Papers, (MS) Number 2383.

Endnotes

58. The Lamar Papers, (MS) Number 2386.
59. The Lamar Papers, (MS) Number 2390. The establishment of Fort McIntosh at Laredo, a cavalry post that was maintained well into the twentieth century, is evidence that Lamar's recommendation was eventually heeded.

Chapter 20. IN SEARCH OF A HOME

1. The Lamar Papers, (MS) Number 2395.
2. The Lamar papers, (MS) Number 2396.
3. The Lamar Papers, (MS) Number 2397.
4. The Lamar Papers, (MS) Number 2399.
5. The Lamar Papers, (MS) Number 2400 indicates that Lamar was in Washington, D.C., in late April.
6. The Lamar Papers, (MS) Number 2402.
7. The Lamar Papers, (MSS) Numbers 2457 and 2459.
8. The Lamar Papers, (MS) Number 2457.
9. The Lamar Papers, (MS) Number 2462.
10. *Loc. cit.*
11. *Loc. cit.*
12. *Ibid*
13. Graham, *op. cit.*, pp. 78ff.
14. *Ibid.*, pp. 257–258.
15. Graham concluded that the wedding occurred between the 1st and the 20th of February basing this conclusion on a letter in the Dienst Collection written by Lamar on February 26, 1851. *Ibid.*, p. 79.
16. *Ibid.*, p. 79, 80.
17. *Ibid.*, p. 79.
18. *Ibid.*, p. 80.
19. Cited by Graham (*Ibid.*, p. 80) from an unpublished letter dated May 6, 1853.
20. Cited by Graham (*Ibid.*, p. 81) from an unpublished letter.
21. Cited by Graham (*Loc cit.*) from an unpublished letter dated January 16, 1855.
22. Graham (*Loc cit.*) cites a letter of Lamar to Edward Hall, August 29, 1854, printed in the *East Texas Magazine*, July, 1929.
23. The Lamar papers, (MSS) Numbers 2474–2479. These letters are in Spanish and were written between February and May, 1852.
24. Cited by Graham (*op. cit.*, p. 83) from an unpublished letter dated June 1, 1852.
25. The Lamar Papers, Number 2491.
26. The Lamar Papers, (MS) Number 2469.
27. The Lamar Papers, (MS) Number 2470.
28. The Lamar Papers, (MS) Number 2471.
29. The Lamar Papers, (MS) Number 2481.
30. The Lamar Papers, (MS) Number 2484.
31. Ruth Reese, "Mirabeau B. Lamar, Father of Texas Education," (unpublished manuscript in the Library of The University of Texas), p. 52.
32. The Lamar Papers, (MS) Number 2486.

33. The Lamar Papers, (MS) Number 2489.
34. Cited by Graham (*op. cit.*, p. 82) from an unpublished letter dated January 18, 1858.
35. Graham (*op. cit.*, p. 92) in his study of Lamar's poetry, notes this fact. He made the following evaluation of *Verse Memorials*: "The occasional spirit of the Eighteenth Century [fused] with the sentimentalism of the Nineteenth" (*op. cit.*, p. 93). He concluded that "his lines are too often lacking in creative energy . . . but the music of his verse during his last twenty years compensates for the lack of pictures" (*op. cit.*, p. 95).
36. Mirabeau Lamar, *Verse Memorials*.
37. The Lamar Papers, Number 2537.
38. *Loc. cit.*
39. These two poems appear in Lamar's volume over the name of Mrs. Ann S. Stephens.
40. *Verse Memorials*, p. 69.
41. *Ibid.*, p. 28.
42. *Ibid.*, pp. 145–147.
43. *Ibid.*, pp. 141–143.
44. *Ibid.*, pp. 179–181.
45. *Ibid.*, p. 59.
46. *Ibid.*, pp. 201–202.
47. *Ibid.*, pp. 193–194.
48. *Ibid.*, pp. 173–175.
49. Even while a military post commander in Laredo, Lamar had been corresponding with others who were involved in the writing of poetry. In a letter to John Veatch, he made reference to Veatch's own "poeticals" that were then "progressing slowly but steadily." The Lamar Papers, (MSS) Numbers 2388 and 2515.
50. The Lamar Papers, Number 2517.
51. *Verse Memorials*, p. 28.
52. The Lamar Papers, (MS) Number 2511.
53. The Lamar Papers, (MS) Number 2512.

Chapter 21.   MINISTER IN RESIDENCE

1. The Lamar Papers, (MS) Number 2594.
2. Mary Baptista Roach. "Diplomatic Relations Between the United States and Central America and the Ministership of Mirabeau Buonaparte Lamar" (An unpublished manuscript in the library of The University of Texas at Austin), p. 164.
3. Day and Ullon, *op. cit.*, Volume V, p. 451.
4. The Lamar Papers, (MS) Number 2521.
5. The Lamar Papers, (MS) Number 2522.
6. The Lamar Papers, Number 2524.
7. *Loc. cit.*
8. Graham stated that Lamar refused the Argentine post in favor of the Central American appointment. However, there is no contemporary evidence of such a refusal: apparently the reassignment was dependent upon the immediacy of the need. The State Department simply needed someone

Endnotes

like Lamar in Central America in the light of the developments there (Graham, *op. cit.*, p. 84).
9. The Lamar Papers, (MS) Number 2520.
10. The Lamar Papers, (MS) Number 2530.
11. The Lamar Papers, Number 2533.
12. The Lamar Papers, Number 2538.
13. The Lamar Papers, (MS) Number 25-45.
14. Graham, *op. cit.*, p. 83.
15. The Lamar Papers, Numbers 2548, 2549, 2551 and 2556.
16. The Lamar Papers, (MS) Number 2566.
17. The Lamar Papers, (MS) Numbers 2558 and 2563.
18. The Lamar Papers, (MS) Number 2570.
19. The Lamar Papers, (MS) Number 2576.
20. The Lamar Papers, (MS) Number 2719.
21. The Lamar Papers, (MS) Number 2587.
22. Roach, *op. cit.*, p. 162.
23. *Ibid.*, p. 166.
24. *Ibid.*, p. 167.
25. *Ibid.*, p. 169.
26. The Lamar Papers, (MS) Number 2657.
27. The Lamar Papers, (MS) Number 2612.
28. Graham, *op. cit.*, pp. 300-302.
29. *Ibid.*, p. 303.
30. The Lamar Papers, (MS) Number 2721.
31. Roach stated that Lamar had "language difficulty" but believed that "his good will and sense of justice prevailed over impatience and discouragement" (Roach, *op. cit.*, p. 187).
32. The Lamar Papers, (MS) Number 2611.
33. The Lamar Papers, (MS) Number 2631.
34. The Lamar Papers, (MS) Number 2627.
35. The Lamar Papers, (MSS) Numbers 2595, 2596, 2597, 2598 and 2599.
36. The Lamar Papers, (MS) Number 2631.
37. The Lamar Papers, (MS) Number 2588.
38. The Lamar Papers, (MSS) Numbers 2575 and 2579.
39. The Lamar Papers, (MS) Number 2656.
40. The Lamar Papers, (MS) Number 2714.
41. The Lamar Papers, (MS) Number 2723, p. 3.
42. *Ibid.*, p. 5.
43. *Ibid.*, p. 15.
44. The Lamar Papers, (MS) Number 2716.
45. Unpublished letter cited by Graham, *op. cit.*, p. 86.
46. The Lamar Papers, Number 2658.
47. The Lamar Papers, Number 2661.
48. The Lamar Papers, Number 2674.
49. The Lamar Papers, (MS) Number 2605.
50. The Lamar Papers, (MS) Number 2630.
51. The Lamar Papers, Number 2700.
52. The Lamar Papers, Number 2685.

53. The Lamar Papers, Number 2690.
54. The Lamar Papers, (MS) Number 2722, pp. 25, 26.
55. *Ibid.*, p. 29.
56. The Lamar Papers, Number 2697.
57. The Lamar Papers, Number 2699.
58. The Lamar Papers, Number 2706.
59. The Lamar Papers, Number 2700. Some of his papers in this period show clear evidence of water damage.
60. The Lamar Papers, Number 2728.
61. The Lamar Papers, (MS) Number 2757.
62. The Lamar Papers, Number 2734.
63. The Lamar Papers, (MS) Number 2745.
64. The Lamar Papers, Numbers 2741 and 2742.
65. The Lamar Papers, (MS) Number 2731.
66. The Lamar Papers, Number 2730.
67. The Lamar Papers, Number 2729.
68. The Lamar Papers, (MS) Number 2737.
69. The Lamar Papers, (MS) Number 2759.
70. The Lamar Papers, Numbers 2783, 2784 and 2785.
71. Roach, *op. cit.*, p. 185.
72. The Lamar Papers, (MS) Number 2769.
73. The Lamar Papers, Numbers 2770 and 2771.
74. The Lamar Papers, (MS) Number 2787.
75. The Lamar Papers, Number 2789.
76. The Lamar Papers, (MS) Number 2791.
77. The Lamar Papers, (MS) Number 2744.
78. The Lamar Papers, Numbers 2746, 2747, 2748, 2749 and 2767.
79. The Lamar Papers, (MS) Number 2792.
80. The Lamar Papers, (MS) Number 2794.
81. The Lamar Papers, Number 2795.
82. The Lamar Papers, (MS) Number 2796.
83. Graham, *op. cit.*, p. 87.
84. *Loc. cit.*
85. Resse, *op. cit.*, p. 66.

Epilogue

1. *Ibid*

Bibliography

A. THE LAMAR PAPERS

In March, 1909, the State of Texas purchased from Mrs. Loretto Lamar Calder, daughter of the second president of Texas, an old chest made of three-fourths-inch pine bound at the corners with heavy iron braces. Inside were 2815 documents arranged in chronological order that constituted the personal papers of Mirabeau Lamar. Today this collection is housed in the Texas State Library Archives building in Austin. These documents have been a major source for this study of the life of Lamar.

The majority of these papers are manuscript, although this assemblage includes numerous printed materials. Some are single sheets and a few are fragments; others are extensive multi-page compilations. Many are in Lamar's own flowing style of penmanship; others were written by the hundreds of persons with whom he came in contact during the six decades of his lifetime. It was his intent to use these records as the basis of writing what he believed would become the definitive account of the Texas Revolution. His death in 1859 prevented him from accomplishing this task.

In 1914 Elizabeth Howard West compiled a highly accurate and invaluable catalogue of these papers that was published under the title, *The Calendar of the Papers of Mirabeau Buonaparte Lamar*. (The State Library, Second Biennial Report, 1911–12. Austin: Von Boechmann-Jones, 1914) In 1920 Charles Adams Gulick, Jr., initiated the publication of these documents. Between 1921 and 1927 printing took place under the title, *Papers of Mirabeau Buonaparte Lamar*. This significant work was republished in 1968 with a biographical statement by Dorman H. Winfrey under the general editorship of John H. Jenkins in the Brasada Series in six volumes (*The Papers of Mirabeau Buonaparte Lamar*. Charles Adams Gulick, Jr., et al., Austin and New York: The Pemberton Press, 1968.)

Although this important publication has made the Lamar Papers available both to personal and public libraries, there is no substitute for contact with the original source. Even the very style of penmanship can often suggest much of the character and spirit of the man; it can mirror both tragedy and triumph; on occasion it may reflect either exuberance and expectation or discouragement and dejection. Because of this fact, these original papers have been the basis of this study.

The Lamar that has emerged from the Lamar Papers is not the Lamar of the modern writing of Texas history. Twentieth-century accounts of the second president of the Republic of Texas have often depended naively on Houston's assessments of his political opponent. By going to the original documents a much more accurate picture of Lamar is now possible.

B. BIOGRAPHIES OF LAMAR

Christian, A.K. "Mirabeau Buonaparte Lamar," *Southwestern Historical Quarterly*, Volumes 23 and 24, 1922.

Gambrell, Herbert. *Lamar: Troubador and Crusader*. Dallas: Southwest Press, 1934.

Graham, Phillip. *The Life and Poems of Mirabeau B. Lamar*. Chapel Hill: University of North Carolina Press, 1938.

Siegel, Stanley, *The Poet President of Texas*. Austin: Jenkins Publishing Company. The Pemberton Press, 1977.

C. UNPUBLISHED SOURCES

Fontaine, Edward. "Biographical Sketch of Mirabeau Buonaparte Lamar." (MS) The University of Texas Library, Austin, Texas.

Reese, Ruth. "Mirabeau B. Lamar, Father of Texas Education." (MS) Thesis for the MA degree, The University of Texas Library, Austin, Texas, June, 1933.

Roach, Mary Baptista. "Diplomatic Relations Between the United States and Central America and the Ministership of Mirabeau Buonaparte Lamar." (MS) Thesis for the MA degree, The University of Texas Library, Austin, Texas, August, 1940.

D. SELECTED BIBLIOGRAPHY OF PRINTED SOURCES

Adams, Ephraim D., editor, *British Diplomatic Correspondence Concerning the Republic of Texas*. Austin: Texas State Historical Association, 1918.

Barker, Eugene. "Mirabeau Buonaparte Lamar," *The University of Texas Record*, Austin, Texas, Volume II.

Barker, Eugene C. *The Father of Texas*. Austin: The Steck Company, 1935.

Brinkley, William Campbell. *The Texas Revolution*. Baton Rouge: The Louisiana State University Press, 1952.

Brown, William H. *The Glory Seekers*. Chicago: A.C. McClung and Company, 1906.

Callcott, Wilfrid Hardy. *Santa Anna, the Story of an Enigma Who Once Was Mexico*. Norman: The University of Oklahoma press, 1936.

Carroll, Horace Bailey. *The Texas Santa Fe Trail*. Canyon: Panhandle-Plains Historical society, 1951.

Castañeda, Carlos Eduardo. *The Mexican Side of the Texas Revolution*. Dallas: The Turner Company, 1928.

Clarke, Mary Whatley. *Chief Bowles and the Texas Cherokees*. Norman: The University of Oklahoma Press, 1971.

Connor, Seymour V. *Adventure in Glory*. Austin: Steck-Vaughn Company, 1965.

Connor, Seymour V. *The Texas Treasury Papers*. Three Volumes. Austin: The Texas State Library, 1955.

Copeland, Fayette. *Kendall of the Picayune*. Norman: The University of Oklahoma Press, 1943.

Day, Donald and Ullom, Harry Herbert, editors. *The Autobiography of Sam Houston.* Norman: The University of Oklahoma Press, 1954.

Dixon, Sam Houston and Kemp, Louis Wiltz. *The Heroes of San Jacinto.* Houston: The Anson Jones Press, 1932.

Dressell, Gustav. Translated by Max Freund. *Gustav Dressell's Houston Journal, 1837-1841.* Austin, The University of Texas Press, 1954.

Falconer, Thomas. *Letters and Notes on the Texan Santa Fe Expedition, 1841-1842.* New York: Dauber and Price, 1930.

Gallagher, Peter. *The Santa Fe Expedition.* Dallas, 1935.

Gambrell, H.P. *Anson Jones: The Last President of Texas.* Austin: The University of Texas Press, 1964.

Garrison, George P., editor. *Diplomatic Correspondence of the Republic of Texas.* Washington: Government Printing Office, 1908-11. Two volumes.

Graham, Phillip. "Mirabeau Buonaparte Lamar's First Trip to Texas." *Southwest Review,* July, 1939, Volume 21.

Green, Thomas. *Journal of the Texas Expedition Against Mier.* Austin: The Steck Company, 1935. (This was a facsimile reproduction of the original published in New York by Harper Brothers in 1845).

Held, John A. *Religion, A Factor in Building Texas.* San Antonio: The Naylor Company, 1940.

Hill, J.D. *The Texas Navy.* Chicago: The University of Chicago Press, 1937.

Hogan, W.R. *The Texas Republic: A Social and Economic History.* Austin: The University of Texas Press, 1964.

Johnson, Frank W. *A History of Texas and Texans. Chicago: American Historical Society, 1914.*

Kendall, George. *Narrative of the Texas Santa Fe Expedition.* New York: Harper and Brothers, 1844. Two volumes.

Lamar, M.B. *Letter from the President of Texas to the Governor of Yucatan.* Texas Archives, n.d.

Lamar, M.B. *Verse Memorials.* New York; W.P. Fetridge and Company, 1857.

Lane, Walter P. *Adventures and Recollections.* Marshall: News Messenger Publishing Company, 1928.

McGraw, William. *Professional Politicians.* Washington: The Imperial Press, 1940.

Major, Mabel and Smith, Rebecca W., editors, *The Southwest in Literature: An Anthology for High Schools.* New York: The MacMillian Company, 1929.

Molyneaux, Peter. *The Romantic Story of Texas.* Dallas: The Cordova Press, 1936.

Newcomb, W.W., Jr. *The Indians of Texas; From Prehistoric to Modern Times.* Austin: The University of Texas Press, Texas History Paperback, 1969.

Newell, Chester. *History of the Revolution in Texas.* New York: Wiley and Putnam, 1838. Reprinted by the Steck Company of Austin, 1935.

Newton, Lewis and Gambrell, Herbert. *A Social and Political History of Texas*. Dallas: The Turner Company, 1935.

Pearson, P.E. "Reminiscences of Judge Edwin Waller." *The Texas Historical Association Quarterly*, Volume IV.

Pratt, Willis W., editor. *The Journal of Francis Sheridan*. Austin: The University of Texas Press, 1954.

Roberts, O.M. "The Capitals of Texas." *The Quarterly of the Texas State Historical Association*, Volume II, Number 2.

Steen, Ralph W. *History of Texas*. Austin: The Steck Company, 1939.

Tolbert, Frank. *The Day of San Jacinto*. New York: McGraw Hill, 1959.

Wells, Tom Henderson. *Commodore Moore and the Texas Navy*. Austin:

Wharton, C.R. *History of Texas*. Dallas: The Turner Company, 1935.

Williams, Amelia W. and Barker, Eugene, editors. *The Writings of Sam Houston*. Austin: The University of Texas Press, 1943. Eight Volumes.

Wynne, Mamie Cox. *The Romantic Flags of Texas*. Dallas: Banks Upshaw and Company, 1936.

INDEX

A

A cultivated, mind is the guardian genius of democracy, 138
Act Adopting Seal; Standard for Republic of Texas, 72
Alabama River, 25
Alabama Indian Lands, 140
Alabama, 11, 20, 23, 24, 25, 26, 51, 58, 150
Alamo (Massacre), 5, 30
Allen, Reverend W. Y., 139
  William, 12
Alvarez, Manuel, 132
American Atlantic, and Pacific Ship Company, 195
American Occupation of Laredo, 178
Amory, Nathaniel, 71, 89
Anaya, General, 112
Anderson, Mr., 28
Annexation, 167
Archer, B. T., 76
  Branch T., 148
Argentine Confederation, 193
"Arms for the Southern Land," 189
Army of Mexico, 5
Army of the Republic, 2, 3
Aropoza, Don Rafael, 170
  Doñna Maria, 170
Arrowhead's Map [of 1841], 126
Atlanta Chronicle, 19
Austin City Gazette, 109, 159
Austin, Stephen, 38
Austin, Texas, 69, 77, 78, 79, 80, 81, 156, 157, 161, 180
Austin, The [Sloop-of-War, Texas Navy], 111, 112, 119
Aztecs, 90

B

Baker, Daniel, 141
Baldwin, Dr. John, 147
Barr, Robert, 69, 70
Bastrop, 157, 158, 161
Battle for Monterrey, 170
Battle of Morales, 96
Baudin, Admiral, 97, 115
Bean's Station, 62
Bee, Barnard E., 39, 43, 70, 71, 92, 93, 94, 95, 98, 142, 156
  H. P., 172, 175
Bell, P. H., 46
Belly Contract, 198, 199, 200, 202
Belly, Felix, 196, 197, 198
Bingham, Benjamin, 35
Birdsall, Attorney General, 56
Black John, [Lamar Slave], 55
Blackrode, Thomas, 123
Bliss, W. W. S., 174
Boliver Point, 30
Borden, Gail, 59, 154, 177
Boston, The U.S.S., 113
Bowles, [Cherokee Tribal Chief], 84, 85, 86
Brantley, Reverend William T., 19
Brazoria, 2, 29, 30, 45, 54, 152
Brazos Courier, 154
Brazos River Plantation, 186
Brazos River, 40, 48, 55, 58, 127, 157, 158
Brewster, H. P., 154
Brown, [Mrs.], 28
Bryan, Moses Austin, 142
Buchanan, President, 190, 193
Buffalo herds, 73, 75, 127
Buford, Thomas, 46
Bullock's Hotel, 77, 78, 101
Bullock, [Mr.], 101, 110
Burleson's Regiment, 5
Burleson, Edward, 155, 156, 165, 168
Burnet, David G., 35, 36, 37, 41, 42, 44, 46, 56, 61, 62, 71, 72, 86, 97, 98, 148, 149, 153, 154, 194
Burton, Isaac, 58, 62

C

Cahawba Press, 12
California, 143
Camargo, 96, 172
Campeche, 119
Canales, Antonio, 95, 96
  General, 112
Capers, Sue, 188
Capital City Site [Austin], 74
Capital of Texas [Moving], 69
Cardenas, Jesus, 95, 96
Cass, Lewis, 193, 194, 195, 197,

199, 201, 202
Cavalry, Texas, 4
Cazneau, J. M., 197, 201
  Mrs. William (See Montgomery), 188
Chalmers, John G., 109, 148
Chapman, R. W., 141
Chattahoochee River, 19
Chenoweth, John, 42
Cherokee Indians, 84, 85, 86, 87, 88, 89, 207, 208
Chihuahua, 130
Christman (Surveyor), 31
Christmas at Oak Grove, 203
Church, Dr. Alonzo, 10
Clay, Henry, 180, 181
Cobb, Howell, 193
Cole's Settlement, 29
Cole, J. P., 25
College and University Lands, 140
Collingsworth, James W., 62
Colorado River Valley, 74
Colorado River, 40, 73, 75, 157
Columbia, 38, 48, 51, 61
Columbus Enquirer, 52
Columbus, 29
Comanche Indians, 87, 88, 89, 171
Comanche Peaks, 127
Confederacy, 182
Cooke, Colonel, 129
  Louis P., 70
Corpus Christi Bay, 90
Coshattie [*sic*] Indian Lands, 140
Costa Rica, 191, 199
Council House Fight, 87
Crawford, Joel, 11, 14
Creek Indians, 14
Criesman, Horatio, 29
Cuba, 185
Cueblo, Calaudio, 197
Cultural Development, Texas's, 207
Curtis, Samuel R., 174

D

Declaration of Independence [Texas], 52
Douglass, General Kelsey, 86, 87
Dryden, William G., 123
Duel [Burnet challenged Houston], 154
Dunlap, Richard G., 70, 142
Dunlop, 95
Dunn [incident], 192

E

Eaton, Academy, 10
Education, 138, 139, 140, 141, 207
Edwards Plateau, 90
Elliot, Charles, 106
Ellis, Richard, 60
El Paso, 92
Enquirer, 20, 21, 22
Everitt, S. H., 38, 59, 60, 62
Ewing, Doctor, 36

F

Falconer, Thomas, 126
Fannin [Spirit of], 42
Fannin, James, 2, 30
Fanning, J. T., 51
"Father of Education in Texas," 141, 207
Feeman, Mr., 28
Fetridge, W. E. Company, 188
Filisola [Italian General in Mexican Army], 34, 35, 84
Fisher, William, 96
Flag [Texas] Adoption, 72
Flash [Schooner], 2
Flint, Cassandra, 163, 164
Flores, Thomas, 176
Fontaine, Edward, 74, 154, 160, 162, 180
Fort Parker, 158
France, in Gulf of Mexico, 97
Franklin Society, 26

G

Gadsden, 193
Gaines, Captain, 24
Gallagher, Peter, 127, 128, 129, 130, 131
Galveston Bay, 30, 64
Galveston Civilian, 61
Galveston Navy Yard, 119
Galveston News, 166
Galveston Weekly News, 203
Galveston, Texas, 40, 59, 60, 61, 65, 88, 99, 114, 119, 154, 161, 183
Garland, R., 177
Georgia Telegraph, 161
Georgia, 8, 9, 18, 19, 20, 22, 23, 24, 30, 43, 50, 51, 58, 160, 180, 183
Gilmer, W. Ray, 62
Goliad Massacre, 5, 30
Gonzales, Ambrosio José, 185

Index

Grand Saline, 85
Gray, W. Fairfax, 56
Grayson, P., 53
   Peter W., 61, 62
Green's Bluff, 142
Green, T. J., 76
   Thomas, 60, 115, 149
   [Mr.], 44, 45
Groce's Plantation, 1
Guadalupe River, 40, 41, 43, 59
Guadalupe, [Mexican Ship], 119
Gulf Coast, 111
Gulf of Mexico, 136
Gulf Squadron [U.S. Navy], 113
Gurrey (Ship's Captain), 27

H

Hall, Col[onel], 24
   Edward, 152
Hamilton, James, 43, 104, 105, 106, 107, 108, 115, 193, 194
Handsford, John M., 72
Handy, Major, 53
   Robert Eden, 54, 55, 158
Harrell [Son of Jake], 74, 75
   Jake, 74
Harrisburg [Texas], 2, 30
Harvey, Evaline (Lamar), 21
Hemphill, John, 70
Henderson, J. Pinckney, 71, 104, 105, 168, 169, 174, 175, 176, 180
Hill Country, 81
Hines, Marquis, 199, 200, 202
Hockley's Artillery, 5
Holford, 113
"Home on the Brazos," 189
Houston Banner, (1837), 60
Houston Morning Star, 78
Houston, Sam, 2, 3, 4, 5, 6, 7, 34, 36, 37, 38, 39, 41, 44, 45, 47, 48, 49, 51, 52, 57, 65, 67, 69, 78, 79, 83, 84, 87, 107, 109, 112, 116, 117, 118, 119, 120, 149, 150, 151, 152, 154, 155, 156, 158, 165, 166, 193
Houston [Texas], 53, 57, 64, 78
Hoxey [Mr.], 31
Hoxton, A. C., 62
Hunt, W. H., 75
Hunt, Memucan, 43, 60, 70, 147, 155, 159
Huston, Felix, 44, 83

I

Indian Policy, 102, 208
Indians [and treaties], 82–102, 127, 129
Irion, Secretary of State, 56

J

Jackson, Alden, 109
   Andrew, 150
Johnson, J. Benton, 177
Johnston, Albert Sidney, 70, 77, 83, 86, 87, 97, 159
Jones, Anson, 29, 56, 70, 78, 79, 109, 131, 133, 148, 151, 153, 159, 165
   James, 60
   Oliver, 118, 152
   Seaborn, 21
Jordan, S. W., 96
   Tabitha B. [see Lamar], 17

K

Karnes, Henry, 87
Kaufman, David S., 56
Kendall, George W., 126, 168
Kendrick, Harvey, 148
Kerr, James, 87
Kilgore, Mr., of Brazoria, 2
Kinney, H. L., 176
Kuykendall, Joe, 186

L

La Grange, 75, 161
Lafayette, Marquis De, 15
Lafitte and Company of France, 107, 108
Lafitte, Jean [the Buccaneer], 24, 111
Laguna Colorado, 129
Lamar Papers, 45
Lamar, Charles, 194
   Evaline [See Harvey]
   Gazaway, 55, 185, 193, 194
   Henrietta [See Moffitt], 183, 184, 185, 186, 188, 194, 203
   Jefferson Jackson, 9, 30, 55, 149
   John, 8, 21
   [Mrs. John], 31, 160
   John T., 30, 143
   Loretto Evaline, 184
   Lucius Quintus Cincinnatus, 9, 11, 14, 21, 22
   Mary Ann, 162

Mirabeau Buonaparte, 9
  Rebecca Ann, 18, 31, 58, 160, 161, 162, 164
  Tabitha (Jordan) 18, 19, 20, 29
  Thomas, 30, 161, 180
  Zechariah, 9
Land Bill [Cherokee], 87
Lane, Walter P., 3
Laredo, 95, 96, 170, 171, 172, 175, 176, 179
La Vert, Mrs. Henry [See Walton], 162
Lewis, Captain, 166
Liken, T. M., 173
Linnville, 87
Lipscomb, Abner S., 71
Little Rock [Steamer], 25
Llano Estacado, 129
Lockhart, Matilda, 88
Lone Star Flag [On High Seas], 120
Long, H. L., 177
  Mrs. Jane, 30, 45, 184
Lopez, General, 186
Louisiana, 26
Louisville, The, [Tender, Texas Navy], 113
Love, James, 147
Lubbock, Francis R., 57

M

Macomb, Colonel, 42
Macon Volunteers, 163
Major Brown, [Steamer], 172
Marks, Richard T., 19
Martiñes, Don Andres, 171, 176
Martinez, Tomas, 192, 195, 196, 198, 200
Matagorda, 61
Matamoros, 168, 169
Mayfield, James, 71, 133, 149
  J. S., 159, 160
McCall, George, 172
McCalls, Reverend, W. L., 141
McLeod, Hugh, 122, 126, 127, 131, 136, 145, 146, 147, 153
Meek, A. B., 188
Memefee, William, 148
Mendez, Santiago, 114
Mendoza, José, 197
  Señorita, 197
Methodist Camp (Texas), 28
Mexico City, 170
Millard's Infantry, 5

Milton, John, 21
Miracle, Pedro, 83, 84
Mobile, 26
Moffitt, Eliza, 182, 183
  Henrietta, (See Lamar), 27, 182, 183
  Matilda, 182
  Reverend John Newland, 27, 182
Monterrey, 169
Montezuma, [Mexican Ship], 119
Montgomery, Cora, [See Cazneau], 163, 188
Morning Star, 78, 155
Moore, Dr. Francis, Jr., 154
  Edwin Ward, 113, 114, 115, 116, 118, 119
Mora, Juan Rafael, 199, 200
Morgan, James, 186

N

Nacogdoches, 28, 29, 62
Natchitoches, 27
Navarro, José, 96
Navy Yard at Galveston, 119
Navy, [See Texas Navy]
Neches River, 86
New Orleans Bee, 107
New Orleans Picayune, 126, 168
New Orleans, 26, 36, 51, 124, 142, 147, 152, 182, 183, 187
New Washington, 29
New York Times, 201
Nicaragua, 191, 192, 194, 195, 196, 197, 198, 199, 200, 201, 202
Nolan's Expedition, 24
Nueces County, 176
Nueces River, 90, 91

O

Oak Grove, 55, 58, 62, 158, 186, 203, 204

P

Packenham, Richard, 94, 98
Palmerston, Lord, 98, 104, 105
Palo Duro Canyon, 128, 129
Panic of 1837, 102
Paso Del Norte, 130
Patton, Alexander, 2
Peraza, Martin Francisco, 117
Perote Prison, 131
Pierce, 193
Polk, James, 165

Index

Polk, President, 168
Powelton Academy, 10
Public Education, 138, 139, 140
Puebla, 131, 174

R

Ramon, José, 178
Red River, 27, 142
Redd, William D., 2, 31, 41
Republic of Mexico, 122
Republic of Texas, 39
Republic of the Rio Grande, 95, 96, 97
Richmond, [Texas], 54, 57, 58, 61, 184, 187, 193, 194, 203
Rio Grande River, 22, 42, 90, 91, 95, 96, 170
Roberts, Samuel, 109
  Willis, 11
Romeo, [Steamboat], 27
Ross, Ruben, 96
Rossignol, Charles, 159, 160
Rowe, Joseph, 56, 62
Royall, Richard, 46
Rusk, Thomas, 3, 41, 43, 44, 47, 50, 59, 60, 71, 153, 166, 190
Russell, Lord John, 144

S

Sabine River, 22, 142
Saligny, Count Alphonse de, 100, 101, 105, 108
Saltillo, 96
San Antonio, 87, 88, 92
San Augustine, 28
San Bernard, [War Schooner, Texas Navy], 111
San Christopher, 131
San Felipe, 29
San Jacinto (Battle), 6, 7, 33
San Jacinto River, 2
San Jacinto, [War Schooner, Texas Navy], 111
San Jacinto, 36, 40
San Luis Potosi, 131
San Miguel, 130
Sandusky, William, 154
Santa Anna, 2, 4, 5, 6, 34, 35, 36, 37, 38, 39, 92, 172
Santa Fe [Expedition], 118, 130, 133, 135, 149, 152, 158, 208
Sante Fe, 125, 181
Sartain, J., 188
Sawyer, Caroline, 162, 163

Scott, General, 174
Seguin, Juan, 96
Settle, Mrs. John, 182
Sherman's Regiment, 5
Sherman, Sidney, 3
Sierra Madre, 92
Slough, R. H., 181
Smith, Ashbell, 56, 165
  Henry, 153
Sommervell, Alexander, 60
Soto, Augustin, 176
Staff, James H., 152
Starr, James, 203
Sturgis, B. B., 129
Susquehanna, 195

T

Taylor, President, 165
Taylor, Zachary, 168, 169, 171, 173, 174
Telegraph and Texas Register, 50, 61
Telegraph, 154
Terrell, A. W., 186, 187
Teulon, George, 109
Texan Army, 2
Texan Military, 42
Texan Santa Fe Expedition, 121
Texas Cavalry, 3
Texas Flag, 72, 166
Texas Flag on high seas, 120
Texas Militia, 46
Texas money, 109
Texas Mounted Volunteers, 168, 170
Texas Navy, 94, 111–120, 207
Texas Republic, 6
Texas Republican, 29
Texas Seal, 72
Texas Sentinel, 108
Texas–U.S. boundary, 149, 168
Travis County, 152
Travis [William B.'s Spirit], 42
Treat, James, 93, 94, 98
Treaty of Velasco, 37
Trinity River, 75, 127
Troup, Governor George MacIntosh, 14, 15, 16, 17, 21
Tucker, L. T., 176
Turner, John, 42
"Twin Sisters" [field pieces], 2

U

Urrea, General, 34, 35

V

Veatch, John, 177, 180
Velasco, 30, 37, 40, 60, 76
Veracruz, 99
Victoria, 40, 41, 44, 87
Vince's Bayou, 33

W

Waco Indians, 127
Walker [American filibuster], 195
Waller, Edwin, 70, 75, 77
Walton, Octavia [See Le Vert], 162
Ward, Thomas William, 148
Washington, 194
Washington, Lewis M. H., 147
Washington-on-the-Brazos, 36, 46
Waters, Major B. G., 85
Watkins, Harry, 166
Watrous, James G., 70
Webb, James, 70, 71, 93, 98, 99, 109, 116, 125, 132, 133, 148, 164, 165
Webster, Daniel, 125
Weekly Texian, The, 132, 159
Wharton, John A., 138, 139
Wharton, The, [Sailing Ship-of-War, Texas Navy], 119
Wilde, Richard Henry, 162
Williamson, R. M., 60
Wilson, Robert, 62
    Thomas, 51
Winfield, E. H., 172
Wood, Colonel George, 170
Woolfolk, Sowell, 19
Wright, A. S., 143

Y

Yrissari, [Ambassador], 195

Z

Zacatecas, 130
Zavala, Lorenzo, 31, 35, 37
Zavala, The, [Supply Steamer, Texas Navy], 111, 113
Zeledon, Pedro, 202

www.ingramcontent.com/pod-product-compliance
Lightning Source LLC
Chambersburg PA
CBHW050550160426
43199CB00015B/2599